ADULT PSYCHOPATHOLOGY CASE STUDIES

ADULT PSYCHOPATHOLOGY CASE STUDIES

Edited By

Irving B. Weiner

WILEY

JOHN WILEY & SONS, INC.

Published by John Wiley & Sons, Inc., Hoboken, New Jersey.
Published simultaneously in Canada.

Library of Congress Cataloging-in-Publication Data:

Adult psychopathology case studies / Irving B. Weiner, editor.
    p. cm.
    Includes bibliographical references and index.
    ISBN 0-471-27340-6 (pbk.)
    1. Psychology, Pathological—Case studies.   2. Psychiatry—Case studies.   I. Weiner, Irving B.

    RC465.A326 2003
    616.89′09—dc21

                                          2003053488

10   9   8   7   6   5   4   3   2   1

CONTENTS

Contributors   ix

Preface   xiii

PART ONE
Normality, Abnormality, and Adjustment Disorder

1 *Defining and Classifying Psychopathology*   3
Irving B. Weiner

2 *Adjustment Disorder*   15
Theodore Millon

PART TWO
Disorders of Personality

3 *Dependent Personality Disorder*   23
Robert F. Bornstein

4 *Borderline Personality Disorder*   29
Charles Swenson and Marsha M. Linehan

5 *Antisocial Personality Disorder*   53
Carl B. Gacono

6 *Schizotypal Personality Disorder*   73
David P. Bernstein

7 *Paranoid Personality Disorder*   79
James H. Kleiger

PART THREE
Anxiety and Somatoform Disorders

8   *Panic Disorder with Agoraphobia*   101
Randi E. McCabe and Martin M. Antony

9   *Obsessive-Compulsive Disorder*   119
Deborah A. Roth and Edna B. Foa

10 *Posttraumatic Stress Disorder*   137
Judith G. Armstrong and James R. High

11 *Generalized Anxiety Disorder*   155
Irving B. Weiner

12 *Pain Disorder*   163
Jeffrey M. Lackner

PART FOUR
Identity Disorders

13 *Dissociative Identity Disorder*   183
Paul M. Lerner

14 *Gender Identity Disorder*   207
Kenneth J. Zucker

PART FIVE
Habit Disorders

15 *Polysubstance Dependence*   233
Peter E. Nathan

16 *Bulimia Nervosa*   239
Peter S. Hendricks and J. Kevin Thompson

PART SIX
Mood Disorders and Schizophrenia

17 *Depressive Disorder*   261
Nancy A. Hamilton and Rick E. Ingram

18 *Bipolar Disorder*   267
        Cory F. Newman

19 *Schizophrenia*   293
        Martin Harrow, Kalman J. Kaplan, and Surinder S. Nand

Author Index   313

Subject Index   315

CONTRIBUTORS

Martin M. Antony, PhD, is associate professor of psychiatry and behavioral neurosciences at McMaster University and director of the Anxiety Treatment and Research Center at St. Joseph's Health Care in Hamilton, Ontario.

Judith G. Armstrong, PhD, is clinical associate professor of psychology at the University of Southern California and in the practice of clinical psychology in Santa Monica, California.

David P. Bernstein, PhD, is associate professor of psychology at Fordham University.

Robert F. Bornstein, PhD, is professor of psychology at Gettysburg College.

Edna B. Foa, PhD, is professor of psychology in psychiatry at the University of Pennsylvania and director of the Center for Treatment and Study of Anxiety in Philadelphia.

Carl B. Gacono, PhD, is in the practice of clinical and forensic psychology in Austin, Texas.

Nancy A. Hamilton, PhD, is assistant professor of psychology at Southern Methodist University.

Martin Harrow, PhD, is professor and director of psychology in the department of psychiatry at the University of Illinois Medical School in Chicago.

Peter S. Hendricks, MA, is a graduate student in clinical psychology at the University of South Florida.

James R. High, MD, is associate clinical professor of psychiatry at the University of Southern California Keck School of Medicine and in the practice of psychiatry in Santa Monica, California.

Rick E. Ingram, PhD, is professor of psychology at Southern Methodist University.

Kalman J. Kaplan, PhD, is professor of psychology at Wayne State University and clinical professor of psychology in the department of psychiatry at the University of Illinois Medical School in Chicago.

James H. Kleiger, PhD, is on the adjunct faculty at George Washington University and in the practice of clinical psychology in Bethesda, MD.

Jeffrey M. Lackner, PhD, is assistant professor of medicine and director of the Behavioral Medicine Clinic in the department of medicine at the SUNY Buffalo Medical School.

Paul M. Lerner, EdD, is in the practice of psychoanalysis and psychotherapy in Camden, Maine.

Marsha M. Linehan, PhD, is professor of psychology at the University of Washington in Seattle.

Randi E. McCabe, PhD, is assistant professor of psychiatry and behavioral neurosciences at McMaster University and associate director of the Anxiety Treatment and Research Center at St. Joseph's Health Care in Hamilton, Ontario.

Theodore Millon, PhD, DSc, is professor of psychology at the University of Miami and dean of the Institute for Advanced Studies in Personology and Psychopathology in Coral Gables, Florida.

Surinder S. Nand, MD, is associate professor of psychiatry at the University of Illinois College of Medicine and director of the Mental Health Service Line for the Veterans Administration Health Care System in Chicago.

Peter E. Nathan, PhD, is University of Iowa Foundation distinguished professor of psychology.

Cory F. Newman, PhD, is associate professor of psychology in psychiatry at the University of Pennsylvania and director of the Center for Cognitive Therapy in Philadelphia.

Deborah A. Roth, PhD, is assistant professor of psychology in psychiatry at the University of Pennsylvania.

Charles Swenson, MD, is associate professor of clinical psychiatry at the University of Massachusetts Medical School in Worcester, Massachusetts, and in the practice of psychiatry in Northampton, Massachusetts.

J. Kevin Thompson, PhD, is professor of psychology at the University of South Florida.

Irving B. Weiner, PhD, is clinical professor of psychiatry and behavioral medicine at the University of South Florida and in the practice of clinical and forensic psychology in Tampa, Florida.

Kenneth J. Zucker, PhD, is professor of psychology and psychiatry at the University of Toronto and head of the Child and Adolescent Gender Identity Clinic in the Child, Youth, and Family Program at the Toronto Center for Addiction and Mental Health.

PREFACE

*A*dult Psychopathology Case Studies is written to provide vivid and personalized accounts of the nature of adult psychological disorders—the symptoms they produce and the adjustment problems they cause, how they are experienced and the kinds of experiences that give rise to them, how they affect the lives of disturbed people and those around them, and methods of identifying and treating them.

The chapters of the book describe the ways in which people with psychological disorders are likely to think, feel, and act. Each case presentation includes basic information about the personal histories of the people being described and about the particular disorder they are showing. The presentations are balanced in this way to allow readers an opportunity to formulate their own impressions of the person's problems, which may or may not coincide in all respects with the authors' views. To this end, the authors provide sufficient discussion to illustrate rational case formulation, but stop short of exhaustive or doctrinaire analyses that would discourage alternative opinions concerning how and why a disturbance has occurred and its likely outcome.

The topics for the case studies were chosen to represent a broad range of the most commonly occurring forms of psychopathology, beginning with Adjustment Disorder and proceeding through five types of personality disorders (Dependent, Borderline, Antisocial, Schizotypal, and Paranoid); five types of anxiety and somatoform disorders (Panic Disorder with Agoraphobia, Obsessive-Compulsive Disorder, Posttraumatic Stress Disorder, Generalized Anxiety Disorder, and Pain Disorder); two types of identity disorders (Dissociative Identity Disorder and Gender Identity Disorder), two types of habit disorders (Polysubstance Abuse and Bulimia Nervosa), and three types of serious or psychotic disorders (Depressive Disorder, Bipolar Disorder, and Schizophrenia). Chapters addressing the life experiences of persons with each of these 18 disorders follow an introductory chapter that discusses issues in the definition and classification of psychological abnormality.

A key feature of this book is its diversity, not only in the range of disorders it covers but also with respect to the theoretical perspectives reflected in its chapters. The authors of the case studies, all of whom are experienced clinicians and well-known authorities in their areas of interest, endorse frames of reference that range across psychoanalytic, psychodynamic-interpersonal, cognitive, and cognitive-behavioral conceptualizations of psychopathology and psychotherapeutic methods. Writing from their own point of view, these authors provide a set of theoretically cohesive case descriptions and evaluations that, by virtue of their diversity, acquaint readers with the currently most prevalent alternative approaches to formulating instances of psychological disorder.

The chapters also diverge in terms of the focus of emphasis chosen by the authors in reporting the case histories of persons they have evaluated and treated. Some authors stress the descriptive features of the disorders they are discussing. Some concentrate on developmental events that appear to have led to the emergence of these disorders. Some pay particular attention to diagnostic procedures for identifying the presence of these disorders. Some delineate the course and outcome of efforts to treat these disorders, including detailed accounts of divergent methods such as psychoanalytic psychotherapy and dialectal behavior therapy. Whatever their focus of emphasis, all of the case presentations are exquisitely attuned to the individual experiences of the disturbed persons with whom the authors were engaged and whose adjustment difficulties they were attempting to alleviate.

For additional variety, 6 of the 18 case studies in the book are written in a brief format: those concerning Adjustment Disorder, Dependent Personality Disorder, Schizotypal Personality Disorder, Generalized Anxiety Disorder, Polysubstance Dependence, and Depressive Disorder. For readers whose purposes are served by beginning to study shorter case studies in psychopathology before proceeding to more detailed reports, or by alternating among these, the brief cases as well as the longer cases address a broad range of types of psychological disorders. For the benefit of readers who would like to pursue additional information on adult psychopathology, each chapter concludes with several recommended sources in the literature.

The confidentiality of the persons whose cases are described in the book has been protected by changing their names or initials and by modifying various demographic or historical characteristics that had little or no bearing on the nature of their psychopathology (e.g., whether the person lived in the South or Midwest, had two or three siblings, was 35 or 38 years old, or worked as a salesclerk or a bank teller). Hence, any apparent resemblance to persons known by the readers is coincidental.

Irving B. Weiner
Tampa, Florida

PART ONE

Normality, Abnormality, and Adjustment Disorder

CHAPTER 1

Defining and Classifying Psychopathology

IRVING B. WEINER

Learning about psychopathology through case studies begins with identifying the nature of abnormal psychological functioning and determining how it differs from normal behavior. This is not a simple matter because normality has traditionally been defined in various ways and from different perspectives. Experts have also disagreed about whether psychologically normal and abnormal conditions are continuous phenomena involving similar dimensions of personality or whether they constitute distinctive states of mind that require separate sets of concepts if they are to be described adequately. The first two sections of this chapter discuss alternative ways of defining psychological normality and some implications of considering it continuous or discontinuous with abnormal functioning. The third section of the chapter addresses the utility of a classification system in grouping and distinguishing among different types of psychological disorders, and the fourth section indicates the basis for choosing the topics of the case studies presented in Chapters 2 through 19.

Identifying Psychological Normality

Psychological normality has most often been defined either as an *average,* an *ideal,* or a *level of adjustment.* Normality as an average is a statistical definition that identifies the typical or most common behaviors among a group of people as being normal for that group. This average perspective on what it means to be normal is what someone means when he or she says to another person, "Why can't you be like everyone else?" or "Get with the program!"

Identifying some large middle percentage of a group of persons as showing normal behavior has the benefit of providing a precise criterion for deciding whom to consider abnormal, namely, those who fall outside this middle range. Attention to typical patterns of behavior also promotes *cultural sensitivity* and helps clinicians avoid seeing psychopathology where none exists. Cultural sensitivity in this regard consists of recognizing that what is normal for a person depends in part on the attitudes and behavior patterns that are valued in the groups to which the person belongs. Being aware of respects in which normality is relative to the customs, traditions, and expectations in a person's sociocultural context helps observers avoid inferring psychological disturbance from seemingly strange characteristics that may be common or even advantageous in a subculture with which the observers are unfamiliar.

Although useful for selecting "normal" comparison groups in experimental studies and for minimizing cultural bias in clinical evaluations, a statistical perspective on normality also has some disadvantages. When being normal is defined as being average, highly intelligent as well as intellectually limited people are considered abnormal, as are extremely happy people as well as those who are despondent, and highly creative as well as unproductive persons. Likewise, in a situation of mass panic or mob violence, the many who are acting impulsively or irrationally are considered normal, while the few who remain calm and clearheaded despite the crisis are labeled abnormal. Thus, being different does not necessarily mean being abnormal, as the statistical approach would imply. Moreover, it is unwise to assume that people who become acutely upset in a traumatic situation have no need for mental health assistance simply because most of the people around them are showing similar signs of distress.

As an alternative to defining normality in statistical terms as what is average or typical, normality defined as an ideal refers to a state of perfection that people aspire to but seldom attain. This utopian perspective, as reflected in the expression "Nobody's perfect," assumes that all people struggle with psychological limitations of one kind or another that prevent them from being as happy and successful as they would like to be. Regarding normality as an ideal way of being avoids statistical decisions that label unusually intelligent, happy, or productive people as abnormal. In addition, by calling attention to the potential for people to become more than what they are, the ideal perspective on normality encourages striving toward self-improvement and the active pursuit of greater happiness and success.

On the other hand, by implying that almost everyone is disturbed to some extent, normality as an ideal is a difficult concept to apply. Scientifically, it provides little help in separating normal from abnormal groups of people for research purposes. Practically, unless you take the questionable stance that everyone is more or less in need of therapy, it provides little help in determining whether a person's psychological limitations call for professional mental health attention.

Level of adjustment as a criterion for normality refers to whether people can cope reasonably well with their experiences in life, particularly with respect to being able to establish enjoyable interpersonal relationships and work constructively toward self-fulfilling goals. When normality is defined in these terms, abnormality becomes a state of mind or way of acting that prevents people from dealing adequately with the social and occupational demands of their daily lives. The adjustment approach to normality is more useful than either the average or the ideal perspective in determining which conditions psychopathologists should study and clinicians should treat. For this reason, normality defined as reasonably good adjustment serves the purposes of this book by providing a clear frame of reference for identifying the presence and severity of psychological disturbance.

Continuity and Discontinuity in Conceptualizing Psychopathology

Normal and abnormal behavior can be regarded as either continuous or discontinuous phenomena. From a continuity perspective, differences between disturbed and well-adjusted persons are *quantitative*. A quantitative approach conceives normal and abnormal behaviors as deriving from the same psychological dimensions or traits, with maladjusted individuals having more or less than the optimum amount of these traits. For example, a moderate amount of self-control contributes to good adjustment, whereas too little self-control can lead to pathological impulsivity and too much self-control, to pathological inhibition and rigidity. Similarly, a moderate capacity to reflect on yourself and your experiences tends to promote good adjustment, whereas insufficient reflection can lead to limited self-awareness, and excessive reflection can lead to paralyzing self-consciousness.

From a continuity perspective, every aspect of a disturbed person's behavior constitutes an exaggeration of normal ways of thinking, feeling, or acting. Any normal person can be expected on occasion to think, feel, or act the way disturbed people do, but the key consideration is one of degree. Normal people show maladaptive exaggerations of behavioral traits less frequently, to a lesser extent, and for shorter periods of time than people who are psychologically disturbed.

From a discontinuity perspective, by contrast, differences between normal and abnormal behavior are considered *qualitative,* that is, as differences in kind rather than degree. A qualitative approach emphasizes the study of abnormal psychology in its own right, rather than as an extension of normal psychology, to focus on the unique circumstances that give rise to psychological disturbance and on the special kinds of care and treatment that disturbed persons require.

Both of these approaches to the relationship between psychological normality and abnormality serve useful purposes. The continuity perspective helps mental health professionals and the general public avoid regarding disturbed persons as "different" from the rest of us. Being able to think of psychologically disordered people as having more or less of certain characteristics that we all have, instead of being in an entirely different dimension, fosters understanding of their problems and enlightened and sympathetic efforts to help them overcome these problems. By contrast, the discontinuity perspective has at times resulted in psychologically disturbed people being viewed as alien and unfathomable, with the regrettable consequence of relegating them to places where they are out of sight and out of mind and treating them with little regard for their humanity.

The continuity perspective on psychopathology also brings with it some downside, however, particularly with respect to minimizing the implications of apparent psychological disorder. Perceiving manifestations of disorder as being only an extension of normal behavior and as something we all have may be a prelude for insensitive advice ("Snap out of it"; "Pull yourself together"), unwarranted expectations ("He'll be okay in a few days"; "She just needs a good vacation, and she'll be fine"), and failure to recommend or seek needed professional care. In this regard, the discontinuity perspective can be very helpful by virtue of its stress on the uniqueness of psychopathology. A qualitative approach has the benefit of increasing the likelihood that disturbed people, their family and friends, and mental health professionals who evaluate them will recognize and respond to their needs for help.

Accordingly, the problems of psychologically disturbed persons and the case presentations in the chapters that follow are best viewed from both continuity and discontinuity perspectives. To what extent can the adjustment problems of these people be seen and understood as exaggerations (too much or too little) of characteristics common to all people? At the same time, to what extent have these tendencies to think, feel, and act in certain ways become sufficiently exaggerated to warrant a diagnostic classification and a treatment recommendation, both of which qualitatively distinguish these persons from most people?

Using a Classification System

Classification of disorders serves important purposes in research and clinical practice. To study the origins and effects of a condition and its course over time, researchers must be able to identify people who have that condition and would be appropriate participants in such studies. To draw on their experience and cumulative knowledge concerning treatment methods that are helpful to people with certain kinds of disorders, practitioners must be able to identify which disorders their patients have. Whether a particular classification system serves these research and practical purposes well depends on how reliable and valid the system is. A reliable classification is one in which (1) the individual categories are reasonably distinct from one another, and (2) knowledgeable professionals can agree reasonably well on which category best describes a patient's disorder. A valid classification is one in which the characteristics used to describe and differentiate among disorders have been confirmed by research findings to be in fact associated with these disorders.

With respect to classifying psychological disorders, the best known and most widely used system is the *Diagnostic and Statistical Manual of Mental Disorders* (*DSM*) published by the American Psychiatric Association. The *DSM* first appeared in 1952 and is now in its fourth edition. *DSM-IV* was published in 1994 and was followed in 2000 by a text revision, *DSM-IV-TR,* which lists the same categories of disorders as *DSM-IV* but includes some changes in how these categories are described. A key feature of the *DSM* is a multiaxial approach, in which a person being evaluated can be described on each of five separate axes, according to the following guidelines:

Axis I is used for reporting clinical disorders, which are conditions defined mainly by the kinds of symptoms people present. Symptoms in this context refer to maladaptive ways of thinking, feeling, or acting that are causing people to feel distressed, that are not a natural or welcome part of themselves, and that they would like to be rid of.

Axis II is used for designating personality disorders and mental retardation, which are conditions defined by the way people are and have been, rather than by symptoms they have developed and that come and go. The maladaptive characteristics of people with personality disorders consist of well-entrenched traits and behavioral dispositions that they are comfortable with and see no need to change, regardless of whatever difficulties may be resulting from them. Personality-disordered individuals would like to see the world change to accommodate their style and preferences, whereas symptom-disordered individuals would like to change themselves to fit more happily and productively into the world around them.

Axis III of the *DSM* is used for reporting any general medical conditions that may be relevant to understanding or treating a patient's mental disorder (e.g., cancer, seizure disorder, ulcerative colitis).

Axis IV is used to report psychosocial and environmental problems that have a bearing on the person's treatment needs and prognosis (e.g., family disruption, stressful work situation, homelessness).

Axis V is used for rating the overall adequacy of a patient's level of functioning from 1 to 100 according to criteria specified in a Global Assessment of Functioning (GAF) scale.

Despite its popularity and the years of effort that have gone into preparing and revising it, the *DSM* has some notable shortcomings. First, many of the criteria that are provided for individual categories of disorders are overlapping rather than discrete. Because some symptoms and personality traits characterize two or more of the disorders classified in the *DSM,* clinicians may have difficulty agreeing in their differential diagnosis of these disorders. To minimize this difficulty, the *DSM* recognizes that a person's disorder may meet criteria for more than one Axis I or Axis II condition, in which case all of the conditions that seem present should be diagnosed. This flexibility takes appropriate account of the fact that most psychological disorders are complex and multifaceted. However, it does not resolve the reliability issue, nor does it resolve how people should be selected for a research sample or some form of treatment on the basis of their diagnosed condition when they have been diagnosed with multiple conditions.

A second shortcoming of the *DSM* resides in its calling for categorical classification. Each *DSM* disorder comes with a list of criteria and instructions to diagnose the condition as present if a certain number of these criteria are met. The clinician decides categorically whether each criterion is met, determines whether the required number of positives is present, and decides on this basis, yes or no, whether the condition should be diagnosed. This categorical approach does not fully capture the variability of the disturbing symptoms and maladaptive personality characteristics that constitute psychopathology, particularly with respect to the degree to which they are present.

The alternative to categorical classification is a dimensional approach that considers not just whether five of eight criteria for a condition are met, for example, but also the differential implications of showing all eight instead of just five of the criteria, or four as opposed to the five necessary for a categorical diagnosis. Similarly, in a dimensional approach, the individual criteria for a condition can be examined not only for whether they are present, yes or no, but also for their severity and pervasiveness. Improved reliability and dimensionality in diagnostic classification are issues for the future in the study and treatment of psychopathology, and the readings recommended at the end of this chapter elaborate the current status and anticipated directions of research and practice in this area.

The *DSM* has, despite its shortcomings, fostered substantial improvements in diagnostic reliability and proved extremely valuable in promoting systematic research and treatment efforts with persons considered to have particular disorders. Empirical findings have also documented the validity of many of the descriptive and predictive statements in the *DSM*. Additionally, as a consequence of its widespread use, the *DSM* has facilitated communication among mental health professionals and between the mental health community and people in other walks of life whose work or interests touch on mental health issues. Among persons who are familiar with the *DSM* terminology or have access to a copy of the manual, reference to a *DSM* condition conveys exactly what is being referred to and why. The *DSM* classification was, accordingly, used to guide the selection of case studies for this book.

Selection of Case Studies

The 18 case studies in this book were selected to represent several broad categories of psychopathology identified in *DSM-IV-TR* and to illustrate some of the most commonly occurring disorders in each of these categories. In keeping with the previously described continuity perspective on psychopathology, in which psychological disturbance is conceptualized as a maladaptive exaggeration of normal ways of thinking, feeling, and acting, the first section of the book moves from normality to Adjustment Disorder in Chapter 2. Of all the conditions codified in the *DSM,* Adjustment Disorder represents the least deviation from psychological normality. Adjustment disorders consist of an abnormal and maladaptive reaction to a stressful situation, but they are typically short-lived and have no implications for persistent or recurring psychopathology.

When psychological traits or dispositions become persistently maladaptive, they result in personality disorders. Chapters 3 through 7 present case illustrations of five relatively common and dramatic types of personality disorder: Dependent, Borderline, Antisocial, Schizotypal, and Paranoid. Turning next to symptomatic disorders, in which people experience distressing and unwelcome thoughts, feelings, and action tendencies, the third section of the text illustrates five types of anxiety and somatoform disorders: Panic Disorder with Agoraphobia, Obsessive-Compulsive Disorder, Posttraumatic Stress Disorder, Generalized Anxiety Disorder, and Pain Disorder (Chapters 8 through 12).

Two specifically focused categories of symptomatic disorder, identity disorders and habit disorders, are the focus of the next two sections. Identity disorders are illustrated by Dissociative Identity Disorder in Chapter 13 and Gender Identity Disorder in Chapter 14. Habit disorders are addressed with a case involving addiction (Polysubstance Dependence in Chapter 15) and a case of eating disorder (Bulimia Nervosa in Chapter 16). The text concludes with case illustrations of the most serious forms of psychopathology, mood disorders and schizophrenia: Depressive Disorder in Chapter 17, Bipolar Disorder in Chapter 18, and Schizophrenia in Chapter 19.

Recommended Readings

Beutler, L. E., & Malik, M. L. (2002). *Rethinking the DSM: A psychological perspective.* Washington, DC: American Psychological Association.

Blashfield, R. K., & Lively, W. J. (1999). Classification. In T. Millon, P. H. Blaney, & R. D. Davis (Eds.), *Oxford textbook of psychopathology* (pp. 3–28). New York: Oxford University Press.

Nathan, P. E., & Langenbucher, J. (2003). Diagnosis and classification. In G. Stricker & T. A. Widiger (Eds.), *Clinical psychology* (pp. 3–26). Volume 8 in I. B. Weiner (Editor-in-Chief), *Handbook of psychology.* Hoboken, NJ: Wiley.

Offer, D., & Sabshin, J. (Eds.). (1991). *The diversity of normal behavior.* New York: Basic Books.

References

American Psychiatric Association. (1994). *Diagnostic and statistical manual of mental disorders* (4th ed.). Washington, DC: Author.

American Psychiatric Association. (2000). *Diagnostic and statistical manual of mental disorders* (4th ed., text rev.). Washington, DC: Author.

CHAPTER 2

Adjustment Disorder

Theodore Millon

It was a quiet Sunday afternoon when I got up from my recliner to answer the telephone. "Jerry," I said, after my caller identified himself, "it's been some time since we spoke last. How have you been? What's up? Are you in town?" Jerry's voice seemed to be trembling, most unlike him, a very accomplished psychologist from another Eastern university, a person of note who I considered to be a mentor of mine. "Yes," he answered, "I'm here visiting my son, Paul. You know he's a student at your college . . . been here since late August, three or four months now."

Speaking slowly and hesitatingly, Jerry began to tell me that Paul "was having trouble, had suicidal thoughts, had difficulty getting up in the morning to go to class, seemed lately to spend the day sitting in his dorm room alone, staring toward the lawn below, crying, thinking of jumping out the window, scared and confused." Jerry asked if it would be all right if Paul called me; would I be willing to talk to him and see if I could be of help? He went on to say that he was very worried about Paul, particularly because Paul's mother, Jerry's wife, had experienced numerous depressive and alcoholic episodes in her life and had periodically been hospitalized.

Paul called me the next morning and came to my university office the following day. There I met a tall, slender, nice-looking young man of 18, dressed more formally than most typical college students—jacket, tie, slacks rather than jeans, well-shined shoes rather than sneakers. We talked casually about the college and his decision to accept its scholarship offer rather than several others he had received elsewhere. At no time during our conversation did he look up at me. His voice was subdued and his eyes invariably downcast.

In light of Paul's sad and constrained manner, his suicidal ideation, and his family history of emotional disturbance, I thought it would be useful to ask if he would be willing to take some psychological tests that afternoon. He agreed, and I had a graduate student of mine administer to him the Rorschach Inkblot Method and a new instrument I had been developing at the time, the Millon College

Counseling Inventory (MCCI). I reviewed the results that evening and called Paul to come by my office the next day, which he did.

The Rorschach results revealed that Paul was an emotionally controlled person, inclined to be somewhat uptight and compulsive in dealing with people and situations. However, there was no evidence in his Rorschach responses of any serious psychopathology, nor did any of the usual indicators of depression appear on this test. The MCCI was very helpful in confirming the positive picture on the Rorschach of Paul's basic psychological stability. There were no MCCI elevations on major clinical scales (e.g., depressive pessimism, reality distortions) nor were there alcohol or drug abuse indicators, which I had anticipated as a possibility. On the other hand, a moderate to severe extent of suicidal thinking was confirmed. In addition, MCCI scales for "Expressed Concerns" identified a markedly low level of self-esteem. Notable in particular were high (problematic) scores on scales designed to measure loneliness, homesickness, romantic difficulties, academic concerns, career confusions, and spiritual doubts.

With these findings in hand, I concluded that Paul was exhibiting a clinically significant impairment in his social and academic functioning that had developed within a short time after he left home and entered what he experienced as a stressful university setting. His degree of anguish appreciably exceeded that which would normally be expected among new college students. In each of these respects, Paul met criteria for Adjustment Disorder with Mixed Anxiety and Depressed Mood, as defined in the *Diagnostic and Statistical Manual of Mental Disorders* (*DSM-IV-TR*) of the American Psychiatric Association (APA, 2000). Two additional characteristics of an adjustment disorder are the absence of any of the other disorders codified in the *DSM*, which was the case for Paul, and the disappearance of symptoms within six months following resolution of a stressful situational problem, which remained to be seen.

As for Paul's developing an adjustment disorder, going away to college had upset the routines and daily certainty to which he was accustomed back home. As a somewhat overorganized, perhaps compulsive young man, he had acquired regular and predictable methods of structuring his days. The demands of establishing new coping methods suitable for dealing with the requirements of college life, and having to do so without readily available support from his family and local friends, led to a degree of disorientation and a temporary shortfall in his usual capacity for self-control. Deprived of his habitual guideposts for how to function effectively, he could not find ways to arrange his life comfortably. He worried in particular about the consequences of being seen as a failure and, hence, a serious disappointment to his parents.

Paul's serious self-doubts resulted in his being unable to take any course of action. His dread of being humiliated and of provoking condemnation from those whose approval he sought generated considerable nervous tension and prominent guilt feelings. His paralysis of action resulted in his procrastinating on all matters and was intensified by fears of taking any potential risks. He became inert, stationary, immobile, and unable even to make an effort to pull himself together. He decided it would be best to withdraw from life, to retreat and no longer have to face the awful reality of his shameful discomfitures, his physical immobility, and his psychic collapse; and he could not help but think that this retreat might call for him to put an end to his very being.

Paul and I spoke several times. I then encouraged him to join a college counseling group for first-year students, a group that one of my graduate assistants had recently begun to co-lead. Within a few sessions, Paul began to see that the shame and guilt he felt were not at all that unusual among his freshman peers. He learned how to budget his time and arrange his schedules more efficiently, and he acquired a few good friends with whom he could talk about college life. He began to attend athletic events, started dating, and, most importantly, was able to reestablish his sense of personal worth and self-esteem. When I next saw Paul on campus two or three months later, he said that his life was going well, and he conveyed best regards and thanks to me from his appreciative father. His rapid recovery and return to normal daily functioning following some relief of his situational stress provided further confirmation that the condition for which he had needed help was an adjustment disorder.

Reference

American Psychiatric Association. (2000). *Diagnostic and statistical manual of mental disorders* (4th ed., text rev.). Washington, DC: Author.

PART TWO

Disorders of Personality

CHAPTER 3

Dependent Personality Disorder

ROBERT F. BORNSTEIN

John came for treatment because, at age 30, he had never had a satisfying romantic relationship. As John related the details of his situation during our initial meeting, the problem became clear: John was so anxious around women, he found it impossible to make even the most minor relationship decision without getting his partner's approval. Even then, John apologized repeatedly for all sorts of minor glitches—long movie lines, crowded restaurants, traffic snarls—though most of these things were hardly his fault. John was preoccupied with the idea that he would be rejected when he got close to someone. As a result, he sought constant reassurance from each romantic partner, trying desperately to convince himself that his partner was not about to abandon him.

The result of all this reassurance-seeking was a sort of self-fulfilling prophecy. John's insecure, overdependent behavior destroyed each of his romantic relationships, as the women in his life eventually tired of taking all the decision-making responsibility on themselves and playing the "mommy" role. His worries about being rejected created a situation that virtually ensured rejection, time and time again.

Interview Behavior

As John described his problems, he certainly seemed insecure. He had great difficulty maintaining eye contact when he spoke, and he hesitated and stammered as he struggled to talk about his feelings. John prefaced many of his statements with self-deprecating comments such as, "I'm not really much of . . . ," and "I've never been very good at . . ." His lack of self-confidence came through loud and clear. John's interview behavior provided important clinical information in two ways. First, it showed that his insecurity was not limited to romantic relationships but arose as well in talking with a mental health professional. Second, John's behavior indicated that the intensity of his dependency was actually greater than he realized. He saw himself as only mildly dependent, but his manner of presenting himself suggested a more severe problem.

Developmental History

Questioning revealed that John's problematic dependency dated back many years. John had developed a serious illness when he was 4 years old, and from that day forward, his mother became extremely over-protective and treated him as if he were fragile and weak. John had difficulty adjusting to school, becoming panicked when his mother tried to drop him off at the start of the day. Even when he did accept the separation from his mother that school required, John never fit in well with his peer group, preferring to spend time with the teacher instead. This pattern continued throughout John's adolescence, with his developing a strong attachment to each new authority figure in his life (teachers, coaches, clergy, etc.), but never establishing close ties with his peers.

Diagnostic Profile

Without question, John fulfilled the criteria for Dependent Personality Disorder (DPD) as specified in the *Diagnostic and Statistical Manual of Mental Disorders* (*DSM-IV-TR*) of the American Psychiatric Association (2000). The *DSM* requires a person to exhibit five of eight particular symptoms to receive a DPD diagnosis, and John exhibited at least six of these symptoms: difficulty making decisions, needing others to assume responsibility, difficulty expressing disagreement, difficulty doing things on his own, feeling uncomfortable when alone, and being preoccupied with fears of abandonment.

In addition to constituting a clear instance of DPD, John's case was intriguing from a clinical perspective because of his lack of insight into his own nature. Although John's dependent behavior was extreme and pervasive, he had little awareness of this behavior and its impact on his life experiences. In this respect, John's case illustrates a limitation in the *DSM* approach to diagnosis. The *DSM* criteria are based largely on patient self-reports, but patients—especially those with personality disorders—do not always perceive their behavior accurately. Even when personality-disordered patients are aware of their symptoms, they are not always willing to describe these symptoms to a psychologist or other mental health professional.

Case Formulation

John's lack of insight into his problematic dependency suggests that, even though he showed a relatively high level of *self-attributed* (i.e., self-reported) dependency, he had an even higher level of *implicit* (i.e., unacknowledged) dependency. From a psychoanalytic perspective, it would be concluded that John's unconscious dependency needs were stronger than his conscious dependency needs. This is a common pattern, especially among men, because in many Western cultures (including ours), men are taught not to admit feeling helpless, needy, and dependent. Some men—like John—do not admit being this way even to themselves.

When patients like John show higher implicit than self-attributed dependency needs, their therapy often begins by helping them gain insight into those aspects of their functioning that they are unable or unwilling to see. Only after DPD patients become aware of the impact that dependency is having on their social and work relationships can they begin to alter this behavior and find better, more adaptive ways to deal with life's challenges.

Recommended Readings

Bornstein, R. F. (1993). *The dependent personality.* New York: Guilford Press.

Bornstein, R. F. (1997). Dependent personality disorder in the *DSM-IV* and beyond. *Clinical Psychology: Science and Practice, 4,* 175–187.

Livesley, W. J., Schroeder, M. L., & Jackson, D. N. (1990). Dependent personality disorder and attachment problems. *Journal of Personality Disorders, 4,* 131–140.

Overholser, J. C. (1996). The dependent personality and interpersonal problems. *Journal of Nervous and Mental Diseases, 184,* 8–16.

Pincus, A. L., & Wilson, K. R. (2001). Interpersonal variability in dependent personality. *Journal of Personality, 69,* 223–251.

Reference

American Psychiatric Association. (2000). *Diagnostic and statistical manual of mental disorders* (4th ed., text rev.). Washington, DC: Author.

CHAPTER 4

Borderline Personality Disorder

CHARLES SWENSON AND MARSHA M. LINEHAN

When initially seen for the present evaluation, JP was a 26-year-old unmarried Caucasian woman who was soon to be discharged from a state mental hospital. She had been hospitalized for the first time while a freshman in college, following a suicide attempt. Over the next seven years, she spent more than 80% of her time in various hospitals, admitted on each occasion for management and treatment of high suicide risk. Now she was being referred for dialectical behavior therapy (DBT), which was to be continued on an outpatient basis following her discharge.

From the perspective of the referring treatment team, JP's main problem was the high frequency and life-threatening nature of her self-injurious behavior. In addition to actual suicide attempts, her history included dangerous but nonlethal instances of overdosing, hanging and self-strangulation, cutting and burning herself, and carbon monoxide poisoning. From JP's perspective, however, these suicidal behaviors were not the problem. Instead, she said, they served as solutions to intense and unbearable feeling states that she repeatedly experienced.

History of Presenting Problem

Although JP recalled feeling depressed during high school, she was able to do well academically. Her academic success continued through her first semester of college, but her level of depression increased as the months passed, along with accompanying anxiety. She did not communicate her distress to anyone because she wanted to avoid burdening others or upsetting her family. When at age 19 her misery became intolerable, she swallowed more than 100 Tylenol tablets with the intention of ending her life. She survived the overdose but was kept in the hospital for 27 days. Only years later did she reveal that this overdose had been an attempt to flee from a flood of intrusive memories and terrible nightmares relating to a childhood history of sexual abuse.

In the three months following this first hospitalization, JP was admitted and discharged from psychiatric hospital units on three separate occasions. At the conclusion of the last of these three admissions, she was transferred to a long-term, psychotherapeutically oriented psychiatric hospital in the Midwest, where she remained for the next two years. During that hospital stay, she remained free of suicide attempts and self-injurious acts and made some progress toward improved adjustment. She worked at a job and had a boyfriend, with whom she twice became pregnant. In her opinion, it was these pregnancies that provided her the motivation and hope she needed to refrain from harming herself. Both times, however, she had abortions at her boyfriend's insistence.

JP eventually broke off her relationship with this boyfriend, and, about the same time, found it necessary for financial reasons to discontinue her long-term psychotherapy. Shortly thereafter, she once more became intensely suicidal. She was hospitalized in the psychiatric unit of a general hospital, where she engaged almost daily (more than 60 times in one month) in apparently determined efforts to injure or kill herself. She swallowed pills, cut and attempted to hang herself, and, on one occasion, set herself on fire. She was desperate to reduce her misery and to die.

Having drained her personal finances and exhausted her insurance coverage, JP next reentered the public mental health system in her home state and spent nine months in a long-term state hospital unit. During this hospitalization, she reported for the first time that she had been repeatedly sexually abused as a child by members of her family and by neighbors and strangers as well. At the end of this nine-month admission, she was discharged to an aftercare program in which her hospital psychotherapist continued to work with her on an outpatient basis. For the next four months, she lived in an apartment, attended therapy, worked in a social services job, and remained free from self-injury and suicide attempts.

JP's interactions with her family became problematic during this time, however, particularly with respect to an uncle who had allegedly had sexual intercourse with her when she was a child. This uncle began making sexual advances toward her, which she hated but felt paralyzed by and unable to oppose. The four months of initially promising aftercare ended with her being hospitalized for suicidal urges and self-mutilation, which had been occurring in the context of flashbacks, nightmares, intrusive thoughts, and dissociative episodes. In the course of the following six months, she was discharged and readmitted to community hospitals for suicidal behavior on at least six occasions. Finally, she was readmitted to the long-term state hospital unit, where this time she remained for seven months. During this hospitalization, she was introduced to DBT through participation in a DBT skills training group. The plan was then formulated for her to begin individual DBT following her discharge, while living in a group home, continuing to participate in a DBT skills training group, and attending a day treatment program not involving DBT methods.

Again, however, careful planning and dedicated professional care proved insufficient to stem the tide of JP's disorder. Two days following this discharge from the state hospital, she was admitted to a medical unit after overdosing with more than 100 Tylenol tablets. During the next eight months, she was discharged and readmitted four more times after only brief stays at home, each time subsequent to harming herself in some way. During the seven years from the time of her initial hospitalization, JP had spent fewer than 12 months out of hospitals, her longest period in the community lasting only four months. She had engaged in hundreds of incidents of suicidal and self-injurious behaviors, many of which proved almost fatal.

Personal History and Diagnostic Formulation

As a patient, JP was frustrating and frightening to those who attempted to understand and treat her. At times, she would present herself in a calm, thoughtful, self-controlled manner and pledge not to harm or kill herself. Shortly thereafter, without warning, she would suddenly become excitable and impulsive and engage in self-injurious behaviors that were at times highly lethal. Staff and therapists, who were convinced by her controlled presentations and believed in her assurances, lost confidence in their ability to predict her actions and protect her from herself.

JP would also talk insightfully about certain kinds of high-stress situations that she should avoid (e.g., movies about sexual abuse, extended visits with her parents) and then expose herself to these situations anyway, usually with the result of being precipitated into self-injurious behavior. Mental health professionals working with her clashed over the question of whether she should be treated at all outside an inpatient setting. Instances of JP harming herself were in reality at least as likely to occur while she was hospitalized as when she was in the community. Facing JP's possible suicide and their liability for it, however, anxious professionals tended to overlook this piece of information. As for JP, she consistently preferred to be out of hospitals, and she repeatedly made commitments to staying safe—commitments that, as already indicated, she rarely kept for more than a few days.

With further respect to the sexual abuse that she alleged, JP said that her aunt and uncle had forced her from the ages of 7 to 14 to engage in sexual acts, including fellatio, cunnilingus, and intercourse, under threat that she would be killed if she refused. She alleged further that they had continued their sexual advances to her in her adult years, even between hospitalizations. Yet, she stated that she still wanted to be near them because she loved them and believed that she was no longer in danger of being abused by them. On the other hand, when JP came to suspect that her aunt and uncle were sexually abusing her cousin, their 14-year-old son, JP reported them to child protective services. In the ensuing investigation, the aunt and uncle denied these allegations. Nothing was said to JP about this episode, but for a time her family treated her as a pariah. When the aunt and uncle were confronted with the sexual abuse allegations by JP's treatment team, they neither denied nor confirmed them. They simply expressed a wish for JP to be able to come to their home on passes from the hospital, and, as far as is known, they did refrain from any sexual advances when she visited them during this particular hospitalization.

JP was the second of two children, who grew up with their parents in a rural area. Her mother worked as an administrator of social service programs and her father as a taxi driver. According to JP's reports, she suffered as a child from prolonged exposure to physical, emotional, and sexual abuse at the hands of family members, friends, neighbors, and strangers. Although she did not provide many details of this abuse, she did say that, between the ages of 4 and 23, she had been raped at knifepoint or gunpoint by perpetrators from all four of these groups. Whenever she mentioned the sexual abuse to any family members, she said, she was met with vigorous denial and harsh warnings to stop stirring up trouble. There was a history of substance abuse problems in her family, and both her mother and her sister were known to have experienced depressive episodes and made suicide attempts.

In JP's own mind, struggling with depression and suicidal thoughts had been part of her life at least since she was age 7. She recalls discovering as a 7-year-old that she could immediately relieve tension and anxiety by cutting herself, and she continued from that time on to use harming herself as a way of feeling less distressed. JP also participated in what was a family pattern of keeping secret from the outside world unmentionable behaviors such as substance abuse and incest. Although she did not allege that her own parents had sexually abused her, her allegiance to the family code of secrecy, as a way of presenting an apparently competent "mask" to the world, included her never telling her parents about what her aunt and uncle had done. JP considered herself to be a highly sensitive but also a loyal person, who joined with others in her family in creating an illusion of apparent competence.

Along with her sensitivity, JP was a highly intelligent person who, as previously mentioned, had been an excellent student. In hopeful moments at age 26, she imagined herself returning to school and becoming a biologist, and she contemplated marrying and having children. More often, however, she anticipated that she would some day die of suicide. Life would only be worthwhile, she said, if she could live with her parents and sister and have frequent contact with her aunt and uncle.

During the course of her many hospitalizations and at the time when she began the treatment program described in this chapter, JP was considered to be showing primarily a Borderline Personality Disorder (BPD). As defined in the American Psychiatric Association (2000) *Diagnostic and Statistical Manual of Mental Disorders* (*DSM-IV-TR*), BPD consists of a chronic, persistent, and maladaptive pattern of unstable mood states, self-images, and interpersonal relationships, combined with potentially self-damaging impulsivity.

More specifically, persons with BPD typically experience intense and rapidly shifting emotions. They are quick to become deeply depressed or highly anxious, and they may be especially prone to irritability and flashes of anger, or even fury. Often, their emotional states result in their being described by others as moody or ill-tempered, but most notable about BPD moods is their intensity, unpredictability, and the suddenness with which they come and go.

Recurrent suicidal attempts, suicide threats, and nonsuicidal self-injuries, including self-mutilating behavior, so apparent in JP's history, are relatively common among BPD persons and contribute to identifying the presence of this disorder. Persons with BPD are also at elevated risk for engaging in a broad range of impulsive and dysfunctional activities without apparent regard for their potential consequences. These include alcohol and drug abuse and binges of spending, eating, gambling, and sexual promiscuity.

The unstable self-images that characterize BPD are manifest in persistent and troubling uncertainty about the individual's sense of identity. Persons with this disorder frequently struggle to answer, with only fleeting success, questions such as: What kind of person am I? What do I believe in? How am I likely to respond in certain kinds of situations? What do I want to do with my life? As for their unstable interpersonal relationships, persons with BPD characteristically show intense involvements with people in which they often vacillate between idealizing them (i.e., thinking they're wonderful) and devaluing them (i.e., thinking they're terrible). The intensity of their relationships, together with their sensitivity to rejection, often leads the borderline individual into alternating urges to approach or separate from these relationships.

Many of these defining characteristics of BPD are apparent in the information presented thus far about JP, and others emerge in the course of presenting her treatment with DBT. In addition, JP had also been diagnosed at various times as showing features of Posttraumatic Stress Disorder, Panic Disorder, and Major Depressive Disorder. Over time, she had reported flashbacks, nightmares, extreme terror, memory lapses, insomnia, numbness, and even some apparent hallucinatory experiences (although not of sufficient duration to suggest schizophrenia). She also showed some features of bulimia, with episodes of bingeing and purging, and her self-harmful behavior since she left college included episodes of alcohol abuse, laxative abuse, abuse of prescription drugs, and excessive gambling. She had been treated at various times with a long list of antidepressant, mood stabilizing, antianxiety, and antipsychotic medications. Although the impact of these medications was difficult to assess, some seemed to lessen her ruminations and reduce her anxieties. Even with these medications, however, she experienced almost constant intense anxiety that was relieved most effectively by her self-injurious behaviors.

As typified in JP's case, persons with BPD are often difficult to treat. The intensity of their affect interferes with their being able to examine themselves and reflect on their behavior in a constructive manner. Their ambivalent attitudes when in intense relationships and their fears of being abandoned are typically as evident with the therapist as with other intense relationships, with resulting alternation between desperately wanting a closer relationship with the therapist than is appropriate and, on the other hand, emotional shutdown and withdrawal from the relationship or angry outbursts toward the therapist when feeling threatened or hurt. Their impulsivity introduces into the treatment a constant risk of ill-advised or dangerous behaviors that undermine the goals of the therapy or prevent it from continuing, with suicide the ultimate instance of such behaviors. These characteristics of BPD patients severely challenge therapists' ability to monitor their own therapeutic behaviors, manage their own limits in responding to cries for help from the BPD individual, ward off potential burnout, and maintain the equilibrium necessary to sustain steady progress in the treatment. DBT, to which we turn next, was developed as a method of meeting these challenges.

Treatment with Dialectical Behavior Therapy

DBT is a staged treatment in which the case formulation consists in part of identifying stages in the patient's disorder and a therapeutic focus appropriate for that stage. The treatment begins with a pretreatment stage devoted to establishing agreements concerning how the patient and the therapist will work together and to strengthening the patient's commitment to this process. Stage 1 of the disorder is characterized by the presence of severe and disabling behaviors that pose a pervasive threat to the treatment, to the patient's life, or to the quality of the patient's life. In this stage, the therapist works with the patient to replace behavioral dyscontrol with behavioral stability and safety.

Stage 2 is characterized by less disordered behavioral patterns than in Stage 1, but by symptoms of stress and the presence of suppressed and painful emotions. In this stage, the therapist helps the patient to process painful emotional experiences that have not been resolved, including episodes of trauma. In Stage 3, the therapist helps the patient work on problems in living, including the establishment of self-respect. In Stage 4, the therapist helps the patient achieve more enduring episodes of joy and a sense of freedom in life.

Each stage has a set of targets, for example, reducing life-threatening behaviors and behaviors that interfere with treatment in Stage 1. Certain treatment strategies are stage appropriate as well, such as strategies for enhancing commitment during the pretreatment stage and exposure procedures for addressing unresolved trauma in Stage 2. Hence, determining the stage of a patient's treatment is crucial in DBT case conceptualization for selecting treatment strategies to be employed.

JP returned repeatedly to suicidal and other Stage 1 behavioral patterns after appearing to make progress beyond them, which led some professionals and friends of hers to doubt her level of commitment.

Nevertheless, her DBT therapist and other professionals closely involved with her were satisfied that she and they were mutually committed to common goals that included the reduction of suicidal behaviors, the strengthening of treatment, and the achievement of higher life quality. In spite of this strong mutual commitment, powerful psychological forces repeatedly superseded her dedication to safety and maintained suicidal behaviors in her repertoire. JP was, accordingly, at the beginning of DBT evaluated as being in Stage 1, with a goal of establishing behavioral control and stability. As a further obstacle to progress in her treatment, JP had shown a passive approach to solving life problems and had occasionally missed sessions of individual therapy and skill groups. In the month of preparatory work with her DBT therapist before discharge from the hospital, considerable attention was paid to strengthening her commitment to treatment and assessing the determining factors in her repeated suicidal behaviors.

Primary Targets

DBT is a treatment for individuals with multiple serious problem behaviors. Attempting to target at the same time all of many such problem behaviors can create chaos in the treatment. The DBT therapist and patient work together to specify a list of treatment goals, which then leads to a list of particular target behaviors. These target behaviors are prioritized so that the most serious problems are targeted early in the treatment. The prioritized target list drives the goals of the overall treatment and of each treatment session, with the therapist targeting the highest priority target behavior that has been occurring since the prior session.

The pretreatment stage for JP targeted increasing the intensity and frequency of her experiencing and communicating commitment to the therapy and its goals. A second target in this stage was the development of a sense of confidence in the therapist that the two could work productively together and that DBT would be an effective treatment. For Stage 1, where her treatment began, the following list of prioritized targets was established:

1. Decrease life-threatening behaviors.

   a. Decrease hanging, overdoses, setting self on fire, carbon monoxide poisoning, neck cutting, swallowing objects, with intent to die.

   b. Decrease nonsuicidal self-injuries (cutting, strangulation, overdosing, purging, with intent to injure herself without intent to die).

   c. Decrease suicidal and self-injurious urges.

   d. Decrease suicidal affect (e.g., "Realizing I could kill myself makes me feel much better").

   e. Decrease suicidal expectancies (e.g., "If I die, my problems will be over").

2. Decrease the patient's treatment-interfering behaviors.

   a. Decrease secret-keeping and lying.

   b. Decrease passivity in collaboration to solve problems.

   c. Decrease hospitalizations that interfere with treatment.

   d. Decrease dissociating in sessions or skill groups.

3. Decrease the therapist's treatment-interfering behaviors.

   a. Decrease disrespectful behaviors toward the patient (e.g., returning phone calls only after unnecessarily long periods of time).

   b. Decrease significant imbalances in the therapist (e.g., excessive nurturance or excessive coldness, excessive flexibility or excessive rigidity).

4. Decrease quality-of-life-interfering behaviors.

   a. Dealing with family—decrease "dangerous" contacts with family members (e.g., contacting her aunt and uncle when lonely or stressed, driving home at a moment's notice, submitting to sexual demands, keeping secrets in the family).

b. Eating disorder behaviors—decrease bingeing, vomiting, laxative use, fasting, overexercising, diet pills, extreme dieting, and mindless eating.

c. School and work problems—decrease procrastination, poor sleep, and being "sick" too often.

d. Social and interpersonal life—decrease isolating, shying away, passivity, staying in the background, leading people on, and saying no too late.

e. Financially irresponsible behaviors—decrease shopping sprees, catalogue shopping with credit card, and over-spending account limit.

f. Sleep-interfering behaviors—decrease computer games and cleaning late at night.

g. Spirituality—decrease confusion about spirituality.

5. Increase use of behavioral skills.

JP's treatment plan following achievement of these Stage 1 targets consisted of efforts to decrease her stress disorder, grief, and misery in Stage 2; attempts to increase her self-respect and effective pursuit of personal goals in Stage 3; and working to increase her enduring joy and meaning in life in Stage 4.

Secondary Targets

In addressing primary target behaviors, the DBT therapist routinely encounters six dysfunctional behavioral patterns that interfere with achieving them. These obstacles to progress constitute secondary targets in the treatment. Specification of the exact nature of these six dysfunctional behavioral patterns in a given case facilitates precise efforts to overcome them in each therapy session. All six patterns were prominent in working with JP, and they are listed next in order from the most to the least prominent.

1. Apparent Competence

JP's manner of presenting herself, including her tone of voice, the content of what she says, and her facial expressions, convey calmness, stability, and safety, when in fact she is intensely anxious, uncertain of herself, and on the verge of acting impulsively. She involuntarily "masks" her distress, so even good observers cannot detect it. This apparent competence prevents other people, including at times her therapist, from recognizing her current emotional state, understanding her ideas and beliefs, and being able to provide validation for her thoughts and feelings. JP's failure to communicate her distress adequately, despite what she often believed was adequate communication, leads her to feel that it is unrecognized by others, which exacerbates her feelings of isolation. Suicidal behaviors that are precipitated by this sense of isolation then catch others by surprise. Accordingly, a secondary target in treating JP consisted of increasing her recognition and effective expression of distress to others in the service of enhanced communication and help seeking.

2. Active Passivity

JP is often energetic but passive in treatment sessions in the sense of actively seeking solutions to her problems from the therapist without making much effort to find solutions for herself. The same pattern could be seen in her daily life, where in the face of problems, she often shuts down emotionally and cognitively rather than actively focusing on what she could do differently to solve the problem at hand. The secondary target for JP was to increase active and effective problem solving as ways of dealing with her negative emotions and uncontrollable impulses.

3. Crisis-Generating Behaviors

JP engages in a variety of behaviors that increase her vulnerability to crises and bad decisions, for example, visiting her aunt and uncle when she is emotionally distressed. She shows poor judgment in this regard, sometimes surprisingly so in contrast to her sincerely expressed determination to avoid situations known to precipitate impulsive dysfunctional behaviors. The secondary target in this instance consisted of increasing use of good decision making as a way of reducing crises even when she is under the pressure of strong emotions.

4. Inhibited Experiencing (Inhibited Grieving)

JP has so many memories and triggers that set off feelings of panic, despair, anger, hopelessness, shame, guilt, and fear that she can barely consider these memories or encounter these triggers without becoming overwhelmingly distressed and drawn to self-injurious acts. She devotes considerable time and energy to limiting her exposure to these triggers, whether internal or external. Over time, she developed a pattern of automatic cognitive and behavioral escape responses to distress cues, leading to an inability to process or experience emotions in a therapeutic manner. Although direct and prolonged exposure to memories and cues associated with childhood abuse were put off until Stage 2 of her therapy, this difficulty called for a secondary target of increasing her capacity to experience without immediately escaping from disturbing memories and the sensations and thoughts associated with negative emotional responses.

5. Emotional Vulnerability

The intensity of JP's emotional reactions to triggering events and the rapidity with which these events cause her to "swirl into the abyss" make it difficult for her to get hold of her mind and put an end to her psychological pain. The secondary target for this problem was to find ways of increasing her ability to regulate painful emotions effectively.

6. Self-Invalidation

JP hates her body, criticizes herself for being weak and disloyal, expects others to evaluate her in a harsh manner, thinks of herself as boring and uninteresting, and generally considers herself a freak and a weirdo. Her reflexive self-criticism helps her at times to avoid feelings of hurt, disappointment, and anger toward others, but it also interferes with her acquiring adaptive social skills. To deal with this problem, a secondary treatment target was reducing her self-deprecating statements and increasing her validation of herself as a worthwhile person.

Behavioral Chain Analysis

The assessment of controlling variables that drives a given repetitive dysfunctional behavior is undertaken in DBT by way of a behavioral chain analysis. Over time, these repeated analyses further build the case conceptualization. The following behavioral chain, spelled out during a therapy session that directly followed a suicide attempt, was typical for JP.

One Monday afternoon at a group home where JP was living shortly after a brief hospital stay, she cut herself and tied a plastic bag over her head in a suicide attempt. The target behavior that was analyzed in her subsequent therapy session was the suicide attempt with the bag. Typically in DBT, the behavioral chain analysis consists of five chronological components: vulnerability factors, prompting event, links in the chain leading from prompting event to problem behavior, the problem behavior itself, and consequences of the problem behavior.

Vulnerability Factors

Vulnerability factors are those contextual events and states of mind that give the prompting event power at the time that it occurs. Several factors rendered JP vulnerable to negative emotional arousal and subsequent suicidal behavior at the time of this incident. She had been out of the hospital for only two days and was anxious about reintegrating into her community residence. She was experiencing constant intense anxiety, bordering at times on panic. She had gained 40 pounds in recent months, perhaps in part because of her mood-stabilizing medication, and she was loathing her body. She had gone to the beach with other residents of her group home on the previous Saturday and had neglected to apply sunscreen, which resulted in a painful sunburn. As a result, she had become dehydrated and required three liters of normal saline at an emergency room. The additional fluid load led her to feel bloated and to hate even more the way her body looked. Her physical pain and discomfort from the sunburn, as well as her hatred of how her body looked to her, led JP to skip her day treatment program that Monday and remain at the home, where there was little structure for her day.

Prompting Event

While watching TV, she turned to a movie that portrayed a family's struggle with sexual abuse. She watched the movie until a staff member at the residence came in, saw what she was watching, and suggested that she turn it off.

Links in the Chain

While watching the movie, JP felt drawn to it and disgusted by it. She found it validating to see in the movie that sexual abuse does happen in families, which helped her to challenge her confusion and intermittent denial about her own abuse and to "feel more real." She felt anxious, ashamed, and disgusted, and yet she did not want to interrupt the experience. Turning the movie off "broke the spell," but during and after the movie, she had flashbacks to her own abuse. She then went to her room to be alone, only to have her fears and intrusive memories become more intense, and in this context she began to think of suicide as a good "way out."

JP then told a staff member at the residence about her anxiety and intrusive thoughts. She paged her therapist twice, with hopes of talking about the pain and anxiety, but he did not call back soon enough to intervene by coaching her in skills for dealing with her distress. Her ruminations continued to the accompaniment of intensified feelings of self-loathing and loneliness. She considered trying to reach her therapist on his cell phone or at home, which he had recommended she do under circumstances like these, but she thought that this would be too intrusive. The particular staff member on duty at the time was someone JP didn't like and whose interventions felt "invalidating" to her. Hence, she decided not to communicate her distress or to seek help from this "on-site coach."

Alone in her room and continuing to think of suicide as a way to end her current intolerable distress, JP took a pair of scissors she had borrowed from the group home office and cut herself superficially on her thumb, arm, and leg, "testing the scissors for sharpness." As she cut, she became afraid that she might actually kill or seriously injure herself and suddenly did not want to die. She called for the staff member and gave her the scissors. While talking with the staff member—which did nothing to reduce her hopelessness and despair—JP decided that she would kill herself to stop the pain and escape from her loathed body. She told the staff member that she would be safe, and the staff member left the room.

Problem Behavior

JP shut the door of her room after the staff member left, emptied the trash bag, placed the bag over her head, and secured it around her neck.

Consequences

JP felt relief as she prepared to die, but immediately after tying the bag tight around her throat, she became intensely afraid of suffocating. She tried frantically to rip the bag from her head, but it stuck fast. She let out a muffled scream for help, just loud enough to be heard by the staff member, who rushed into the room and helped rip the bag off JP's head. The crisis team was called, JP was assessed at the residence, and the decision was made to hospitalize her. Although JP regretted that she had "panicked" and thereby aborted her suicide attempt while trying to die, she felt some relief at being back in the hospital. Of importance as likely rewards or reinforcers for the suicide attempt, JP had anticipated relief from killing herself and did experience relief from preparing to die as well as from being back in the hospital. Thus, the act of hospitalizing her following the suicide attempt served as an unintended positive reinforcement for her having made the attempt.

Assessment of Controlling Variables

To continue with JP's suicidal behavior as the example, the review of history and examination of links in various behavioral chains are followed in DBT by identifying variables that maintain suicidal behavior in the chain and thus serve as controlling variables. The chain in the incident just described includes a wide array of dysfunctional behaviors and a corresponding wide array of possible points of intervention. Perhaps the chain leading to this suicide attempt could have been averted early on, by better self-care of her body on JP's part or by a therapist's challenging her thoughts and feelings about her "loathed" body. Had she and the staff of the residence addressed more effectively the problem of the structureless day, the links leading to her suicidal behavior may not have arisen. And if JP had been alert to the hazardous impact of watching even a small bit of a movie about incest and had immediately weighed the pros and cons of watching that program as measured against her larger goals, she might have avoided such an evocative prompting event.

What if JP had worked further with her therapist on her fears about being too intrusive to call his secondary phone numbers? What if she had kept trying to reach her therapist or had decided to communicate her difficulties to the staff member on duty? What if the consequences of her behavior, which she could understandably anticipate on the basis of her previous experiences, were different? Which of these are the most important variables?

In DBT, which is an integrative treatment that borrows from a wide range of cognitive-behavioral therapies, these questions fall into several categories, each related to various possible problem-solving interventions. What is the role of skills deficits that could be addressed by skills training? What is the role of dysfunctional cognitions that could be addressed in cognitive modification? What is the role of classically conditioned overwhelming emotional responses that could be addressed with exposure procedures? What is the role of contingencies that reinforce the targeted dysfunctional behavior or that extinguish more adaptive alternative behaviors that could be changed by modifying environmental responses to her behavior? And in DBT in particular, what is the role of any or all six of the previously mentioned behavioral patterns, the dialectical dilemmas involving active passivity, apparent competence, emotional vulnerability, self-invalidation, crisis-generating behaviors, and grief inhibition?

Case Formulation

Based on the preceding information, JP's psychological disorder can be formulated in terms of several prominent characteristics that laid the groundwork for a potentially effective treatment plan. First and most critical, she is subject to experiencing overwhelming emotions often set off by cues linked to the contexts in which she was sexually abused during her developmental years. It is in the context of these overwhelming emotions that her maladaptive behavior chains ensue. These emotions include fear, panic, shame, and disgust, and they trigger as well flashbacks and intrusive thinking.

Second, certain contingencies operate to perpetuate her maladaptive behavior. Most significantly, her attempts to kill herself prompt rescue responses by staff members, resulting at times in hospitalizations that confirm to her that she is being taken seriously. However, these responses, thought at the time to be necessary, ultimately reinforce the life-threatening behaviors. Additionally, JP's efforts to come forth more adaptively with her overwhelming feelings and intrusive thoughts have at times been extinguished or punished by staff members who have failed to recognize the potential benefit of these efforts.

Third, various skill deficits have made it extremely difficult for JP to overcome or escape her recurrent cycles of distress. She lacks skills in self-management, as shown in neglecting care of her body (e.g., getting sunburned) and poor judgment in structuring her day (e.g., staying out of treatment all day). She lacks skills in emotional regulation that would make it possible to let her intense emotions wax and wane as a means of reducing her suffering without having to harm herself. She lacks skills in distress tolerance that would help prevent her from engaging in behaviors obviously dangerous to her, such as watching a movie about sexual abuse; and she is unable or unwilling to distract herself from experiences that offer short-term satisfaction but long-term danger, such as cutting herself. She lacks skill in interpersonal effectiveness, as exemplified in her failures to ask for help and her difficulty saying no in a variety of circumstances. All of these skill deficits minimize her ability to calm her mind and body and to slow down events in her life sufficiently for her to take charge of them.

Fourth, dysfunctional cognitions play a significant role in fostering and sustaining her maladaptive behavior. Her failing to contact her therapist when crises approach, even though she has been instructed to do so, and her reluctance to call his phone numbers when he does not return a page, are based on thoughts that she is too intrusive and a burden. Her hatred of her body is based on judgments about having gained weight. She has thoughts that she is alone in the world in having been sexually abused in her family, which made the watching of the movie compelling for her despite its traumatic impact.

Fifth, her determination to wear a mask of apparent competence at times and her inability to communicate distress effectively when she does attempt to do so hides her distress and feelings of being overwhelmed, but at the same time interferes with her expressing her concerns and asking for help. This mask of competence also makes it difficult for others to recognize her level of internal distress at a given moment.

Additionally playing a part in perpetuating JP's disordered behavior are her previously mentioned active passivity, in which she behaves in a manner that prompts rescue and caretaking actions by others; her own crisis-generating behaviors; her inhibited grieving, particularly the ongoing and unprocessed impact of a life history of sexual abuse that leaves her susceptible to negative emotional reactions to a wide range of cues; her emotional vulnerability, with very high levels of sensitivity and intense reactions that dissipate slowly; and self-invalidating and self-critical thoughts about herself that undermine her sense of identity as a worthwhile person.

Treatment Plan and Outcome

This formulation of JP's psychological disorder led to a multifaceted treatment plan that centered on developing a collaborative working relationship in psychotherapy that could provide a source of reinforcement for adaptive alternative behaviors on her part. In the context of this relationship, the therapist would emphasize and encourage dialectical patterns of thinking, feeling, and acting, which consist of avoiding polarized, rigid, black-and-white perspectives and, instead, identifying and appreciating the value of opposing points of view and appropriate syntheses or compromises between them. The therapist would then use a good working relationship and a dialectical perspective as the backdrop for engaging in behavioral chain analyses of JP's dysfunctional behaviors, one after the other, in a search for their crucial controlling variables.

JP's DBT therapy was undertaken in hopes that these procedures would be successful in identifying and helping her address vulnerability factors such as her neglect of her body, her poor eating and sleeping habits, and her inadequate structuring of her time. The therapy would also focus on expanding her recognition of prompting events that set off overwhelming emotions and guiding her in using stimulus control strategies for avoiding or minimizing the impact of these events. Other specific skills would be taught and reinforced to enhance JP's ability to communicate interpersonally, tolerate and manage stress, and block self-injurious behaviors. As the therapy proceeded, she would be encouraged to become more open about distressing thoughts and feelings in her sessions and more aware of her nonverbal presentation style, she would be challenged to replace her self-invalidating cognitions with more positive and realistic attitudes toward herself, and she would be helped in the therapy relationship to weaken her attraction to suicidal acts by strengthening the appeal of adaptive alternatives.

The therapist instituted this plan and reinstituted it after each hospitalization, and progress was made on the major Stage 1 targets. Suicide crisis behaviors and hospitalizations have now been absent for the past year, and self-injurious behaviors were eliminated, with the exception of one occurrence that followed an unusually stressful incident and did not require hospitalization. JP's attendance, collaboration, and compliance in the treatment grew stronger, and she was able to take positive steps toward building a higher quality life with a job, two new friendships, a course in school, and the reestablishment of selective relationships with family members who are "safe" for her.

As is often the case in working with persons who have a well-entrenched and life-threatening BPD, therapy for JP has been an extraordinarily difficult treatment that has elicited strong reactions in the therapist from time to time, including fear, frustration, anger, and sadness. The therapist relied on a mindful appreciation and management of his own emotions, which was made possible by a consultation team of DBT colleagues, who validated his reactions and helped him identify problem-solving strategies. In the past year, the treatment came to feel like treatment of JP by the team, with the therapist as the instrumental intermediary, which had a liberating and supportive effect on the therapist. The therapist is currently orienting JP to the goals and procedures of Stage 2 of DBT, which will involve systematic and prolonged exposure to her memories of the traumas of her life. It will be her choice whether to enter Stage 2 and her therapist's task to strengthen her commitment to it should she decide in favor of proceeding.

Recommended Readings

Linehan, M. M. (1993). *Cognitive-behavioral treatment of borderline personality disorder.* New York: Guilford Press.

Linehan, M. M., & Kehrer, C. A. (1993). Borderline personality disorder. In D. H. Barlow (Ed.), *Clinical handbook of psychological disorders* (2nd ed., pp. 396–441). New York: Guilford Press.

Paris, J. (1999). Borderline personality disorder. In T. Millon, P. H. Blaney, & R. D. Davis (Eds), *Oxford textbook of psychopathology* (pp. 628–652). New York: Oxford University Press.

Robins, C., Ivanoff, A. M., & Linehan, M. M. (2001). Dialectical behavior therapy. In W. J. Livesley (Ed.), *Handbook of personality disorders* (pp. 437–459). New York: Guilford Press.

Reference

American Psychiatric Association. (2000). *Diagnostic and statistical manual of mental disorders* (4th ed., text rev.). Washington, DC: Author.

CHAPTER 5

Antisocial Personality Disorder

CARL B. GACONO

D ave was a married Caucasian man in his mid-20s. During his childhood and adolescence, he was involved in shoplifting, fighting, truancy, and drug and alcohol use. As an adult, Dave continued to abuse drugs and alcohol. His substance abuse resulted in his being fired from his job, and drug-related offenses led to his being arrested and incarcerated in a state prison. It was while serving a seven-year sentence for selling marijuana that Dave volunteered to receive psychological treatment.

When first seen for an evaluation in the prison setting, Dave's presenting problems included anxiety, depression, sleep disturbance, anger outbursts, abuse of cannabis (marijuana) and amphetamines, and feeling that he was a socially isolated person who did not fit in. During the initial interview, he expressed concern that he might be "going crazy." His artwork was exceptional in quality, but portrayed repetitive themes of demons and other bizarre, surrealistic fantasies. He stated that this artwork had evoked comments from other inmates concerning "my mental stability."

Background Information

Dave was raised by his mother. He never knew his father, and his mother had withheld from him any information about him. Dave denied having been abused as a child, but he gave a history consistent with neglect. According to his report, he was "pretty much on my own" because his mother "worked all the time." Dave hung out with the neighborhood kids, with whom he got into drinking, petty theft, and other kinds of delinquency. Holiday celebrations for Dave and his pals took the form of drinking stolen beer and starting a fire in an empty lot to roast hot dogs.

Dave reported having been a stubborn and oppositional child and frequently getting into fights with other boys. Concerning his fights as a child and as an adult, however, he said, "I don't start them; I just finish them." Dave had never been arrested for assault and had never used a weapon in a fight. His violence was apparently reactive and driven by emotions, rather than being planned and purposeful.

His use of marijuana, amphetamines, and alcohol helped to keep him "calm." Drug sales literally involved "pedaling" marijuana. He did not own a car and rode a bicycle to distribute drugs to his customers. Despite his problem behavior, Dave had enjoyed working as he grew up and had held a steady job in a factory. He had been promoted to a supervisory position in the factory and was apparently doing well in this position until declining performance related to his substance abuse resulted in his being fired. Dave had been married for several years, and despite a substance abusing lifestyle, he had been sexually faithful to his wife.

Assessment Data and Case Conceptualization

Dave was dressed in army fatigues and combat boots for his initial interview. He was unshaven and emitted an unpleasant body odor, and his personal hygiene was generally poor. He was heavily tattooed and wore his hair in a Mohawk. He seemed anxious and ill at ease, especially while he was showing me his artwork and asking me if I thought he was crazy. He appeared to be motivated to receive treatment, not only because he had volunteered for it, but also because of the anxiety he was experiencing.

Dave was open in revealing his personal history and presenting his complaints, perhaps too much so. Premature sharing of personal information had apparently been causing some problems for him. According to his report, he had been inclined to talk a great deal about himself to other inmates, only to have this information used against him in various ways.

For whatever reasons patients present for mental health treatment, a thorough assessment aids clinicians in understanding their individual problems and adjustment difficulties. Typical assessment methods include a detailed clinical interview and administration of standardized tests designed to measure intellectual, personality, and behavioral functioning. Such comprehensive assessment procedures facilitate accurate inferences about a patient's diagnostic status, treatment needs, and amenability to intervention. A thorough assessment before initiating treatment was particularly important in Dave's case since it was suspected that he had an Antisocial Personality Disorder (ASPD). ASPD patients present with a diverse array of personality styles and personal issues, and assessment plays an important role in ferreting out their individual psychological strengths and weaknesses.

Dave's assessment included the Psychopathy Checklist-Revised (PCL-R), the Millon Clinical Multiaxial Inventory-III (MCMI-III), the Rorschach Inkblot Method (RIM), and the Shipley Institute of Living Scale, which is a measure of intellectual functioning that yields an IQ estimate (Zachary, 1986). The Rorschach administration was repeated 12 and 16 months after treatment was begun to monitor Dave's progress.

The PCL-R (Hare, 1991) uses a record review and a clinical interview to quantify certain traits, attitudes, and behaviors that define psychopathy, including self-centeredness, interpersonal exploitiveness, and an antisocial lifestyle. In addition to indicating an overall level of psychopathy, the PCL-R provides information about treatment needs and treatment amenability. The MCMI-III and the RIM measure numerous facets of personality functioning. The MCMI-III (Millon, 1994, 1997) is a self-report instrument that is particularly helpful in identifying the presence or absence of various personality disorders. The Rorschach method (Exner, 2003) is a relatively unstructured and performance-based measure that provides information about how people pay attention to their surroundings, think about their experiences, express feelings, manage stress, regard themselves, and relate to other people.

Dave's assessment indicated above-average intelligence, a moderate level of anxiety and depression, and little in the way of psychopathic personality traits. Each of these findings is usually associated with a favorable treatment prognosis. Particularly informative were the

PCL-R results, which are shown in Table 5.1. The PCL-R involves rating 20 items as to whether they are absent (score of 0), present (score of 1), or pronounced (score of 2). Eight of these 20 items refer to personality traits (e.g., callousness, lack of remorse, a grandiose sense of self-worth) and are listed as Factor 1 in the table. Nine other items measure an antisocial lifestyle (e.g., irresponsible, impulsive,

Table 5.1   Dave's PCL-R Protocol

Item	Factor 1 (Traits)	Factor 2 (Behaviors)	Total Score
1. Glibness/superficial charm	0		0
2. Grandiose sense of self-worth	0		0
3. Need of stimulation/proneness to boredom		1	1
4. Pathological lying	1		1
5. Conning/manipulative	0		0
6. Lack of remorse or guilt	1		1
7. Shallow affect	0		0
8. Callous/lack of empathy	1		1
9. Parasitic lifestyle		0	0
10. Poor behavioral controls		1	1
11. Promiscuous sexual behavior	x	x	0
12. Early behavioral problems		2	2
13. Lack of realistic long-term goals		1	1
14. Impulsivity		1	1
15. Irresponsibility		1	1
16. Failure to accept responsibility for own actions	1		1
17. Many short-term marital relationships	x	x	0
18. Juvenile delinquency		1	1
19. Revocation of conditional release		2	2
20. Criminal versatility	x	x	1
Total	4	10	15

stimulation-seeking, and unconventional behavior) and are listed as Factor 2 in the table. Three items load on neither factor.

With respect to diagnostic classification, the behavioral characteristics included in Factor 2 of the PCL-R closely parallel the criteria specified for ASPD in the *Diagnostic and Statistical Manual of Mental Disorders* (*DSM-IV-TR*) of the American Psychiatric Association (2000). Generally, persons who receive high scores on the behavioral items but not on the personality trait items (Factor 1) of the PCL-R are likely to have a relatively mild form of ASPD. On the other hand, persons who receive high scores on both the behavioral and the personality trait items of the PCL-R often have a relatively severe form of ASPD that includes some maladaptive traits shared with other personality disorders, including being histrionic, narcissistic, borderline, and paranoid.

Consistent with this distinction between behavioral and trait characteristics, ASPD patients vary considerably in their amenability to treatment. Those who show both significant behavioral and personality trait characteristics, when compared to those who show only the behavioral characteristics of ASPD, tend to be less responsive to treatment, more likely to participate in institutional misbehavior if incarcerated, and at higher risk for recurrent violent and nonviolent offenses. There is as yet no empirically validated treatment for ASPD patients who are psychopathic. The prognosis for ASPD patients who have a history of behavior problems but are not psychopathic is more promising.

With these considerations in mind, some individual items of the PCL-R were helpful in ruling out histrionic and narcissistic personality traits in Dave's case. His scores of 0 on glibness, grandiosity, and shallow affect (items 1, 2, and 7) and scores of only 1 on lack of remorse, lack of empathy, and failure to accept responsibility for his own actions (items 6, 8, and 16) were relevant, as were low scores he received on the Histrionic and Narcissistic scales of the MCMI-III. Also of note were indications in his Rorschach responses of low self-esteem, rather than grandiosity or an inflated sense of his value and entitlement as a person. The Rorschach findings were also helpful in demonstrating a desire and a capacity on his part for forming close and mutually supportive relationships with other people, which is consistent with his previously mentioned low scores on items 6, 7, and 8 of the PCL-R.

These Rorschach and PCL-R markers of receptivity to interpersonal attachments are seldom found among repeat felons. In Dave's case, his need to make connections with other people may help to account for three previously noted characteristics that are also unusual to find in a prison population: his expressed interest in seeing a therapist, his having had a stable long-term relationship with his wife, and his proclivity for being more forthcoming than was advisable in talking about himself to other people. As a further clue to his tendency to share more information than he should with his fellow inmates, his Rorschach responses also identified susceptibility to exercising poor judgment in interpersonal relationships.

Dave's desire and capacities for attachment, together with his being anxious and depressed, had positive implications for his being able to form a helpful relationship with a therapist. Although he was inclined to avoid affect, he did not appear to be lacking in feelings. His capacity for interpersonal bonding was reflected further in his scores of 0 on PCL-R items 11 (promiscuous sexual behavior) and 17 (short-term marital relationships). Like his being by nature receptive to attachments, his having been sexually involved for a decade with just one partner (who became his wife) is an unusual finding among incarcerated offenders.

The PCL-R also captured the origination of Dave's behavioral problems in childhood (items 12 and 18) and his demonstrated ability to work (as shown in a score of 0 on item 9 for parasitic lifestyle). He appeared to be more impulsive than would have been desirable, but not markedly so (item 14). The PCL-R additionally indicated some problems Dave was having in managing anger (item 10).

Other features of Dave's life history and his test results identified him as a person who was easily overwhelmed by emotions. His difficulty in handling his feelings had caused him interpersonal problems, because being involved in relationships inevitably stimulates emotions. Dave, in fact, described some strains in his marriage related to his inability to deal comfortably with his wife's expressions of feelings. He appeared to be frightened of her affect as well as of his own, and the Rorschach results indicated further that becoming overwhelmed by emotion was likely to interfere at times with his being able to think clearly and perceive his experiences accurately. There was also evidence that he had difficulty showing anger directly and was inclined instead to find passive ways of expressing resentment toward people he felt had not treated him well. Finally, the neglect that Dave had experienced as a child appeared to have resulted in his having little expectation of positive interactions with other people, despite his interest in having such interactions.

Taken together, then, Dave's juvenile and adult behavioral history and the test findings were consistent with his having diagnoses of amphetamine abuse, cannabis abuse, and Antisocial Personality Disorder (ASPD), Mild. Unlike many ASPD patients, he did not show histrionic and narcissistic personality characteristics features, but he did give evidence of prominent anxiety and depression. The assessment data were additionally consistent with his being an avoidant, passive-aggressive, and inadequate individual whose adjustment had been compromised by low self-esteem and a basic sense of being a damaged person.

Treatment

The preceding assessment of Dave, particularly with respect to his being anxious, depressed, self-denigrating rather than narcissistic, and capable of working steadily and forming personal relationships, offered more promise for a favorable response than is often the case in working with ASPD patients. His problems with anxiety, depression, low self-esteem, passivity, and stress and anger management provided accessible targets for intervention. In addition, the planning for his treatment took into account his probable need for a father figure in his life, which he never had. The treatment plan for Dave involved three components:

1. Small doses of medication to alleviate his anxiety and depressive symptoms.

2. Participation in a comprehensive life skills training program in which group-based cognitive-behavioral methods were used to enhance his coping skills, help him think more realistically and less like a criminal, improve his anger management, and minimize the risk of his becoming a repeat offender.

3. Individual therapy with a male therapist intended to support his skills training program and provide him a relationship with a father substitute.

Dave attended 10 months of intensive skills training followed by an additional 12 months of group work focused on criminal thinking and relapse prevention. He remained in individual therapy throughout this 22-month period. As expected from the assessment data, Dave showed signs of forming an attachment to his individual therapist, and he often expressed feelings and attitudes toward this therapist of a type typically experienced by men toward an older brother or father figure. Such feelings are rarely shown by psychopaths, but they are often encountered by therapists working with nonpsychopathic conduct-disordered adolescents. It is interesting that Dave's hairstyle and his manner of dress varied considerably during his treatment. These shifts in his appearance seemed to reflect some ongoing struggles with his identity (i.e., the kind of person he thought he was or wanted to be) and some testing of his therapist to see whether outlandish behavior would result in his being abandoned or rejected.

In his group training programs, Dave cooperated fully and completed all of the therapeutic assignments. Although he was initially passive in the group situations, he became increasingly active during the course of the treatment. Before beginning the treatment program, Dave had been receiving numerous incident reports for institutional misbehavior. These infractions of rules and regulations ceased entirely after the first nine months of his treatment.

Dave's progress was also reflected in 12- and 16-month follow-up Rorschach testing. Compared with the pretreatment findings, his 12-month Rorschach responses indicated improved perceptual accuracy and reality testing, better affect tolerance, less hostility, increased self-esteem, greater assertiveness, more interest in other people, and better judgment in assessing interpersonal relationships. At 16 months, the Rorschach data confirmed these treatment gains but also identified areas needing further work. Although perceiving his experiences more accurately than before, he was still inclined to see the world in unconventional ways. He had learned to exercise better judgment in interpersonal relationships, which was helping him reduce the extent of his avoidant and passive-aggressive interactions with people, but he was still not well adjusted in these respects.

Nevertheless, Dave's growing confidence in his ability to handle his emotions and his interpersonal relationships effectively had contributed to his feeling better about himself and his future prospects. He gradually became a more active participant in group sessions, where he reported feeling less anxious than before, less like he didn't fit in, and less like he was crazy. More than before, he began to associate positive attributes with interpersonal interactions. Taken together, the test data and his self-reports confirmed considerable progress in his being able to manage his feelings, tolerate affect, and avoid becoming depressed. At the same time, the follow-up evaluations identified anger management problems and passive-aggressive tendencies as continuing treatment targets for the future.

In summary, Dave's assessment resulted in an individualized treatment plan based on his unique personality strengths and weaknesses, and follow-up assessments provided a means of monitoring his treatment progress. Of particular importance in the course of his treatment was the previously mentioned fact that, although Dave's childhood behavioral history was typical for ASPD patients, his personality style was not. He did not show the narcissistic and histrionic personality characteristics that are frequently found among persons with ASPD, and he had a low level of psychopathic personality traits. Instead, despite his antisocial lifestyle, he was basically an avoidant and inadequate person with frustrated but nevertheless existent capacities for interpersonal attachment. When present, these nonpsychopathic characteristics improve the prognosis for ASPD patients, who otherwise are rarely responsive to psychological interventions. Dave was considered initially to have some potential for a favorable treatment outcome, and this prognosis was confirmed by the progress he made in response to a carefully planned and multifaceted intervention program.

Discussion

The frequency of ASPD patients in a given setting varies considerably. ASPD patients are rarely found in nonforensic community outpatient settings, whereas the diagnosis is common in forensic and correctional settings, particularly among men. The extent to which this diagnosis is based on behavioral rather than personality trait criteria also distinguishes ASPD from other personality disorders codified in the *DSM-IV-TR*. The number of different criteria combinations that can lead to an ASPD diagnosis is very large. ASPD persons are not a homogenous group, but instead a group of people who are diverse in personality structure and behavioral functioning. As previously mentioned, then, thorough personality assessment and a detailed diagnostic formulation are especially important in ascertaining the treatment amenability of an ASPD patient.

Treatment Considerations: To Treat or Not to Treat?

Before beginning treatment of an ASPD patient, the clinician must have an understanding of antisocial dynamics and develop a clear picture of the individual patient's psychology. Training, experience, and supervision can facilitate understanding of antisocial dynamics, and psychological assessment is necessary to clarify the patient's psychology.

Most important, the clinician must first determine whether the structure of the treatment setting can contain the patient's manipulation and violence. Outpatient centers are suitable for treating nonviolent ASPD patients who present with anxiety and other neurotic problems. Inpatient psychiatric facilities and minimum security forensic psychiatric hospitals are advisable for ASPD patients who display concurrent major mental illness and exhibit low levels of psychopathy. Maximum security forensic hospitals and prisons are best for managing chronic offenders and the criminally dangerous. Several personality and historical factors, including the presence of sadistic aggressive behavior, a complete absence of remorse, extremely high or low intelligence, the lack of any attachment capacity, and very negative reactions on the part of the clinician, also diminish an ASPD patient's treatment amenability.

After ensuring the safety of staff and other patients, the clinician must determine whether the available services in a treatment setting match the clinical needs of an ASPD patient. The staffing and treatment modalities must be adequate to provide the indicated treatment program. Staff must be capable of managing extreme negative emotional reactions to these volatile patients. Because staff emotional reactions mirror a patient's inner life, they often furnish valuable information concerning the patient's personality functioning, provided they are identified and understood. On the other hand, it is not uncommon for staff working with ASPD patients to feel frightened, controlled, or even totally unable to have any positive impact, and, in response, to form unwarranted negative attitudes toward them. Empirical assessment data can help to identify whether patients really have certain negative characteristics that are being attributed to them by staff members or whether these attributions have been derived from emotional reactions among the staff. Becoming able to manage emotional reactions to ASPD patients and to some of the crimes they have committed so that these reactions will not interfere with perceiving these patients accurately and treating them effectively requires adequate training, good supervision, and personal growth.

As shown in the case of Dave, psychological assessment data can also aid in determining treatment amenability and treatment needs in

ASPD patients. Specifically, PCL-R data, combined with other assessment findings, are useful for estimating violence risk. In-depth assessment of cognitive and personality functioning helps to identify areas in need of remediation and characteristics that may have a favorable or unfavorable bearing on a patient's responsiveness to therapy. Like Dave's pretreatment evaluation, an initial assessment should include measurement of psychopathy level, identification of symptomatic or personality disorders other than ASPD, functional analysis of personality characteristic and situational influences that have led to the patient's antisocial behaviors, and determination of the appropriate security level of the treatment setting where the patient will be seen.

It cannot be emphasized enough that effective treatment of ASPD patients can occur only when the skill level of the treatment team and the physical structure of the treatment setting are sufficient for their intended purpose. Without the proper staff and structure, treatment of these patients typically becomes a series of disjointed crisis interventions. In the absence of adequate staff and structure, management strategies take priority over treatment, and clinicians find themselves continually putting out fires and not doing much else. When staff and structure appear sufficient to support effective therapy, the decision to treat a particular patient is followed by obtaining the patient's informed consent to participate. The informed consent procedure is used to outline the expectations, rules, structure, and goals of treatment, and this procedure results in a document that serves as a prelude to the formal treatment plan.

Psychology of the Antisocial Personality Disorder Patient: Treatment Methods

Unlike Dave, who was interested in receiving treatment for relief of his anxiety and depression, most ASPD patients enter treatment involuntarily, having been mandated by the courts to do so. It is critical to understand the patient's motivation for seeking treatment. ASPD patients seldom begin treatment wanting to change their character structure.

Rather, they believe that their problems are external and that it is other people and rules that are problematic. The typical belief of ASPD patients that they are victims rather than victimizers runs counter to the premises underlying traditional treatment methods for persons with a social conscience, who seek help to change themselves and not the world around them.

The basic character pathology of ASPD patients is *ego-syntonic,* which means that they are satisfied with what they are like and see nothing wrong with how they behave. However, they may also present with some *ego-alien* symptoms, including manifestations of anxiety, depression, and schizophrenia, that they do not consider a natural or acceptable part of themselves and want to get rid of. Often these ego-alien symptoms can be reduced with medication and other brief treatments, which also help to foster participation in the therapy and to inhibit violent behaviors. At the same time, however, competent clinicians recognize that the underlying ego-syntonic personality disorder in many, if not most, ASPD patients is typically refractory to brief treatment. Modification of personality disorders usually requires long-term and intensive treatment that goes beyond alleviation of symptomatic disorder.

Allowing for the previously mentioned heterogeneity of persons diagnosed with ASPD, certain particular features of disordered personality functioning are commonly present in these patients. These features include problems with self-esteem regulation (whether grandiose or inadequate), deficits in attachment capacity, difficulties containing anxiety and affect, impaired empathy, poor frustration tolerance, impulsiveness, remorselessness, and suspiciousness. ASPD patients typically place a high premium on power as well. They loathe being vulnerable or dependent, and they view emotions and kindness as signs of weakness.

Awareness of these and other aspects of the psychology of ASPD patients helps clinicians understand and be empathic in working with them. For example, given the worldview of ASPD patients, active confrontation of their inconsistencies, rather than more passive reflections or silence, constitutes an empathic interaction. Insightful confrontations help these patients experience the therapist as a strong figure who is worthy of their respect, is not frightened by them, and can be trusted not to disappoint, abandon, or reject them. Trust is always a major issue in working with ASPD patients, who devote an enormous amount of energy to sizing up their therapists. Having often come from backgrounds of neglect or abuse, antisocial patients are particularly likely to mistrust naive and gullible therapists and authority figures who fall prey to their manipulations.

Treatment requires ASPD patients them to give up many of the basic beliefs and behaviors that define their character style. Recognizing this premise helps therapists to appreciate the enormity of their task. Real involvement in therapy can be a very anxiety-producing experience for an ASPD patient, and their anxiety may be acted out through violence, drug use, and criminal behavior within the walls of a secure prison setting as well as in the community. Because ambiguity in the therapeutic process tends to heighten this anxiety, successful treatment usually calls for providing as much structure and as little uncertainty as possible.

ASPD patients typically think in criminal ways about being entitled to take whatever they want from other people or to harm anyone who gets in their way, or both. Cognitive-behavioral interventions are often necessary in the initial phases of treatment to change these criminogenic thinking patterns. Group therapy and educational programs can also be used to help ASPD patients monitor and alter their thinking, including their belief that the right thing to do is: (1) whatever serves their immediate needs and (2) whatever they can get away with. As noted in Dave's case, cognitive-behavioral interventions can also be useful in promoting improved coping skills, such as better anger management and decreased impulsiveness. Following this initial cognitive phase of treatment, psychodynamic approaches in the treatment can be helpful in exploring the origins of the ASPD patient's maladaptive belief system and relieving the distress that originally led to it.

Anger is usually a treatment issue in working with ASPD patients. Typically, they use anger consciously as a way of intimidating and controlling others. At the same time, without their being consciously aware of it, their anger serves as a defense against inner feelings of worthlessness and supports a grandiose self-image and sense of entitlement. By confronting their criminal thinking, the therapist first stimulates and then counters the ASPD patient's escalating anger while concurrently interrupting its defensive functions. Interruption and restructuring of this defensive process provide a foundation for subsequent more intensive therapy addressing issues such as childhood abuse, affect tolerance, and identify formation.

Cognitive confrontation coupled with exploratory psychotherapy can help ASPD patients become gradually better able at tolerating their feelings of worthlessness and boredom, especially if, like Dave, their psychopathy level is low. Becoming increasingly tolerant of dysphoric affect and reducing negative self-attitudes diminishes the likelihood that either will contribute to a relapse into antisocial conduct. Enhanced mastery over emotions also decreases the need of ASPD patients for defensive grandiosity, while at the same time fostering actual gains in self-worth. True self-esteem, as opposed to defensive grandiosity, cannot be given to ASPD patients, but instead must be earned. When antisocial individuals begin to behave responsibly and stop hurting other people, genuine self-worth increases because of their altered lifestyle.

The essential ingredients of treating nonpsychopathic ASPD patients like Dave can be summarized as follows:

1. Clear and unambiguous program rules and consequences must be established at the beginning of treatment, considered nonnegotiable, and consistently enforced. This treatment philosophy assumes that these patients have abused their status and privileges in society. Therapeutic confrontations are then used to expose maladaptive and irresponsible patterns of behavior. These interventions contront specific dysfunctional behaviors, penetrate justifications for them, stimulate self-evaluation of behavior, promote acceptance of responsibility, challenge patients to mobilize their coping resources, and define paths toward personal growth and development.

2. Practical life skills and cognitive skills must be taught in a manner that is congruent with an individual patient's psychosocial developmental levels. Life skills deficits in reading and working, handling finances and sexuality, and taking care of

health and personal hygiene can be remediated through specific curricula designed for offenders. The same can be said
for improvement of cognitive skills related to problem recognition and problem solving, goal setting and motivation, social perspective taking, and empathy.

3. There must be a heavy emphasis on identifying and modifying patients' cognitive distortions and criminal lifestyle
patterns. Specific treatment targets include antisocial values
and attitudes, association with criminal peers, impulsivity,
substance abuse, and insensitivity to aversive consequences.

4. The treatment should foster increased appreciation for
the emotional impact of the patients' behavior on their family and victims. Because this kind of awareness typically
evokes distressing affect, the treatment must also prepare
the patient for increasing levels of anxiety.

5. Treatment should be available throughout a patient's time
in prison, supervised release, and subsequent community
aftercare.

6. Early in treatment, action-oriented interventions aimed
at consciousness-raising, symptom relief, and environmental reevaluation maximize the receptivity of ASPD
patients to change. Later in treatment, attention to relapse
prevention techniques helps these patients identify potential high-risk situations and develop specific strategies for
preventing relapse. Postrelease, community resources, including mentoring by volunteer ex-offenders, can provide
a helpful supportive adjunct to the treatment.

Conclusion

Dave's case reminds us of the great diversity among individuals who
are diagnosed with ASPD. His uniqueness highlights the importance of

a thorough personality assessment in ferreting out individual differences among persons with this disorder. Dave's avoidant style, attachment capacity, low psychopathy level, lack of sexual deviation, and adequate impulse controls were prognostically favorable in his case, but atypical for most ASPD patients. More commonly, clinicians working with people who have received an ASPD diagnosis will be confronted with an arrogant, glib, and abrasive patient with many narcissistic or histrionic qualities. Whatever their clinical presentation, however, the treatment amenability of ASPD patients should never be judged solely on the basis of their diagnosis or the clinician's subjective opinion, but should instead be determined through a detailed psychological assessment.

Treating ASPD patients is often an arduous task. Nevertheless, many of these patients can be successfully treated, as in Dave's case. Others, unfortunately, can only be managed. Aside from evaluating treatment amenability on the basis of a patient's personality functioning, the clinician must determine whether the treatment setting is capable of containing and modifying the patient's aggressive and manipulative tendencies. If the treatment setting can match the patient's clinical needs, treatment should be instituted; if not, the patient should be transferred to a more secure setting where control is sufficient to support a treatment program. When an adequate treatment setting is not available, management will have to take priority over treatment.

Recommended Readings

Cleckley, H. (1942). *The mask of sanity.* St. Louis, MO: Mosby.

Gacono, C. B. (1998). The use of the Psychopathy Checklist-Revised (PCL-R) and Rorschach for treatment planning with antisocial personality disordered patients. *International Journal of Offender Therapy and Comparative Criminology, 42,* 49–64.

Gacono, C. B. (Ed.). (2000). *The clinical and forensic assessment of psychopathy: A practitioner's guide.* Mahwah, NJ: Erlbaum.

Gacono, C. B., & Meloy, J. R. (1994). *The Rorschach assessment of aggressive and psychopathic personalities*. Hillsdale, NJ: Erlbaum.

Gacono, C. B., Nieberding, R., Owen, A., Rubel, J., & Bodholdt, R. (2001). Treating conduct disorder, antisocial, and psychopathic personalities. In J. Ashford, B. Sales, & W. Reid (Eds.), *Treating adult and juvenile offenders with special needs* (pp. 99–129). Washington, DC: American Psychological Association.

Lykken, D. T. (1995). *The antisocial personalities*. Hillsdale, NJ: Erlbaum.

Meloy, J. R. (1988). *The psychopathic mind: Origins, dynamics, and treatment*. Newbury Park, CA: Sage.

Walters, G. (1990). *The criminal lifestyle: Patterns of serious criminal conduct*. Newbury Park, CA: Sage.

References

American Psychiatric Association. (2000). *Diagnostic and statistical manual of mental disorders* (4th ed., text rev.). Washington, DC: Author.

Exner, J. E. (2003). *The Rorschach: A comprehensive system. Volume 1: Basic foundations* (4th ed.). Hoboken, NJ: Wiley.

Hare, R. (1991). *The Hare Psychopathy Checklist-Revised*. Toronto, Ontario, Canada: Multi-Health Systems.

Millon, T. (1977). *Millon Clinical Multiaxial Inventory*. Minneapolis, MN: National Computer Systems.

Millon, T. (1994). *Manual for the MCMI-III*. Minneapolis, MN: National Computer Systems.

Zachary, R. A. (1986). *Shipley Institute of Living Scale, Revised manual*. Los Angeles: Western Psychological Services.

CHAPTER 6

Schizotypal Personality Disorder

DAVID P. BERNSTEIN

James is a young man whom I saw in psychotherapy for four years from ages 12 to 16. His parents brought him to see me because of problems at school, including temper outbursts, social isolation, and uneven academic performance. According to his parents, James had always been a peculiar and difficult child. As an infant, he had been difficult to soothe, and as a toddler, he had frequent temper tantrums. The parents described James as being extremely bright and creative, a gifted artist and voracious reader with many esoteric interests, but a boy who had always been socially awkward. His peers teased him mercilessly, taking particular pleasure in provoking him into infantile fits of rage. He had never managed to form a close friendship. He seemed desperately unhappy, and his parents worried that he might be suicidal.

When we met for the first time, James' appearance struck me as more akin to that of a befuddled old man than a teenage boy. He wore thick glasses and frequently pulled out an overused handkerchief to blow his nose, which was a longstanding nervous habit. He openly discussed his unhappiness at school, especially his frustration at being picked on, and his embarrassment at his outbursts of rage. In one of our first sessions, he told me of a dream he had had the night before in which he was carried down a raging river—a metaphor, I thought, for his own inner turmoil and tenuous self-control. As we got to know each other better, he revealed more of himself to me. He drew me beautifully rendered pictures depicting legions of angels and demons waging war against each other. He had an almost obsessive interest in Native American culture and religious practices, a topic on which he had read widely, and he engaged me in lengthy discussions of Shamanism.

James was also fascinated by the 1960s and the hippie movement. His discourses on these subjects were often rambling and hard to follow. He could be quite an astute observer of people, and he had an acerbic wit, which I openly enjoyed. We developed an easy rapport, yet he could become enraged with me if I disappointed him or failed to understand him. On such occasions, he would seize objects and hurl them across the room, prompting me to set limits on his behavior. Moreover, despite our developing relationship, he made no progress in forming friendships outside the therapy. He confided that he wanted to form friendships but had no idea of how to do so. He shared very few "normal" interests with his peers, he said, and experienced social interactions as awkward and uncomfortable.

Diagnostically, John met the criteria specified in the *Diagnostic and Statistical Manual of Mental Disorders* (*DSM-IV-TR*) for Schizotypal Personality Disorder (SPD; American Psychiatric Association, 2000). SPD shares many genetic, developmental, and behavioral features with Schizophrenia and is often conceptualized as a "schizophrenia-spectrum" condition. Unlike Schizophrenia, however, SPD does not involve being out of touch with reality or the presence of other psychotic symptoms such as delusions or hallucinations. Of nine *DSM* criteria for SPD, James showed the following five: He held odd beliefs; his thinking and speech were circumstantial, overly elaborate, and metaphorical; his behavior and appearance were peculiar; he had no close friends; and he experienced excessive social anxiety.

James also displayed some of the diagnostic features of Borderline Personality Disorder (BPD), a condition that often occurs in combination with SPD. His BPD features included unstable interpersonal relationships marked by alternating idealization and devaluation of others; identity disturbance, as reflected in an uncertain self-image; and difficulty controlling his anger, as displayed in his frequent temper outbursts.

Although caution must be exercised in diagnosing personality disorders in adolescence, which is often a period of personality instability, James' schizotypal features appeared to be longstanding and to have preceded his becoming a teenager. My only unresolved diagnostic question was whether his schizotypal features represented the early or prodromal phase of a schizophrenic disturbance that would become manifest later in life. Neither his parents nor his siblings had shown signs of Schizophrenia, which reduced somewhat the likelihood of his developing this disorder. On the other hand, his mother had a diagnosed Bipolar Disorder that was being controlled by medication, and there was a history of mental illness on both sides of his family. For the time being, however, James was not presenting any evidence of psychosis or mood disorder.

Over the four-year course of James' treatment, he gained control over his temper and eventually managed to form a few friendships, albeit with other socially marginalized adolescents. He deliberately cultivated more typical adolescent interests and began to dress and behave in a less conspicuously peculiar manner. In time, his overused handkerchief became a thing of the past. Three years after his treatment ended, James contacted me, and we met for a few times to help him with his adjustment to college. He still showed no signs of psychosis. However, despite having made considerable progress in improving his social and emotional adaptation, he remained am odd and eccentric young man.

Recommended Readings

Lenzenweger, M. F. (1999). Schizotypic psychopathology: Theory, evidence, and future directions. In T. Millon, P. H. Blaney, & R. Davis (Eds.), *Oxford textbook of psychopathology* (pp. 605–627). New York: Oxford University Press.

Meehl, P. E. (1990). Toward an integrated theory of schizotaxia, schizotypy, and schizophrenia. *Journal of Personality Disorders, 4,* 1–99.

Siever, L., Bernstein, D., & Silverman, J. (1995). Schizotypal personality disorder. In J. Livesley (Ed.), *The DSM-IV personality disorders* (pp. 71–90). Washington, DC: American Psychiatric Association.

Reference

American Psychiatric Association. (2000). *Diagnostic and statistical manual of mental disorders* (4th ed., text rev.). Washington, DC: Author.

CHAPTER 7

Paranoid Personality Disorder

JAMES H. KLEIGER

When this quiet and charming gentleman requested an evaluation, he seemed like a good candidate for a treatment process designed to provide him some support while helping him express and come to grips with his concerns. He complained of conflicts in his family and said he wanted to talk with someone. An apparently obsessional man, whose underlying paranoid personality structure did not fully emerge until he became involved in psychotherapy, Mr. K agreed to begin treatment with a focus on his sense of estrangement from his family.

How did this bright and motivated man with seemingly neurotic concerns come to reveal another aspect of his personality, a paranoid core that would eventually lead to the disruption of his treatment in the context of mistrust and feelings of persecution? What follows is an extensive case study of this complex individual, whose functioning at a fairly high level belied an underlying paranoid personality structure.

Presentation

Mr. K was 55 at the time he arrived for his first appointment. A quiet man with a serious demeanor, Mr. K indicated that he had previously received some biofeedback training for tension headaches, which he said had been helpful. Now, he said, he felt dissatisfied with his life, in particular with his relationships in his family.

A long-time resident of a small New England community, Mr. K owned and operated a chain of convenience stores with his wife and two grown children. He made a comfortable living but spent most of his waking time at his stores involved in all aspects of his family business. It was not unusual for Mr. K to rise at 3:30 A.M. to open his stores, which was long before the doors were open for business, and to lock up well after 10:00 P.M.

Mr. K focused initially on his deteriorating relationship with his 22-year-old daughter, Alice, whom he had recently fired from one of his stores, and he talked about how his wife and son had formed an alliance against him. His wife accused him of being too harsh with both of his children and distant from and secretive with her, he said. He accordingly spent long hours at work, not only to attend to the myriad demands of small business ownership, but also to find refuge in his office, by himself and away from what he perceived as a hostile environment at home.

It was the firing of his daughter that precipitated his request for an evaluation, along with an urgent message from his wife that he needed to do something about his anger. It was not that he had a volatile temper; it was more that he would withdraw in a silent, icy manner, refusing to speak to those whom he felt had crossed him or let him down. Such was the case with Alice, his older child. Alice had managed his busiest store until Mr. K abruptly fired her one month before his first psychotherapy consultation. Mr. K accused Alice of embezzlement and deceit. Although his wife, daughter, and son, who managed another store, tried to reason with him, presenting another side of the story that made the daughter look like a naïve victim of circumstances, not a crook, Mr. K would hear nothing of this. Firing her one day without notice, he refused to speak with her thereafter, despite the fact that she would frequently come over to their house to talk with her mother. Mr. K could not be budged, despite his wife's imploring him not to turn his back on his flesh and blood and an integral member of the family business. Growing increasingly isolated (although the theme of isolation was not new in his life), Mr. K agreed to seek a consultation, if for no other reason than to preserve the family business.

Family Background and Developmental History

The second of six children in an intact family, Mr. K was 15 when his father left their family home. He and his older brother, Vic, were two years apart, followed by four younger siblings, two girls and two boys, each at roughly a two- to three-year interval between births. Because he and his older brother were several years older than the younger siblings, Mr. K felt that there were, in effect, two sets of children in his family—he and Vic and then all the rest.

When Mr. K was growing up, his father was frequently gone, sometimes for several days at a time. He worked as a laborer for the railroad, earning barely enough to keep the children adequately fed and in decent clothes. Mr. K remembered his father as a quiet, passive man, who seldom spoke when he returned from long days at the train yard. Perhaps it was both the father's infrequent time spent at home and his quiet, distant demeanor that contributed to Mr. K's having few memories of his father from early childhood. His father had apparently grown up in an orphanage, served briefly in the army, and returned to a rural New England community, where he met and married his first wife. Details about this first marriage were sparse. Mr. K's father never spoke about it, leaving it to his mother to fill in the gaps with stories about how this woman had been unfaithful and stole money from his father.

His father died of a stroke when Mr. K was 31. He had kept in occasional contact with his father, seeing him perhaps every three or four months for short, near wordless visits. When Mr. K was a sophomore in high school, his father had suddenly cleared out his belongings and moved away. Again, in the absence of a coherent explanation provided by his father, Mr. K was left to rely on his mother's version of events, which consisted of venomous descriptions of his father's weakness as a father, husband, sexual partner, and man.

Recalling his mother as an extremely strict, controlling, and critical woman who formed a strong alliance with his older brother and her mother, Mr. K felt that he had no allies in his family. He said that he was given enormous responsibilities at home for the care of his younger siblings. Recounting his cooking dinner, doing chores around the house, and washing the family's laundry, Mr. K bitterly described himself as a "house servant." His story had a Cinderella theme, with him in the role of the suffering slave-child, while his "wicked" mother, "spoiled" brother, and his aloof grandmother did not lift a finger. Regardless of whatever additional dimensions and other truths there may have been, this is how Mr. K recalled his early life in his family.

Mr. K went on to portray his mother in a most unfavorable light. Not only did she demean his father, but she also reportedly criticized everything Mr. K did. No one in this small and conservative community would ever seek psychiatric treatment, but Mr. K suspected that his mother had been hospitalized when he was around the age of 10. It had been a particularly difficult summer, with his mother flying into rages more often than usual. After breaking all of the dishes in the kitchen one morning, his mother suddenly disappeared for an extended "visit" to relatives in a neighboring town. After returning, he recalled, she was taking some kind of medicine for her headaches and nerves. She died of emphysema when he turned 50, but not before filling him with chronic resentment over the miserable way in which he felt she had treated him throughout his life. Her harsh treatment included not only verbal abuse and emotional neglect, but also physical violence, with frequent use of the belt or, according to Mr. K, "anything else she could get her hands on." To his shame, memories of his mother's harshness and emotional deprivation were juxtaposed with fragmentary images of her seductiveness. For the most part hidden from conscious recollection, these memory fragments concerned an anxious sense that his mother may have fondled him or gotten him to fondle her when she had him sleep in her bed. The thought that this might be true disturbed Mr. K no end. He had grown accustomed to viewing his mother as an angry and ungiving woman, but to imagine her as an incestuous seducer as well filled him with revulsion.

Mr. K was pretty sure that his mother had carried on an incestuous relationship with his older brother, Vic. Although this was a closely guarded family secret, he remembered seeing Vic's bed empty on many nights when he awoke to some strange sound in their old house. Vic had always been his mother's (and grandmother's) favorite. He was the oldest and, according to his mother, the best looking, most intelligent, and gifted. More than anything, it was the fact that Vic resembled her side of the family, while Mr. K happened to look more like his ineffectual father.

Vic and Mr. K had reportedly never gotten along. They were close in age but distant in every other way imaginable. Vic was outgoing, whereas Mr. K was introverted; Vic was aggressive, whereas Mr. K was passive, like his father. Furthermore, whereas Mr. K reportedly worked and studied throughout school, Vic never opened a book and cheated his way through high school. Petty thievery in high school escalated to grand theft larceny in his 20s. After spending five years in prison, Vic returned to live off his mother's inheritance. He had chronic difficulties maintaining steady work, frequently getting fired or laid off because he had gotten into fights or been accused of taking things that were not his. Both his brother and mother had reputations in the community as freeloaders who ran up tabs at local businesses. As an adult, Mr. K reportedly tried to help them out financially, only to end up feeling that his big brother, like his mother, was cheating or somehow taking advantage of him financially. He said that he was often ashamed whenever he came into contact with other business owners who had known his mother and brother as people who did not pay their bills.

Mr. K's younger siblings were a faceless and nameless montage of hardworking people who had families and jobs and lived at great distance from him, both emotionally and geographically. He occasionally saw one or two of them but was never close to any.

In the context of his distant and seemingly ungratifying home environment, Mr. K recalled one benign and positive influence. His Uncle Terry, his mother's half-brother, was interested in him and seemed aware of the negative manner in which Mr. K's family treated him. Unlike his father, his uncle did not shy away from an argument with Mr. K's mother, nor did he miss an opportunity to try to stick up for Mr. K. Unfortunately, he was killed in the Korean War when Mr. K was 12.

Mr. K got married in his early 20s, while a student in business school. He had known his wife casually for several years before they decided to marry. "She was quiet and didn't pry," said Mr. K about the reasons that he decided to marry her. Roughly one year after marrying, they had their daughter, followed two years later by the birth of their son. Mrs. K became ill following the son's birth. According to Mr. K, their home became a combination of a nursery and infirmary. For more than a decade, the family maintained a precarious balance. Mrs. K was preoccupied with her health and the lives of her children, which enabled Mr. K to manage his discomfort with intimacy by spending most of his time at work. Like his own father, Mr. K worked long hours and was largely absent from his home and his children's lives. Although his distant relationship from his wife and children served a purpose for Mr. K, it also helped consolidate an extremely close bond between Mrs. K and the children. Mr. K recalled that there was something familiar about coming home at night to see the three of them sitting together on the couch, then suddenly falling silent when he entered the room. Mr. K acknowledged that, on more than one occasion, he had lost his temper with the children and been "too harsh" in his punishment of them.

Educational and Occupational History

Mr. K said that he "got by" in school. No one apparently took an interest in his studies, so school became a way to keep away from the house, his brother, and his mother. In fact, Mr. K remembered spending most of his time by himself, on his bicycle away from the house. He did not recall what he had been doing, only that he preferred to be alone. Being a loner made it difficult for him to make friends.

He graduated from high school with his class and attended the city college until he was drafted into the military at the age of 20. Like many veterans, he spoke little about his experience in Viet Nam. When the subject came up, he would become even quieter than usual. His only reference to his war experience was a cryptic comment about how you should never light a cigarette in the dark because this was the way that snipers could get a mark on their targets. When asked to expand on his combat experience, Mr. K smiled inwardly and said, "Yes, let's just say that I know a little something about that and leave it there."

Finishing college after his release from active duty, Mr. K attended a local business school and went to work for a manufacturing company in his hometown. He referred to himself as a middle manager, who gained a reputation as the "hatchet man" of the corporate community. Whenever the senior executives wanted to terminate an employee, they turned to Mr. K, who had become adept at finding ways either to fire people or "motivate" them to quit. When he discussed this phase of his professional life, he did not seem particularly proud, nor did he seem filled with remorse or shame. He spoke unemotionally about ruining people's lives and of playing the role of the "good soldier" who carried out his orders from his superiors.

A dispute over his bonus eventually led Mr. K to leave this company and go into business for himself. He maintained that the CEO was going to cheat him out of the bonus he had coming to him. Although he had received a bonus that year, it had come late and was smaller than Mr. K believed he was owed. He concluded that the CEO and board members did not like him and that others in comparable positions had received more than he had. He began to suspect that they were conspiring to remove him from his position, so he took protective action. Almost from the time he began working for the company, Mr. K had copied and kept all of the internal memos in a series of black binders, meticulously catalogued and locked in his bookcase. He made oblique reference to these in numerous discussions with his superiors, who he believed knew that he had amassed a great deal of "incriminating evidence" against them. When he finally decided to resign, he was able to negotiate a sizeable settlement, which he attributed to the superior bargaining position afforded him by his black notebooks that he had kept in plain view, under lock and key (with copies hidden where no one could find them). Whenever he spoke about his triumph over corporate greed and suspected deceit, Mr. K seemed pleased with his cleverness.

Mr. K had saved enough to purchase a chain of convenience stores, which he decided to operate as a family business. Despite his emotionally distant relationship with his wife and two children, he believed their business was no one else's business and was best kept in the family. The stores provided well for his family, and each member took on a different role in managing and operating the business. Mr. K's long hours of work grew even longer because he insisted on opening and closing each store. He described the eeriness of waking at 3:30 A.M., parking his car, and walking through the dark streets alone to open his stores. It was in this context that he brought up his enigmatic reference to never lighting a cigarette in the dark.

Over time, tension arose in the family. Mr. K felt little trust for his older child, Alice, whom he began to suspect of stealing from the cash drawer. Mrs. K would hear nothing of this and vigorously defended Alice against her father's accusations. Mrs. K also told Mr. K that she thought that he had been physically abusive with both children when they were young. The schism that existed in the family grew more pronounced, but their considerable dependency on one another for their mutual livelihoods kept them together in a fragile equilibrium.

Mr. K began feeling anxious whenever he came home at night and on the weekends. He and his wife did little together, but something about being home became associated with a vague sense of dread. He started having difficulties sleeping and keeping up with the heavy demands of his schedule. A respected acquaintance revealed that he had gone to a therapist once and found it helpful. Although Mr. K had said nothing about his own mounting stress, he thought about whether he should seek professional help. The idea of talking to someone about his private life made him feel uncomfortable; however, he felt some comfort at the notion that the therapist would be a "stranger." After ruminating privately about this for more than a year, Mr. K called to make an appointment.

Initial Diagnostic Understanding

Growing up in an environment in which feelings were not well tolerated and dissent was reportedly punished, Mr. K developed a character style dominated by a need to seek security by avoiding conflict at all costs.

Through behavioral, interpersonal, and intrapsychic means, he managed to ward off the awareness and expression of strong emotion that might threaten his security. Consequently, he became an overly constricted individual who was initially unable to muster any three-dimensional, affect-enlivened memories from his abusive past, nor could he access current feelings abut his life, other than reporting a vague sense of unhappiness and episodic attacks of anxiety. His ability to focus solely on his work was adaptive in allowing him to fend off troubling feelings from the past, avoid current family conflicts, and build a successful family business, but it was no longer the refuge for him that it once was. He had grown increasingly dissatisfied with his life and reacted toward his wife as if she were the controlling mother of his childhood. On one hand, he wanted to keep his distance from her; on the other hand, he wished he could stand up and resist her control, as he had been unable to do with his own mother when he was a boy.

Evaluation for Psychotherapy

Mr. K initially presented himself in a manner inconsistent with the history that he revealed over time. He was a quiet and soft-spoken gentleman, whose sardonic wit seemed to be offset by an ability to poke fun at himself in a manner that lightened his reported emotional distress. He wore thick, tinted glasses that made it difficult to get a clear view of his eyes. He spoke slowly and deliberately, without any trace of a local accent. Although an articulate spokesman, he at times became somewhat vague and oblique, especially when attempting to describe his feelings. During the initial sessions, his thought processes appeared grossly intact, with no evidence of delusional beliefs, phobic concerns, obsessional ruminations, or illogical reasoning.

Mr. K's manner of expressing himself, his grasp of concepts, and his ability to connect ideas and discern meaning, together with his educational level and success in business, all suggested that his intellectual functioning was superior. Despite his vagueness when attempting to express his feelings, he demonstrated an ability to use words to express himself and to contain his impulses without taking flight into action. He described his mood as apprehensive and increasingly despondent. However, his expressed mood was incongruent with his calm and impassive demeanor when narrating his experience. He denied suicidal thoughts or impulses. Despite his reported history of physical abuse and neglect, his primary defenses were obsessional and relatively mature in nature, based on isolation of affect and intellectualization. More primitive defenses involving projection did not become apparent until psychotherapy was underway.

The quality of Mr. K's relationships with family members, though distant and conflict-ridden, had been stable over a long period of time. He had been married for 32 years. Contrary to his apparent emotional distance from his wife, he expressed great concern about her chronic emphysema. He denied a history of infidelity or thoughts of separation.

Mr. K gave no indication of alcohol or substance abuse. Occasionally, he drank a beer by himself before going to bed, but he denied other circumstances in which he would drink. He suffered from hypertension and was taking antihypertensive medication. A recent physical examination had uncovered no other medical conditions, and his overall health was good.

Although he had always preferred solitude, Mr. K realized how isolated he had been. He said that he hoped he could lessen the conflict in his family and his sense of isolation. Mr. K showed some interest in understanding himself more fully and was initially open to the idea that his present malaise might have roots in his childhood experiences. Despite his concerns about his family problems, he indicated that he was not interested in a treatment process that would include his wife or other members of his family.

Course of Psychotherapy

Mr. K said that he was comfortable meeting weekly for a "period of time" to explore the psychological underpinnings of his symptoms of anxiety and depression. Initially, he preferred to talk exclusively about his unsatisfying relationships with his family members. He seemed to respond surprisingly well to observations concerning how his conflictual relationships with family members reflected his unwitting identifications with his own parents. In both his physically abusive behavior and subsequent withdrawal, Mr. K related to his children as he felt both of his parents had related to him. He spoke fondly about summers with his Uncle Terry, who had been the only person who he felt had cared about him.

What emerged over the first three months of therapy was Mr. K's underlying feelings of resentment over his daughter's irresponsible behavior and, more importantly, his wife's growing invalidism. For a long time, he had attempted to suppress his growing rage and disappointment in his daughter's irresponsibility because, in the past, venting his anger had cast him in the role of "bad guy" and "odd man out" in the family. He was also able to see that he was resentful toward his wife, whose illness he felt he had so dutifully attempted to manage. For all his perceived sacrifice and concern, he felt she responded by forming a conspiracy with the children against him. Although he commented that he must sound paranoid, he said that he felt increasingly uncomfortable with his estrangement from his family members.

Mr. K eventually decided that he would like to talk with someone together with his wife, and he requested referral names for a couples' consultation. The couple saw a marital therapist for roughly two months, but decided not to pursue therapy because "it was too intense." Which of them found this intensity to be problematic was not clear; apparently neither felt comfortable with the openness required by the couples work.

Mr. K continued to attend weekly individual sessions, which he seemed to use effectively. Although he reported that his relationship with his wife had improved slightly, he voiced greater awareness of feeling misunderstood, devalued, and scapegoated by her. He complained how she had turned the children against him, leaving him feeling alone in his family. Feeling ignored and disrespected by his wife, he remained increasingly bitter about the years that went by in which he felt unheard and ignored. These angry feelings of being ignored dovetailed with earlier experiences in his own family, in which his mother and older brother had excluded him. Making the connection for him between how he felt isolated and beleaguered in his current family and in his family of origin seemed to pique his interest in looking more broadly at his life and chronic feelings of isolation.

Viewing me as a surrogate for his supportive and concerned uncle, Mr. K was receptive to the idea of deepening the psychotherapeutic work. Despite a less than optimal early life history that would not seem to augur well for a more intensive approach, Mr. K placed a high value on the psychotherapy process and demonstrated increased motivation to deepen and intensify the work of the treatment. The chronic nature of his unhappiness, the positive nature of the treatment relationship, and his demonstrated ability to use psychotherapy to understand himself better all suggested that he had the capacity to benefit from more frequent psychotherapy sessions.

The transition to a more intensive therapeutic process occurred over several months. Mr. K talked openly about his anxiety regarding more frequent sessions. He admitted that he had grown to depend on therapy but was not sure how he felt about depending too much on any one person. As the time for adding another session drew near, he began to bring in long-forgotten memories of his childhood and family relationships. Previously, Mr. K had claimed to have forgotten large chunks of his early life. He seemed intrigued by the return of these long-forgotten memories. However, the nature of these recovered memories had to do with specific instances of emotional neglect or physical abuse. At times, he appeared almost flooded with memories of his early family life and told vignettes that vividly portrayed his experience of being victimized, exploited, or ignored by his mother. As he began to talk more openly about his history of abuse, his perception of me shifted from that of a benign ally to one of a critical, controlling judge. Much of this shift crystallized around his resistance toward paying his bill. He suddenly stopped paying his bill and complained bitterly about a billing error he felt I had made.

Failing to pay his bill became a central issue in treatment. Not paying was treated as both a manifestation of resistance and a reality-based issue. We discussed the meanings that he had attached to paying the bill. In particular, he feared that paying would lock him into therapy and that he would eventually either go crazy or end up killing himself. His perception of me changed from being his ally to becoming a money-grubbing figure, who was only interested in what I could get from him. Further, it seemed that, in refusing to pay, Mr. K had unconsciously identified with his antisocial brother and daughter, both of whom had rebelled against authority figures and manipulated the system.

The sessions were dominated by his angry assertions that I did not have his best interests at heart. I had become for him a representation of corporate greed, showing little interest in his needs and feelings and wanting only what I could extract from him. He reacted strongly to almost every comment I made, even to benign statements that were intended to be supportive. I had long since shifted away from offering interpretations of his behavior because this only fueled his increasingly paranoid attitudes toward me, and I invited him to share more about his changed perceptions of our interactions. I was careful not to challenge the negative characteristics that he attributed to me, believing that to do so would reinforce his growing sense that I, like his mother and former bosses, was trying to mislead and deceive him. He began to focus narrowly on my gestures and the words I used, making what seemed to be cryptic references to his "documentation" and "clear vision" of how things were. Using highly charged descriptions of the treatment process, Mr. K said that he felt "beat down" and "shafted" by therapy. Veiled references to homosexuality surfaced when he wondered whether most of the men who became therapists were gay.

His negative attitudes in the treatment relationship had thus taken on a distinctly paranoid and psychotic quality. No longer did Mr. K speak about his feelings of betrayal and abuse at the hands of others. Instead, his perception of me as an exploitive, self-serving figure dominated our sessions, often leaving me both to question why he continued to come and to wish that he would not. This entrenched relationship paradigm continued for several months and was finally interrupted by my unplanned absence for a week. When I returned, Mr. K called to tell me that he had decided that he could no longer take time off from his business and that therapy was no longer helpful. He agreed to come in for a final session to talk about his feelings and review our work together.

During this final encounter, Mr. K's paranoid stance softened slightly. He said that the billing error I had made several months earlier had awakened him to the fact that I only wanted his money. This insight coincided with another realization he reluctantly shared that he had come to depend too much on his sessions and that this was unhealthy and uncomfortable. He said that he had gotten all that he wanted out of therapy and was not interested in continuing under any circumstance. Somewhat surprisingly, he promised to pay his unpaid balance and he left abruptly. Several weeks later, I received in the mail a clipping from a local newspaper about a corporate scandal in a nearby town, along with copies of all of his unpaid statements. That was the last thing I heard or received from him.

Final Formulation: Reassessment of Initial Diagnosis and Assessment of Change

Despite a painful ending that seemed to recapitulate his view that others are not to be trusted and to unveil his underlying paranoid structure, Mr. K actually derived some benefit from psychotherapy. At our final meeting, he reported feeling less depressed and more resigned to living with the emotional distance in his marriage. Clearly, however, what had appeared as a benign, positive treatment relationship in the early months of therapy had given way to more negative, persecutory perceptions, which rekindled old paradigms of abuse and exploitation.

Mr. K's active resistance to paying his bill involved a number of such issues. In particular, not paying perpetuated a sadomasochistic paradigm, in which he perceived me as a critical and controlling authority figure, who, like his mother and corporate bosses, was only interested in what I could get from him. His emergent perception of me as an untrustworthy and avaricious parent, ready to pounce on him, was depicted in a dream following our initial discussion of his failure to pay his bill. In this dream, Mr. K was being viciously beaten by his mother (an event he had previously disclosed to me). He could not get away from her; no matter what he tried to do, she kept coming at him. He went on to describe how he was on his grandmother's couch, which was cluttered with figurines (he had once commented that my office seemed cluttered to him). When I asked him about the couch in his dream, he glanced at the couch in my office and said, "Maybe you're like her [mother], coming after me and brow-beating me about this bill."

The perpetuation of this paranoid, sadomasochistic type of relationship acted not only as a defense against painful feelings of loss and deprivation, but also as a way of attributing an exploitive and abusive orientation to someone else. In this way, he could retain an image of himself as a victim and thus not have to grapple with his uncomfortable identification with his own abusive and exploitive mother. Identification with his mother had been a very disturbing idea that he never wanted to accept. Although he had talked about his history of being "cut throat" and "ruthless" in business and "harsh" with his children, he rejected any implication that he may have unwittingly identified with aspects of his own abusive mother.

Mr. K's ability to think psychologically, make connections, and explore meaning collapsed not only around the discussion of his unpaid balance, but equally in the context of his growing feelings of dependency. In this increasingly uncomfortable setting, when issues of payment and a billing error surfaced, all traces of a treatment alliance evaporated. Mr. K then shifted to a perception of me as an adversary from whom he needed to protect himself. His long-standing belief that he must remain on guard against others who would deceive or abuse him was reinforced. As a consequence, he felt less depressed and dissatisfied with himself. The focus of his distress returned, once again, to the external world.

In summary, Mr. K was a complex individual who was capable of functioning at a high level and initially working effectively in a supportive psychotherapeutic relationship. However, his underlying personality weakness and paranoid structure emerged when he found himself becoming dependent on the therapist. When this happened, he began to feel threatened and retreated into an overly suspicious, referential mind-set, in which he perceived the therapist as a critical, unsupportive, and exploitive figure who did not have his best interests at heart.

Conclusion

Typically, individuals with a paranoid personality structure would not be considered to be interested in consultation and self-examination. Paranoid characters are thought to represent an immature level of personality organization in which primitive defenses preclude self-reflection and acknowledgment of internal emotional distress. Mr. K was unusual in many respects. In addition to demonstrating a paranoid core in his personality structure, he had a number of personality strengths that made him initially amenable to psychotherapy. Being able to contend with manageable feelings of depression, self-dissatisfaction, and loneliness are desirable outcomes in working with individuals who employ primitive defenses that involve seeing people as all good or all bad (*splitting*) or without justification attributing to them undesirable and unrecognized characteristics in themselves (*projection*). After all, no personal change is possible unless individuals are in some way dissatisfied with themselves.

Mr. K arrived for therapy voicing dissatisfaction and a wish to change himself. Unfortunately, despite appearing ready to risk taking a look at his life and his relationships, he found the intimacy of increased therapeutic contact and emerging feelings of dependency to be threatening. Threats to autonomy, dependency feelings, and passivity are widely recognized as dangerous risks that paranoid individuals need to ward off at all costs. The arousal of these feelings as therapy progressed made exposing Mr. K's vulnerability intolerable for him, necessitating that he revert back to a character style that had served a self-protective function in the past. The price he paid was feelings of isolation, which sometimes became acutely uncomfortable but, for this man, were far less threatening than the alternative.

Recommended Readings

Gabbard, G. O. (1990). *Psychodynamic psychiatry in clinical practice.* Washington, DC: American Psychiatric Press. (See pp. 305–316 on Cluster A personality disorders: Paranoid, schizoid, and schizotypal.)

Kleiger, J. H. (1999). *Disordered thinking and the Rorschach.* Hillsdale, NJ: Analytic Press. (See pp. 304–310 on disordered thinking associated with other conditions.)

Meissner, W. W. (1978). *The paranoid process.* New York: Aronson.

Meissner, W. W. (1981). The schizophrenic and paranoid process. *Schizophrenia Bulletin, 7,* 611–631.

Shapiro, D. (1965). *Neurotic styles.* New York: Basic Books. (See Chapter 3 on paranoid styles.)

PART THREE

Anxiety and Somatoform Disorders

CHAPTER 8

Panic Disorder with Agoraphobia

RANDI E. McCABE AND MARTIN M. ANTONY

Jason S was a 21-year-old college student and varsity hockey player from a small town in Michigan, who was referred by his college health center to an urban anxiety clinic for evaluation and treatment of anxiety symptoms. At the time of his evaluation, Mr. S was living with a teammate in a college residence. He had played on the varsity hockey team for the past three years and was a senior majoring in political science. He was in the process of applying to enter law school the following year. Mr. S described his schedule as grueling, and he reported struggling with trying to balance his academic load with the demands of playing right wing on the starting line-up of his hockey team. Mr. S said that he enjoyed playing hockey and found his coursework interesting. He was in a steady relationship and described his girlfriend as being "very supportive."

Mr. S described his childhood as having been uneventful. However, he did report that money was scarce when he was growing up, and sometimes his family had struggled to make ends meet. His father was 46 years old and worked in a manufacturing plant. His mother, age 42, had worked in administrative jobs on and off over the years. Mr. S reported being especially close with his father, and he spoke to his parents regularly on the telephone. He described his parents' relationship as loving and supportive. Mr. S had a younger brother, age 19, who was working as an auto mechanic. He described having a "good" relationship with his brother.

Since he was age 8, hockey had played an important role in Mr. S's life, and he was currently attending college on a hockey scholarship. He described himself as a high achiever. He reported that he had always had high expectations for himself and that this had been a source of stress and pressure for him. He described his parents as being very proud of him, but he denied that they had ever set high standards for him. He stated instead that his parents' major priority was having him be happy.

Mr. S reported a family history of depression and alcoholism on his father's side and anxiety on his mother's side. His paternal grandfather was an alcoholic, who died of liver complications. His father's brother had a long history of depression. His maternal grandmother was always a "worrier," he said, and did not like to leave the house.

Presenting Problem

Mr. S reported experiencing problems with anxiety since childhood. He recalled sitting in the gym at age 10 during an assembly at school when, all of a sudden, he felt extremely anxious and thought he was going to be ill. He ran out of the gym to the bathroom. He was sweaty, his heart was racing, and he thought he would vomit, although he never did. His teacher came to check on him and called his mother, who took him home. Mr. S reported that he felt much better once he got home. After this episode in the assembly, he said, it was very difficult for him throughout school to sit in large gatherings where he could not leave easily because of his fear that a similar episode would occur and that he might become sick in public. Aside from this difficulty with sitting in assemblies, however, anxiety did not become a problem for him until he started high school.

During the summer before entering high school, Mr. S felt very anxious about doing so. He was moving from a small middle school to a large high school and was concerned about not knowing anyone and not being able to manage. While riding on a bus, he experienced another episode of physical symptoms. He suddenly began to feel sweaty, lightheaded, and very nauseous. He managed to stay on the bus until he arrived at his destination, but at each stop, he had to fight a strong urge to get off. Once he reached his destination, he felt much better. At this point, Mr. S reported, he started thinking that something was really wrong with him, and he began to worry about having future episodes, especially while at school. He also started to avoid using public transportation.

Mr. S reported that he, nevertheless, managed the transition to high school adequately, often pushing himself to do things despite feeling very anxious and being concerned about future episodes of physical symptoms. He engaged in subtle avoidance strategies, such as sitting on the aisle during an assembly or when in a movie theatre and eating minimally before entering anxiety-provoking situations. For example, he would eat a very small lunch on days when there was an afternoon assembly, so that he wouldn't have anything in his stomach in case he became nauseous. After the first few months of high school, Mr. S's anxiety subsided somewhat, and his fear of having physical symptoms was no longer foremost in his mind. However, he continued to avoid public transportation, and he engaged in safety behaviors during assemblies (i.e., sitting on the aisle) and in other situations that he could not leave easily without attracting attention to himself. He played hockey throughout high school and was offered an athletic scholarship to the college he attended.

The transition to college went well for Mr. S. He enjoyed his coursework and playing on the hockey team. Partway through his first year, Mr. S experienced an episode of physical symptoms during a hockey practice. While on the ice, he felt a wave of nausea, accompanied by a hot flash and dizziness. He thought he was going to throw up. He left the ice and sat on the bench until these feelings passed. He continued with the practice but reported thinking, "Why is this happening again?" and "Is something really wrong with me?" For the rest of his first year and throughout his second year of college, Mr. S struggled through such occasional episodes of intense physical symptoms. He developed ways of coping with anticipatory anxiety by trying relaxation techniques and avoiding situations such as sitting in the middle of an aisle at school or in the middle of a room. When out with friends, he would avoid drinking or using marijuana in case it triggered one of these episodes. He also tried to eat only minimally before games and before entering other anxiety-provoking situations so that, if he had an attack, he could be sure that there was nothing in his stomach that he could throw up.

During the first part of his third year of college, Mr. S's anxiety became significantly worse. He was having attacks of physical symptoms several times per week. It became increasingly difficult for him to sit in class and to attend hockey practices and games. He lost 10 to 15 pounds because of his anxiety. He also reported feeling anxious all of the time, even in situations that he had previously enjoyed, such as going out with friends, going out to eat, and going to the gym. He started to avoid a number of activities. Mr. S's girlfriend let him know that she was very worried about him and wondered what she could do to help. She encouraged him to see a doctor. Mr. S's coaches noticed that he wasn't well and were concerned about his weight loss. They thought that he might be physically ill and instructed him to visit a doctor at the college health center.

The physician at the health center ordered a number of blood tests and a complete medical investigation. Not finding any physical cause for Mr. S's symptoms, the physician suspected that they were due to anxiety and referred him to a specialized anxiety clinic.

Clinical Assessment

Mr. S was pleasant and cooperative when interviewed at the anxiety clinic, although at times he appeared distressed. He seemed motivated to get help for his anxiety symptoms, which were indicative of suffering recurrent, unexpected panic attacks. These panic attacks occurred suddenly, "out of the blue," when Mr. S was not expecting them. During a typical panic attack, he experienced a rush of physical symptoms that included dizziness, nausea, lightheadedness, hot flushes, depersonalization (feeling detached from himself), and derealization (feeling detached from things going on around him). He also reported a number of cognitive symptoms during his panic attacks, including fears of losing control and vomiting. At the time of his assessment, Mr. S's panic attacks were occurring frequently, several times per week.

In addition, Mr. S reported fearing the consequences of his panic attacks, and he displayed significant worry about future attacks. He described "checking in" with his body when he awoke each morning and wondering how he would feel that day. He related frequent thoughts of

"What if I have an attack?" and "Will I be able to make it through the day without having an episode?" He reported being overly aware of how he was feeling on a daily basis and being extremely sensitive to fluctuations in his physical symptoms. He stated that it had become difficult for him to distinguish his usual excitement before a hockey game from the physical signs of an impending panic attack. He also had become reluctant to make any plans, in case he would not be feeling well.

Mr. S had also changed his behavior markedly in response to his episodes of panic. He avoided a number of situations, including waiting in line, crowded places, restaurants, and formal gatherings where it would be hard for him to leave undetected. He also continued to engage in subtle avoidance behaviors, such as sitting next to the aisle in a movie theatre, avoiding movie theatres on crowded nights, and sitting near the back of the class so that he would be close to the door and could leave without being noticed.

Mr. S also reported safety behaviors that he engaged in to control his anxiety. For example, he avoided wearing sweaters or warm clothing because feeling hot was one of his feared symptoms. Depending on how he was feeling, he would carry a brown paper bag in his backpack, particularly if he were going to be in situations that would be difficult to leave, just in case he needed to throw up. Mr. S had never actually vomited during a panic attack. He also reported that, when he needed to enter unfamiliar or anxiety-provoking situations, he felt more comfortable when his girlfriend was with him. He had additionally been adjusting his eating when anticipating an anxiety episode. He would eat minimally and stick to bland foods, which had resulted in his weight loss.

Because of his recent weight loss, Mr. S was feeling increased fatigue and decreased energy. He reported that his mood was starting to worsen as he wondered about how long he could go on feeling the way he did. In the previous month, he had experienced several days of depressed mood. Although he denied any thoughts of suicide, he described his life as having been a struggle since his anxiety had worsened, and his anxiety was making it increasingly difficult for him to enjoy his activities. However, he did not report feeling worse about himself, he was sleeping normally, about seven hours a night, and he denied any other symptoms of depression.

Mr. S reported that he previously had been an outgoing, independent, energetic, and self-confident person. Since his anxiety had worsened, however, his confidence in himself had *disappeared,* he said, and he no longer felt sure about himself or his ability to do things, mainly because he never knew how he would feel. He described a sense of having become *a different person* since his anxiety had begun to interfere with his life. In the past, he felt that he could handle things, although sometimes it was a *struggle to push through.* Now he felt *desperate* to get help because he could no longer function effectively. He also indicated that he had kept his anxiety a secret until now and had been able to confide only in his girlfriend. He worried that his friends and family would think less of him if they knew about his anxiety because they had always viewed him as a confident high achiever.

Mr. S reported drinking sparingly and only at parties because he had always been afraid of how alcohol would affect his anxiety. He did not smoke or drink coffee or tea, and his caffeine intake was minimal. As an athlete, he had always tried to eat well, and he drank caffeinated soft drinks only a few times per week. He was not taking any medication, he had never had any serious illnesses or surgeries, and he had not received any previous treatment for his anxiety.

Diagnostic Impressions and Case Formulation

Mr. S's symptoms were consistent with a primary diagnosis of Panic Disorder with Agoraphobia, as this condition is defined in the American Psychiatric Association (2000) *Diagnostic and Statistical Manual of Mental Disorders (DSM-IV-TR).* He also reported depressive symptoms, but these symptoms were not sufficiently severe or pervasive to meet diagnostic criteria for a depressive disorder. It may be that, if his anxiety had remained untreated, his depressive symptoms might have escalated into full-blown depressive episodes. He denied any other symptoms of mood disorder (e.g., sleep disturbance, loss of interest or pleasure in his activities) or of other anxiety disorders, somatoform disorders, substance use disorders, or eating disorders. He did not exhibit any psychotic symptoms, and there was no evidence of any diagnosable personality disorder. As previously mentioned, there was also no known general medical condition that could have been causing or exacerbating Mr. S's symptoms.

At the same time, Mr. S described several personality characteristics that may have increased his vulnerability to experiencing panic. He was perfectionistic and had high personal standards for success. He displayed a high level of *anxiety sensitivity,* a general tendency to report fear over experiencing the physical symptoms of anxiety. He also reported a family history of anxiety and mood problems, possibly suggesting a biological vulnerability to becoming anxious. Also relevant was the financial stress in his family when Mr. S was young. It is likely that Mr. S's personality style, a biological vulnerability to anxiety, and financial stress in his family combined to precipitate the initial panic attack he experienced at age 10.

Subsequent panic attacks occurred in a fluctuating course over the years, with exacerbations at times of significant stress (e.g., the transition to high school, managing the demands of a full college course load and the hockey team, and, most recently, his application to law school). After his initial panic attack, Mr. S's fear of physical symptoms intensified, and he developed a number of behaviors and maladaptive coping strategies to manage his anxiety, including subtle and overt avoidance and safety behaviors. Over the years, these behaviors had fluctuated along with the intensity of his anxiety and the frequency of his panic attacks.

Numerous personality strengths may have buffered Mr. S against an earlier worsening of his anxiety symptoms, including his high self-esteem, intense determination to *push through* symptoms, and a good social support system that included close family ties and a dependable network of friends. In the last year of his college program, however, Mr. S's stress was heightened as he began to make application to law schools, worried about whether he would get accepted anywhere, and became concerned in general about his future life after college. As Mr. S's stress intensified, his panic attacks and consequent agoraphobic avoidance also intensified, resulting in significant emotional distress and interference with his school and social functioning.

Treatment Recommendations and Prognosis

Several treatment options were reviewed with Mr. S. He had never known that the symptoms he was experiencing had a name, and he expressed great relief to know that he was not crazy, but instead that he had an anxiety disorder that affects up to 3% of the population. Relevant self-help readings on panic disorder and agoraphobia were recommended to Mr. S to help him learn about his symptoms and about strategies for overcoming the anxiety disorder with which he was struggling. A course of cognitive-behavioral therapy (CBT) was recommended as the first step in his treatment. CBT is a type of psychotherapy that has proved highly effective in the treatment of Panic Disorder with Agoraphobia. CBT involves education about panic symptoms and agoraphobia, development of strategies to change anxious thoughts, and behavioral strategies aimed at reducing situational avoidance (situational exposure) and reducing fear of physical symptoms (interoceptive or symptom exposure). It was recommended that Mr. S attend weekly therapy sessions for approximately 12 sessions, followed by maintenance sessions held one month, three months, and six months posttreatment. Mr. S was given the option of individual or group therapy, and he chose to participate in group therapy.

The prognosis for Mr. S was very good. He was highly motivated to engage in treatment and was receptive to the idea of doing homework assignments between therapy sessions, which is an integral part of CBT that facilitates treatment change. He was also eager to meet others who were dealing with symptoms similar to his.

If Mr. S's symptoms were still significantly interfering in his life following the group CBT program or if his symptoms worsened to the extent that he had difficulty engaging in CBT, the addition of a medication would be considered. Several commonly used antidepressant medications have been identified, as well as first-line pharmacological treatments, for Panic Disorder with Agoraphobia, including Prozac, Paxil, Zoloft, and Celexa.

Treatment Course

Mr. S attended all of his scheduled group treatment sessions. Session 1 consisted of discussing the cognitive-behavioral model of Panic Disorder with Agoraphobia, the difference between fear and anxiety, and understanding the cognitive, behavioral, and physical components of anxiety. Mr. S reported that, from the time of the assessment to the first treatment session, he had noticed a significant decrease in his anxiety just from the knowledge he had gained about his anxiety disorder. Although he was anxious about having to sit in a room for a two-hour group therapy session with people he did not know, he managed to tolerate his anxiety and participate in the session. Over the course of the first session, he noticed that his anxiety diminished with time.

In Session 2, Mr. S stated that he felt better about himself after meeting others who were coping with the same problem. Session 2 focused on examining cognitions (thoughts, beliefs, predictions, interpretations, and images) and the major role they play in the exacerbation and persistence of anxiety and panic. Mr. S readily identified his anxious thoughts and was able to grasp the link among thoughts, feelings, and behavior. He identified numerous thoughts involving overestimation of the probability of negative outcomes. For example, he reported that his panic attacks were accompanied by expecting a 90% chance that he would vomit. However, his own experience indicated that the realistic probability of his throwing up during a panic attack was 0%, inasmuch as he had never actually vomited during a panic attack. Mr. S also identified a tendency to engage in *catastrophizing* about the consequences of panic, which consisted of thoughts such as, "If I panic, it will be the worst thing ever and I will not be able to cope," or "If people see that I am anxious, they will think there is something seriously wrong with me," or "If I vomit in public, I will not be able to stand it."

Mr. S additionally described certain beliefs he had about anxiety and about himself that were unrealistic and maladaptive, including "Anxiety is a sign of weakness," "Anxiety is dangerous," "I must always be in control," and "I must be perfect." Mr. S noted that his anxiety had increased from Session 1 to Session 2 after completing homework assignments in which he monitored episodes of panic and anxiety instead of trying, as he usually did, to avoid thinking about his anxiety. He was reassured that this was a normal part of the treatment process and that it was typical for anxiety to increase before it decreases, primarily because treatment focuses on monitoring anxious feelings and thoughts and on decreasing avoidance and safety behaviors.

Session 3 focused on shifting thoughts from anxiety-related cognitive distortions to more realistic, balanced thinking. At first, Mr. S had some difficulty generating evidence against his anxious thoughts. After practicing this task for a week, he began to develop some skill in it. For example, he became able to counter the thought "I am going to panic and throw up" with the following more realistic thoughts: "I have panicked many times before and have never vomited. The chances of something bad happening during a panic attack are 0%. The worst thing that will happen is that I will feel horrible and uncomfortable, but these feelings will pass. The more I practice sitting through the panic feelings, the less scary they will become."

Sessions 4 to 6 were devoted to situational exposure, which involves gradual and repeated confrontation of anxiety-provoking situations. An exposure hierarchy, which is a list of anxiety-provoking situations arranged in ascending order of the distress they are causing the persons, was created for Mr. S and is shown in Table 8.1. Mr. S began with the least anxiety-provoking situation on the list, practiced each step until his anxiety decreased to a minimal level, and then moved up to the next step. When practicing a situation, Mr. S was encouraged to use his cognitive strategies to counter anxious thoughts and to avoid distraction and the use of other subtle avoidance strategies.

Table 8.1   Pretreatment Exposure Hierarchy Ratings for Mr. S

Situation	Anxiety (0–100)	Avoidance (0–100)
Go alone to student center when it is crowded.	100	100
Go to a restaurant and eat a large meal.	95	100
Eat a regular meal the day of a hockey game.	80	90
Go to practice after eating a normal meal in the day.	75	85
Eat a full lunch and then go to class.	75	80
Sit in the middle of the classroom.	70	100
Go to crowded student center with girlfriend.	60	90
Stand in a long line at the bank.	50	70
Sit on the aisle in class.	50	0
Go to class without vomit bag.	40	100

Sessions 7 to 9 were concerned with interoceptive exposure, which consists of repeated confrontation of anxiety-provoking physical symptoms. During the symptom-testing phase, Mr. S attempted a series of exercises designed to trigger various physical symptoms similar to those that occur during panic attacks. The purpose of this initial symptom testing phase was to determine which exercises induced physical symptoms that were both anxiety-provoking and similar to those that Mr. S customarily experienced during his panic attacks. Spinning in a chair for 60 seconds triggered nauseous feelings similar to those that accompanied his panic attacks. Wearing a heavy sweater or turtleneck triggered flushing and anxiety symptoms resembling his experiences when panicky. The third exercise that was anxiety-provoking for Mr. S was staring at himself in a mirror for three minutes. This exercise induced feelings of depersonalization, derealization, and visual disturbance that were similar to his panic symptoms. Over the course of these treatment sessions, Mr. S continued to repeat each of these exercises until he no longer experienced anxiety in response to the intense physical sensations they produced.

Sessions 10 and 11 focused on combining situational exposure with interoceptive exposure. For example, Mr. S would practice wearing heavy clothing into anxiety-provoking settings, such as a movie theatre and his classes. He also practiced spinning in a chair before walking around campus to practice feeling nauseous when in public situations.

Session 12 was devoted to helping Mr. S maintain the gains that he had made during treatment and prevent recurrence of anxiety symptoms and avoidance behavior. Strategies learned during the treatment were reinforced and reviewed. Goals to continue working on were identified. A review of Mr. S's posttreatment hierarchy ratings, shown in Table 8.2, indicated that he should continue to practice eating regular meals before going to class and on game days. He was also encouraged to continue practicing being in crowded situations. The improvements he had achieved were emphasized, but plans were also put in place to prepare him for a possible return of his symptoms. Specifically, Mr. S was instructed to review the materials that had been handed out during the course of treatment, to resume using the strategies taught in the group, to monitor his anxious thoughts and symptoms, and to review his self-help manual for Panic Disorder with Agoraphobia. He was offered the opportunity to schedule a booster session at the clinic to help him get back on track if the need were to arise. Mr. S stated that he was ready for the weekly sessions to come to an end but was glad that he could have some follow-up treatment sessions in the future.

Table 8.2 Posttreatment Exposure Hierarchy Ratings for Mr. S

Situation	Anxiety (0–100)	Avoidance (0–100)
Go alone to student center when it is crowded.	5	0
Go to a restaurant and eat a large meal.	0	0
Eat a regular meal the day of a hockey game.	10	5
Go to practice after eating a normal meal in the day.	5	0
Eat a full lunch and then go to class.	25	15
Sit in the middle of the classroom.	20	10
Go to crowded student center with girlfriend.	10	0
Stand in a long line at the bank.	5	0
Sit on the aisle in class.	0	0
Go to class without vomit bag.	0	0

Treatment Outcome

By the time of his 12th and last treatment session, Mr. S had made significant gains. The frequency of his panic attacks had decreased from several attacks per week to one attack in the past month. His fear of panic also decreased markedly, although he reported that he was still somewhat worried about the panic resurfacing in the future. His agoraphobic avoidance behavior had decreased substantially as well. Mr. S's pre- and posttreatment hierarchy ratings showed a reduction in anxiety and avoidance scores that illustrated further the progress he had made in the course of his treatment.

Mr. S's scores on measures of panic disorder symptom severity that he completed before and after treatment also decreased markedly. On the Panic Disorder Severity Scale (PDSS; Shear et al., 1992), he went from a 2.70 pretreatment score down to 0.71 posttreatment. The PDSS is a clinician-rated scale that measures panic disorder severity on the basis of panic attack frequency, degree of distress during panic attacks, severity of anticipatory anxiety, presence of agoraphobia, fear of panic-related physical sensations, impairment in work or school functioning, and impairment in social functioning. Mr. S's score on the Anxiety Sensitivity Index (ASI; Peterson & Reiss, 1993; Reiss, Peterson, Gursky, & McNally, 1986) decreased from 32 pretreatment to 19 posttreatment. The ASI is a measure of anxiety sensitivity, which, as described earlier, is the fear of experiencing anxiety-related symptoms. Finally, Mr. S's level of impairment, as measured by the Illness Intrusiveness Rating Scale (Devins et al., 1983), diminished markedly from a pretreatment score of 52 to 15 posttreatment.

At the conclusion of Mr. S's treatment, he had reengaged in his regular activities and had begun trying out new activities that he had previously avoided because of his anxiety, such as eating in restaurants. His subtle avoidance strategies had disappeared, and he was able to sit comfortably in a crowded classroom in the middle seat of a row. His safety behaviors had also been reduced. He no longer relied on carrying a bag in case of vomiting, and he was able to normalize his eating.

He reported that his mood had improved substantially and that he was hopeful about his future. He also had increased confidence in his ability to manage any recurrence of anxiety symptoms, using the skills he had developed in the CBT program.

Mr. S expressed interest in continuing some treatment at his college counseling center to address some of the beliefs that made him vulnerable to experiencing stress and anxiety. In particular, he wanted to work on his perfectionism and high standards, his tendency to take on more tasks than he could manage, and his difficulty in setting limits for himself. Mr. S was eager to explore ways of using CBT to get at these underlying issues. He felt very positive about the treatment process he had experienced at our clinic, and he still felt that way when he was seen for follow-up visits one, three, and six months after termination. These follow-up visits were devoted to reviewing his progress, identifying obstacles to continued progress, assessing any current symptoms, and helping him refine and revise his goals for the future.

Recommended Readings

Antony, M. M., & McCabe, R. E. (2002). Empirical basis of panic control treatment. *Scientific Review of Mental Health Practice, 1,* 189–194.

Antony, M. M., & Swinson, R. P. (2000). *Phobic disorders and panic in adults: A guide to assessment and treatment.* Washington, DC: American Psychological Association.

Baker, S., Patterson, M., & Barlow, D. H. (2002). Panic disorder and agoraphobia. In M. M. Antony & D. H. Barlow (Eds.), *Handbook of assessment and treatment planning for psychological disorders* (pp. 67–112). New York: Guilford Press.

Craske, M. G., & Barlow, D. H. (2001). Panic disorder and agoraphobia. In D. H. Barlow (Ed.), *Clinical handbook of psychological disorders* (3rd ed., pp. 1–59). New York: Guilford Press.

Taylor, S. (2000). *Understanding and treating panic disorder: Cognitive and behavioral approaches.* Chichester, UK: Wiley.

White, K. S., & Barlow, D. H. (2002). Panic disorder and agoraphobia. In D. H. Barlow (Ed.), *Anxiety and its disorders: The nature and treatment of anxiety and panic* (pp. 328–380). New York: Guilford Press.

References

American Psychiatric Association. (2000). *Diagnostic and statistical manual of mental disorders* (4th ed., text rev.). Washington, DC: Author.

Devins, G. M., Blinik, Y. M., Hutchinson, T. A., Hollomby, D. J., Barre, P. E., & Guttman, R. D. (1983). The emotional impact of end-stage renal disease: Importance of patients' perceptions of intrusiveness and control. *International Journal of Psychiatry and Medicine, 13,* 327–343.

Peterson, R. A., & Reiss, S. (1993). *Anxiety Sensitivity Index Revised test manual.* Worthington, OH: International Diagnostic Systems.

Reiss, S., Peterson, R. A., Gursky, D. M., & McNally, R. J. (1986). Anxiety sensitivity, anxiety frequency and the prediction of fearfulness. *Behavior Research and Therapy, 24,* 1–8.

Shear, M. K., Brown, T. A., Sholomskas, D. E., Barlow, D. H., Gorman, J. M., Woods, S. W., et al. (1992). *Panic Disorder Severity Scale (PDSS).* Pittsburgh, PA: University of Pittsburgh School of Medicine, Department of Psychiatry.

CHAPTER 9

Obsessive-Compulsive Disorder

DEBORAH A. ROTH AND EDNA B. FOA

David was a 26-year-old man who presented for treatment of Obsessive-Compulsive Disorder (OCD) at the University of Pennsylvania Center for the Treatment and Study of Anxiety. His two primary complaints were anxiety about contamination and fears about inadvertently harming others or behaving inappropriately to others. David came to our center savvy about the nature of OCD, having already read about the disorder and having tried to work on the problem himself using self-help books. Yet, despite a great deal of effort and motivation, he continued to be plagued by intrusive thoughts and time-consuming rituals.

At the time of the assessment, David was holding a temporary job after having to leave his job as a journalist because of his OCD symptoms. Specifically, David feared that he would inadvertently write insulting or offensive things in his articles. He frequently missed deadlines because he spent far too much time checking his articles before turning them in. Once they were submitted, he would be plagued by intrusive thoughts about what he had written until the articles came out and he could check them.

When David presented for treatment, he was living with his girl friend of six years. Although their relationship was strong, David reported that his OCD often interfered with it. He frequently asked his girlfriend for reassurance about his concerns and had strict rules for cleanliness in the house that he expected her to follow. Furthermore, David was bringing in much less money than he had in the past, which was causing additional stress inasmuch as the couple had recently purchased a new house.

David came across as a pleasant, open, and friendly young man. Despite his struggles with OCD, he was positive about his future, was extremely committed to treatment, and refused to "let OCD win."

History and Assessment of Problem

David recalled having had symptoms of OCD since age 8 or 9. As a child, he was nicknamed "Doubting Thomas" by his mother because he worried so much about doing the wrong thing or making mistakes. His contamination fears also began in childhood. At the time of his evaluation at our center, David had been seeing a therapist weekly for more than a year, but the treatment had not been focused specifically on OCD symptoms. He had also been prescribed Zoloft, an antidepressant medication used in treating OCD, which he said had led to minimal improvement in his symptoms.

David was assessed with the Yale Brown Obsessive Compulsive Scale (YBOCS; Goodman, Price, Rasmussen, Mazure, Delgado, et al., 1989; Goodman, Price, Rasmussen, Mazure, Fleischmann, et al., 1989) to measure his OCD symptoms and the Structured Clinical Interview for *DSM-IV* (SCID-IV; First, Spitzer, Gibbon, & Williams, 1997) to help determine the full extent of his current difficulties.

Assessment of Obsessive-Compulsive Disorder Symptoms

The YBOCS is the most commonly used clinician-administered measure of the symptoms of OCD. It includes a checklist of commonly experienced obsessions and compulsions as well as 10 items that assess the severity of obsessions and compulsions. YBOCS scores range from 0 to 40; before treatment, David's score was 25, reflecting OCD of moderate severity.

Before administering the YBOCS, it is important to discuss with patients the YBOCS definitions of obsessions and compulsions and to help them recognize the functional relationship between them. Obsessions are thoughts, impulses, or images that are experienced as intrusive, unwanted, and distressing. Patients with OCD engage in compulsions, which can take the form of behaviors or mental acts, as a means of alleviating obsessional distress. Compulsions are meant not only to relieve anxiety, but also to ward off consequences that are feared by patients with OCD.

As previously mentioned, one of David's main concerns was behaving inappropriately. When having conversations with people, he worried that he had cursed, said something offensive, or given incorrect (wrong) information. At times during his evaluation interview, David seemed lost in his own thoughts and sometimes missed questions that were asked of him. When asked about this behavior, David indicated that he had been reviewing his previous responses to make sure that he had not said anything wrong. This clarification was helpful for the therapist because it allowed her to see in action how the OCD symptoms were affecting David in his daily life. Furthermore, being asked whether his symptoms were making it difficult to attend to the interview made David feel understood by the therapist and, subsequently, more comfortable in admitting that he had failed to hear some of the questions he had been asked.

As already noted, David presented with two main complaints. First, he had contamination obsessions. Some of these obsessions, such as getting dirty or being exposed to germs while using public bathrooms and cleaning up after his dog, are fairly common concerns among obsessive people with OCD. Other cues for his contamination obsessions were more idiosyncratic, such as walking by street people and "sick-looking people" while out in public. David was also preoccupied with concerns about bugs (mostly maggots), which he constantly worried he would find in his food, at the bottom of his glass, or even in his clothing.

When inquiring about patients' obsessions, it is essential to ask what they fear will occur if, when confronted with situations that cause them to worry, they do not engage in their customary compulsive rituals. David said that he feared contracting illnesses, most notably AIDS and other sexually transmitted diseases, but that he was also concerned about how exposure to these situations made him feel. For him, disgust was just as much a part of the experience as anxiety, and he reported often feeling "grossed out" when he came into contact with people or objects that he perceived as contaminated.

As to how these concerns affected David's behavior in terms of compulsions, he did a great deal of washing and checking. He frequently washed his hands, not only after using public restrooms or cleaning up after the dog, but also when he felt dirty (e.g., after walking by a street person). David checked his body for bugs after cleaning up the dog's droppings or taking the trash out; checked his clothes for bugs before putting them on in the morning; and checked his food, dishes, and glasses for bugs. He also avoided many things. He would cross the street to avoid street people or people who looked ill, would not go to hospitals, often avoided public bathrooms, and sometimes threw away food in the middle of a meal if he thought that there were bugs in it.

David's other main OCD complaint involved fear of accidentally harming others or accidentally behaving inappropriately. Included in this category was concern about harm coming to his dog if he failed to make sure that all of the appliances were turned off and the door was locked before he left for work each morning. Concerns about harm coming to others were particularly severe at times when David was not paying careful attention to what he was doing. For example, as David left work each day and walked home, he would worry that he might have touched someone inappropriately in the elevator, pushed someone into traffic in the street, or cursed at a neighbor in his building. At work as well as in his personal life, David worried constantly that he had said or written something obscene when communicating with others (e.g., phone calls, e-mails, letters) or that he had put a dangerous substance such as anthrax in something that he mailed.

In response to these obsessions, David engaged in a great deal of compulsive checking (of locks, appliances, plugs, etc.), but his major compulsion was mental reviewing. When David realized that he had been walking along the street or doing something at his work without paying attention, he would begin to retrace his steps in his head and try to make sure that he had not harmed anyone or done anything inappropriate. Even after checking his e-mails and letters many times before sending them, he would still mentally review them after they had gone out in an effort to remember if he had inadvertently written something inappropriate or potentially harmful. David also avoided being in touch with people unless it was absolutely necessary, and he tried to have his girlfriend always accompany him to social events so that she could monitor what he was saying.

David's evaluation also included the SCID-IV, a semistructured clinical interview that assesses for the presence of anxiety disorders, mood disorders, substance use disorders, somatoform disorders, and eating disorders and includes a screen for psychotic symptoms. The purpose of administering the SCID was to get a more complete picture of David's current difficulties to devise an appropriate treatment plan. The SCID interview helps therapists assess whether OCD is a patient's main psychological disorder and whether the presence of other forms of psychopathology (e.g., severe depression, thought disorder, substance use disorder) might impede treatment for OCD. David gave evidence only of OCD in his responses to the SCID.

Exposure and Ritual Prevention

David decided to participate in exposure and ritual prevention (EX/RP), a treatment designed to target OCD symptoms. The EX/RP program used with David was delivered in 17 twice-weekly sessions, each lasting between 90 minutes and two hours. EX/RP is based on the behavioral theory that obsessions are maintained through avoidance of situations, objects, and thoughts that evoke obsessional distress and through engaging in compulsions, which are conceptualized as escape behaviors. According to this behavioral theory, compulsions are maintained by negative reinforcement, that is, by the manner in which compulsions can temporarily terminate obsessional distress. The treatment involves exposing patients to cues that provoke their obsessions, while at the same time encouraging them to refrain from engaging in compulsive rituals. The goal is to help patients learn that their anxiety will diminish on its own without their engaging in rituals and, most importantly, that the feared consequences of failing to perform these rituals will not occur. Considerable evidence has been gathered for the efficacy and durability of EX/RP as a treatment for OCD (see Franklin & Foa, 2002).

Information Gathering

Before getting started with exposure and ritual prevention, David's therapist spent two sessions gathering information on David's OCD symptoms. During these sessions, David and his therapist reviewed the definition of obsessions and compulsions and discussed their functional relationship. They also discussed avoidance behaviors and how, like rituals, they serve to maintain OCD symptoms over time.

A hierarchy of feared situations was created to guide the progress of treatment (see Table 9.1). David identified the triggers that led to his obsessive thoughts and rituals and rated each according to how much anxiety it caused, using the Subjective Units of Distress (SUDS) scale. The SUDS scale ranges from 0 (no anxiety) to 100 (extreme anxiety). David's therapist explained that they would start treatment by working on items at the lower end of the hierarchy and gradually move up the hierarchy as he succeeded in experiencing a decrease in distress and a change in his beliefs that he had to engage in rituals to gain a sense of safety.

One crucial aspect of these first sessions was conceptualizing correctly David's mental rituals. Before coming to our center, David had not viewed mental reviewing as a ritual. Like many patients with OCD (and many clinicians as well), David assumed that rituals had to be overt behaviors, such as hand washing. In fact, compulsions can also take the form of mental acts such as saying a prayer, counting up to a certain number, and, as in David's case, mental reviewing. Before coming for treatment, David and his other therapists had viewed this constant rush of thoughts as obsessions.

To conduct effective EX/RP, it is necessary to identify which repetitive thoughts are obsessions and which are mental compulsions. This distinction is important because the goal of treatment is to expose patients to the obsessions and to situations that evoke them and to have

Table 9.1   David's Hierarchy of Feared Situations

Situation	Subjective Units of Distress
Visiting a hospital.	50
Leaving house without checking appliances.	60
Walking along street where there are lots of people.	60
Taking meds without checking for bugs.	60
Walking by a sick-looking person.	70
Calling people on phone.	70
Brushing teeth without checking toothpaste for bugs.	80
Writing e-mails.	80
Touching trash cans.	80
Shaking hands with a sick-looking person.	90
Drinking water while walking through hospital.	90
Leaving house without checking doors.	90
Drinking from glass that has been out of my sight.	90
Taking dog out and not checking face and body for bugs.	90
Answering the phone.	90
Using toilet paper without checking for bugs.	95
Sitting directly on toilet seat.	95
People spitting near me.	100
Leaving house without checking plugs.	100
Drinking from the tap without rituals (checking glass for bugs, pouring water out, and refilling repeatedly).	100
Sealing envelopes at work without checking.	100

them refrain from mental rituals as well as overt compulsions. Attempting to push obsessions out of the mind can actually have the paradoxical effect of increasing the frequency with which the thought subsequently occurs (see Abramowitz, Tolin, & Street, 2001).

Once the information gathering was completed, David was taught how to monitor his obsessions and compulsions by recording activities or thoughts that evoked the urge to engage in rituals, the discomfort caused by these activities or thoughts (using the SUDS scale), and the amount of time spent on rituals. The therapist explained to David that the need for such monitoring is dictated by the fact that, for patients who have had OCD for many years, rituals often become so automatic that they are difficult to identify and quantify. Self-monitoring increases self-awareness and thus provides patients and therapists a clearer sense of the cues that trigger obsessions and how much time is being taken up by rituals in a typical day. It also helps patients identify rituals that they might not have recognized in themselves and that were consequently overlooked during the information gathering.

Implementing Exposures and Ritual Prevention

In the third session of EX/RP, the first exposures are done and ritual prevention is implemented. One of the major challenges in this third session is to help patients understand how to stop their rituals. It is unrealistic simply to tell them to stop; if it were that simple, they would have done so on their own. In David's case, he had also tried, very hard but unsuccessfully, to control his OCD symptoms with the aid of self-help books. For patients to accept that they must deliberately expose themselves to their obsessions and at the same time stop their rituals, they must have a clear grasp on the functional relationship between obsessions and compulsions. Within this conceptual framework, it becomes apparent that the goal of EX/RP is to demonstrate that anxiety decreases on its own during exposure exercises without the person having to resort to rituals and that feared consequences are unlikely to happen even if the protective rituals are not performed. It is important to emphasize that, as long as patients give in to the urge to ritualize and do not expose themselves systematically to obsessional cues, the OCD symptoms will continue. Because the OCD symptoms are very distressing, the knowledge that they can be decreased through systematic exposure and ritual prevention can be very motivating for patients. Although stopping rituals is typically a frightening prospect for patients, many are also motivated by the idea of what life would be like without OCD. David was one such patient—he very much wanted to get back to his journalism career, wanted to marry his girlfriend, and hoped to have children. He felt that all of these goals were impossible if so much of his time and mental energy continued to be taken up by OCD.

As in the case of many patients, David's OCD was complicated and required decisions about which symptoms to work on first. As mentioned, David had two main obsessions, both of which were very distressing and time consuming. The idea of stopping his washing and checking rituals and his mental reviewing at the same time was overwhelming to him. Although his mental rituals were the more distressing of the two, ritual prevention with his washing and checking compulsions was implemented first. Although it is typically ideal to target the most distressing and impairing rituals first, mental rituals can be very hard to stop. To increase David's confidence in the treatment approach, it was decided that the best place to start would be with his washing and checking.

Paralleling this decision, the first in-session exposures were focused on David's contamination fears. During the session, David took his medication without checking it for bugs and drank from a bottle of water that he considered to be contaminated (it had been sitting on his desk at work, and he had walked past some street people while holding it). David continued to drink from the bottle of water until his SUDS went from an 80 to a 30. For homework, he was asked to continue drinking from that same bottle of water, and he was also asked to refrain from all compulsions related to drinking (e.g., checking every glass of water for bugs and pouring it out before finishing it if he thought it was contaminated) as well as to getting dressed and using the bathroom (e.g., by dressing without checking his clothes for bugs, sitting directly on the toilet seat, and washing his hands briefly after defecating or taking the dog out).

The third and fourth sessions were also focused on David's contamination-related concerns. In the fourth session, David and his therapist visited the hospital. David was instructed to walk to this hospital with his bottle of water open, which was difficult for him because he feared it would get contaminated. On arriving at the hospital, David followed instructions to drink from his water bottle, and he had a snack in the cafeteria while sitting near some "sick-looking" people. For the fifth session, David's therapist visited him at his home. Home visits are an important part of treatment for OCD patients whose disorder lives at home. At the beginning of David's home session, he poured a bowl of cereal and left it on the counter while he and his therapist turned their attention elsewhere. David became concerned that bugs would get into the cereal, and he also experienced feelings of contamination when asked to take his dog outside and then to carry out the trash. The therapist instructed him to wash his hands briefly and to refrain from checking to see if there were any bugs on him. He was then brought back to the kitchen, where he followed instructions to drink some glasses of water and eat the cereal without checking for bugs.

This fifth session concluded with the therapist's helping David leave the house without checking any appliances or locks. In working with patients like David who are obsessively concerned with being responsible, clinicians doing exposure treatment take care to avoid being assigned responsibility. Ritualistic checkers can often minimize their anxiety by leaving their house in the company of another person, particularly if that other person checks the locks and appliances or watches them do so. This arrangement allows the patient to share responsibility with the other person. When making home visits with OCD patients, therapists should not allow themselves to become such a "safe person." At the end of David's home visit, his therapist stood on the driveway with her back turned as he left the house and locked up. Had David been unable to leave without checking, the therapist could have encouraged him to go back into the house, turn the appliances on and off without checking, and then lock up again. In this way, the therapist would have served as a coach, but not as a safety signal.

Knowledgeable therapists recognize, however, that total ritual prevention cannot be expected right from the start of treatment. Even in eventually effective treatment, lapses in ritual prevention occur, especially in the beginning, and patients must be forewarned about these lapses and helped to accept and tolerate them. Often, patients feel ashamed about doing rituals after they have been encouraged to discontinue them, and it is accordingly important for therapists to convey that recurrent rituals are not signs of failure or grounds for punishment, but rather a basis for working further on the skills that are taught in EX/RP.

Early in David's treatment, he continued to have problems with not putting paper on the toilet seat when using the bathroom. He also continued to have difficulty refraining from checking for bugs on his face and hands after taking his dog out. His reporting these violations led to fruitful discussions about how to get past such sticking points. David decided that it would be helpful to call his therapist a few mornings in a row when he came in from walking the dog, so that she could help him over the telephone to refrain from his rituals. The therapist encouraged him to wash his hands at the kitchen sink instead of in the bathroom (where there was a mirror) to reduce his temptation to check his face for bugs. If David gave in to the OCD and put paper on the seat before using the toilet, the therapist encouraged him to remove the paper and sit on the seat for a few minutes until his SUDS came down, even if he no longer felt a need to move his bowels.

Once David appeared to have a good grasp of ritual prevention related to his contamination fears and was frequently initiating exposures on his own between sessions, the treatment focus turned to his mental reviewing. Diminishing his mental reviewing proved to be a more challenging task than curtailing his washing and checking rituals. Treatment of his mental rituals included teaching him how to deal with intrusive thoughts and how to use imaginal exposure for this purpose.

As already noted, OCD patients need to recognize the paradoxical effect of stopping obsessions. When David experienced intrusive thoughts (e.g., "I might have killed my boss today" or "Maybe I cursed when I left that phone message"), he would often try to stop them. When this failed, he would engage in mental reviewing, retracing his steps or what he said to make sure he hadn't done what he feared he had done. Dealing with the thoughts in this way made it very difficult for David to concentrate on anything else. Furthermore, despite reviewing his experience sometimes for days at a time, David rarely came to an answer that satisfied him and reassured him that he had not done something wrong. He had never considered simply letting the thought be in his head. His therapist told him that he did not have to pay attention to the thought, but rather that he should "go about his business." In other words, even if the thought was still running in the back of his mind, David was told to refrain from attending to it, either by trying to stop it or by engaging in mental reviewing.

The other crucial part of the treatment for David's mental reviewing involved imaginal exposure. In imaginal exposure, scripts are created that tell the story of the patient's most feared consequences in vivid detail. After scripts are written, a tape recording is made of the therapist reading them, and patients are instructed to listen to these tapes repeatedly, until the stories no longer bother them. This technique was very helpful to David. A highly creative person who enjoyed writing, he was very diligent about writing vivid and detailed scripts as homework assignments. However, his SUDS ratings for the first few imaginal exposures were only moderately high on the first listening and decreased after only a few repetitions, which suggested that the scripts had not adequately tapped his fear structure. The stories in these scripts told of David actually doing bad things, such as killing his boss after a stressful day at work. When David and his therapist gave further thought to the scripts they had created so far, they determined that what David truly feared was not doing something bad, but not knowing whether he had harmed someone or done something inappropriate.

From that point, the imaginal exposures consisted of stories in which David would lose track of what he was doing (e.g., daydreaming when he was walking home from work) and then get arrested by the police and charged with a crime he could not remember committing. These stories always ended with David losing his girlfriend and his livelihood and spending the rest of his life in prison. David's SUDS ratings were very high on the first few repetitions of these stories, and it took many repetitions at home between sessions for David to reach a point where the stories began to sound ridiculous to him.

Tackling the mental reviewing aspect of David's OCD proved difficult for him, and he frequently became frustrated with his inability to banish intrusive thoughts and refrain from rituals. This difficulty was dealt with in three ways. First, David's therapist continued to emphasize the functional relationship between obsessions and compulsions, namely, that each time he gave in to the OCD and engaged in mental reviewing, he kept his disorder alive. Second, David and his therapist discussed being able to accept uncertainty. Although they could be confident that he had never done and was unlikely ever to do any of the terrible things he feared doing, they discussed how perfect certainty is impossible to accomplish. The need for perfect certainty leads to the need to engage in mental rituals; by contrast, accepting that something bad might have occurred but that the likelihood is extremely low precludes the need for extensive reviewing of what did or did not happen. Finally, David's therapist spoke to him about having reasonable expectations for the outcome of treatment. Some people with OCD continue to experience intrusive thoughts even after successful treatment. These intrusive thoughts are likely to be less frequent and less intense than before, but they may, nevertheless, recur from time to time. When they do recur, patients should have been helped to learn how to deal with the thoughts. Instead of resorting to rituals, patients must know how to allow an intrusive thought just to be there, while they go about their business.

Termination

Near the end of treatment, David and his therapist spent some time talking about the maintenance of gains and how to continue working on whatever OCD symptoms continued to be problematic for him. By the end of treatment, David realized that he would continue to experience some intrusive thoughts for the rest of his life, but that what was important was how he dealt with them. He recognized that resorting to rituals could lead to a relapse, and, given how much he was enjoying his life with less severe OCD symptoms, he was highly motivated to maintain his new patterns of behavior. David and his therapist also discussed what he should do if new OCD symptoms developed in the future. He recognized that the techniques he had learned could be used regardless of the nature of the obsessions and compulsions he experienced, and he was prepared to do in vivo exposures and imaginal exposures as a way of dealing with new symptoms if they arose. He also left therapy realizing that it was very important for him not to start avoiding the types of situations that had brought on his OCD symptoms.

By the 17th session of treatment, David was doing very well. He had overcome most of his problems in the area of contamination concerns. He was getting ready for work much more quickly in the morning because he no longer had to do his washing and checking rituals. Although he still felt some anxiety after walking the dog and when leaving the house in the morning without checking the plugs, locks, and appliances, he felt confident that this anxiety would decline on its own, without his having to resort to behavioral rituals. David had slightly less success in stopping his mental rituals. He still experienced intrusive thoughts about harming others or doing something inappropriate a few times a week. This was very frustrating for him, even though the intrusions were occurring much less frequently than they had before the treatment. Occasionally, David found himself doing mental reviews, and he realized how important it was for him to do away completely with mental reviewing. He also recognized that, when he did review, he was able to shut off the reviewing process sooner than had previously been the case. He accomplished this improvement by quickly reminding himself that mental reviewing rarely resulted in a satisfying solution to his concerns, and this reminder often proved sufficient to shift his attention to other matters. David was also able to do imaginal exposures on his own when he was having difficulty with some particular intrusive thought.

To obtain some objective measure of David's improvement, he was given a second YBOCS following the 17th session. His YBOCS score was found to have dropped from its pretreatment level of 25 to only 10, thus confirming a substantial decrease in his OCD symptoms. He was continuing to experience some intrusive thoughts that were causing him mild distress, and he was still engaging in rituals from time to time. However, he was clearly feeling better about himself and about his ability to exert self-control. Moreover, there was good reason to believe that, as David continued to apply the skills he had learned in his treatment, his condition would continue to improve and his YBOCS score decline.

Recommended Readings

Foa, E. B., & Kozak, M. J. (1997). *Therapist's guide for the mastery of your obsessive compulsive disorder.* New York: Psychological Corporation.

Goodman, W. K., Rudorfer, M. V., & Maser, J. D. (Eds.). (2000). *Obsessive-compulsive disorder.* Mahwah, NJ: Erlbaum.

Swinson, R. P., Antony, M. M., Rachman, S., & Richter, M. A. (Eds.). (1998). *Obsessive-compulsive disorder: Theory, research, and treatment.* New York: Guilford Press.

References

Abramowitz, J. S., Tolin, D. F., & Street, G. P. (2001). Paradoxical effects of thought suppression: A meta-analysis of controlled studies. *Clinical Psychology Review, 21,* 683–703.

First, M. B., Spitzer, R. L., Gibbon, M., & Williams, J. B. W. (1997). *Structured Clinical Interview for* DSM-IV, *Axis I Disorders (SCID-I), Clinician version.* Washington, DC: American Psychiatric Press.

Franklin, M. E., & Foa, E. B. (2002). Cognitive behavioral treatment of obsessive-compulsive disorder. In P. Nathan & J. Gorman (Eds.), *A guide to treatments that work* (2nd ed., pp. 367–386). Oxford, England: Oxford University Press.

Goodman, W. K., Price, L. H., Rasmussen, S. A., Mazure, C., Fleischmann, R. L., Hill, C. L., et al. (1989a). The Yale-Brown Obsessive

Compulsive Scale. I: Development, use, and reliability. *Archives of General Psychiatry, 46,* 1006–1011.

Goodman, W. K., Price, L. H., Rasmussen, S. A., Mazure, C., Delgado, P., Heninger, G. R., et al. (1989b). The Yale-Brown Obsessive Compulsive Scale. II: Validity. *Archives of General Psychiatry, 46,* 1012–1016.

CHAPTER 10

Posttraumatic Stress Disorder

JUDITH G. ARMSTRONG AND JAMES R. HIGH

Posttraumatic Stress Disorder (PTSD) is one of the few psychological conditions whose very name implies that we know its cause, namely, a psychologically traumatizing event. A traumatizing event causes two reactions: first, the belief that you or another person will be seriously injured or killed; second, feeling terrorized or helpless in the face of this situation. Nearly everyone has had a traumatic experience. After a short period of turmoil, most people can move past the experience and even grow from it. For a few people, however, vivid disturbing memories of trauma continue to plague their sleeping and waking lives as they relive the experience again and again. Seeking escape from continual emotional pain, they close off their feelings and withdraw from relationships. Yet, as though an inner alarm had sounded, their minds and bodies remain on high alert. They are easily startled, sleepless and irritable, and ever vigilant for the next danger. Avoidance and emotional numbing, alternating with overwhelming reexperiencing and hyperarousal, were all problems for Jack when we first met.

The Traumatic Event

Jack had always been someone special. A charismatic leader and star athlete in college, he was now head coach of a university football team. Using his charisma to recruit highly prized prospects, he had rescued the program from mediocrity and won considerable respect. It was a recruiting trip that put him on Flight 1739 as it made its rocky descent through a spring thunderstorm into his home airport. He had made this flight often enough to realize that today the approach was not routine. Passing over the supermarket he used as a landmark, he saw that they were far too high, and he expected a hard landing. The plane slammed down just as he had predicted. However, with growing alarm, he saw that their landing point was halfway to the end of the runway. He was prepared for being thrown forward as the brakes grabbed, but not for the plane's sudden sharp right turn. It threw him hard against the left bulkhead and pinned him there. He watched helplessly as the plane crashed through a fence and skidded toward a wall at the end of the runway. Ceiling panels clattered down, oxygen masks dropped, and the cabin filled with an acrid cloud of smoke. He remained immobilized as the scene took on a surreal quality. Everything now seemed to move silently, in slow motion. He expected the plane to strike the wall, killing everyone in a fiery blast, but he felt surprisingly calm about it all. Suddenly, the horrifying sounds, smells, and sense of rapid motion returned. Somehow, the plane stopped a few feet short of the wall.

Panic overtook most of the passengers, but not Jack. Typical of the leader he was, he controlled his feelings and helped others evacuate. When he reached the tarmac, he even had the presence of mind to phone his wife to reassure her that he was safe, should she see coverage of the crash on TV. Then, thinking of his fellow passengers, he calmly called the local news station to report that no one had been seriously hurt. Jack's call was recorded and broadcast repeatedly that evening. The following morning, he was contacted by national news sources. As the most famous passenger on the plane, he was seen as the best interview. He gave several interviews in which he recounted his story, but he then suddenly refused further requests to talk about what had happened.

When football practice began, he seemed to attack the new season with even greater dedication than usual. His assistant coaches noticed that he was uncharacteristically irritable and aggressive, but he was also more prepared and organized than was ordinarily the case. The team started the season winning. Jack's wife, Lenore, was accustomed to his long work hours during football season. This time, she sensed something disturbingly different about him. He seemed almost to resent her presence. She would wake up in the middle of the night and find him in the study, drinking. Their once active sex life became nonexistent. Her efforts to reach out to him seemed to irritate him and drive him farther away. She hoped the end of football season would bring things back to normal, but it didn't. Jack remained distant and aloof, unable to enjoy having had a successful season.

The following spring, Jack threw himself once more into recruiting, but he seemed to have lost his touch. Returning home from an unsuccessful recruiting trip, he again experienced flying into a storm. His plane shook violently, and the pilots elected to abort their intended landing and divert to an airport 150 miles away. After landing uneventfully, they announced that the storm had passed and that they would soon take off for their original destination. Jack became enraged. Trembling and sweating, he demanded to be allowed to disembark. He left the plane, rented a car, and drove the long distance home. That evening, he refused to discuss the incident with Lenore, but at midnight he woke her, complaining of crushing chest pains and difficulty breathing. For the first time ever, she saw terror on his face. Paramedics transported him to the university hospital, where doctors initially assumed he was having a heart attack. However, blood tests and electrocardiograms showed no evidence of cardiac problems. His only abnormalities were an elevated blood pressure and rapid pulse, both of which returned to normal when he was given a tranquilizer.

Confident that Jack's heart was fine, his doctor suggested he had suffered an anxiety attack. He asked Jack if he were under unusual stress. Jack laughed and said, "I'm always under unusual stress. That's coaching." His doctor persisted and strongly recommended that Jack consult a university psychology professor who specialized in anxiety. Lenore was relieved to learn that her husband had not suffered a heart attack and would get help for something that was going on with him psychologically. Jack, on the other hand, was irritated. He refused to believe that his symptoms could be psychologically based.

The following week, Jack was packing to fly to recruit another top prospect. Suddenly he felt the return of chest pain, rapid pulse, and shortness of breath. This time the symptoms were so severe he thought he would faint. A quick trip to the emergency room resulted in the same negative test findings as before and another recommendation that he seek psychological help. Jack now recognized that the attack had cost him a chance at a top player. This convinced him that he had a real problem that he had better fix. He sought the advice of the dean of the medical school at his university, who referred him to our diagnostic and treatment unit.

Evaluating the Traumatic Reaction

Jack strode into our interview room. He told us he was certain that we had read his file and, therefore, needed no further explanation from him. He just wanted to know our game plan for eliminating his attacks. We gently suggested there might be more to him and his attacks than was contained in his chart. He then admitted that he was worried. He said that he had lost his touch in connecting with recruits and felt distant from people, even his wife and his son Michael. We asked him if he could recall any of his actions, thoughts, or feelings immediately preceding his attacks. At first, he said that his attacks came "out of the blue." Pressing him further, we asked more specifically what he had been doing when the last attack struck. Jack froze. A terrorized look resembling a deer caught in the headlights came over his face. He remained silent and immobile for a while. Then he angrily muttered, "I was packing for another damn plane trip!"

This reaction by Jack led to a sudden shift in our perspective. We now recalled his well-publicized plane accident the spring before. We began to suspect that his symptoms were not panic attacks, but instead a delayed reaction to a very traumatic life experience. When we presented him with this possibility, Jack hesitantly told us that he had been having nightmares since the accident. His first attack came after he woke from a dream of sitting paralyzed at the wheel of his car as it hurtled off an embankment. Suddenly Jack's demeanor shifted. His expression of frightened vulnerability disappeared. With self-assured determination, he demanded that we give him "home exercises" to "rebuild my strength." We sensed that he was retreating from the terror. We asked his permission to invite Lenore to join us for the next session, and he agreed. We invited her participation because partners are often aware of subtle but important changes in their loved ones. Moreover, we hoped that Lenore would help Jack recognize symptoms he was not yet able to talk about.

Lenore came in looking painfully tense. When we asked what was worrying her, she burst into tears and blurted out, "I've lost my husband! For months I've been trying to reach him." Turning now to Jack, she bitterly added, "The more I reach out to you, the more you hide." Jack looked astounded by the force of his wife's emotion and her accusation that he was hiding. First, he just stared at her. Then he slumped in his chair and said, "It's not just you." He told us that he had been feeling "like something inside me died." He added that success as a coach this past season had come from a need to fill his mind with work, not from any real enthusiasm. "I even had myself fooled until after the season. Then I realized I hadn't enjoyed it a bit. My players and assistants don't respect me anymore. They're just afraid of me." Lenore broke in, "You can include me and Michael in that." His voice cracking with anguish, Jack quietly said, "Don't you realize? I thought I'd never see you again." Now it was Lenore's turn to be astonished. "What are you talking about?" she asked. At this point, we intervened to explain, "He's talking about the plane crash."

Lenore's outburst had forced Jack to link his irritability and withdrawal to his horrible thoughts and feelings during the accident. His treatment now had a sense of direction. After this interchange, he recalled that his eerie calmness during the plane crash dissolved suddenly when he realized that he was going to die and never see his wife and child again. Lenore recalled her shock when he called from the crash site. She expressed the hurt she felt when he brushed aside her need to hold him and be held after nearly losing him. She now realized that he was dismissing his own feelings, too. Jack recalled feeling tortured by the reporters' demands to relive the accident and then feeling relief when he refused to continue doing so. He admitted that he found the same relief by avoiding everyone now, even Michael and Lenore.

We told the couple that avoiding memories and dismissing feelings can provide relief from pain and turmoil, but at a cost. Jack and those around him had been paying these costs this past year. We also explained that people avoid trauma memories because they are not only unpleasant but also painful. His anxiety attacks could actually consist of reexperiencing the way he felt when he thought he was going to die. Jack now recalled that, during his attacks, he kept thinking, "I'm gonna die! I'm gonna die!," thus echoing his thoughts during the crash just before the eerie calm descended. We told him that we believed his anxiety attacks were caused by the crash and that he might be suffering from PTSD. His nightmares, irritability, and withdrawal from meaningful relationships also suggested this condition. Jack expressed relief that we could name what he was experiencing. At the same time, he was apprehensive when we told him that this was a wound that time alone might not heal. We suggested that he return in a few days to take some psychological tests useful in assessing posttraumatic conditions and discuss the possibility of medications. Jack agreed to our plan, and we set an appointment for later that week.

Course of Treatment

The appointment time for continuing Jack's treatment planning arrived, but Jack did not. Toward the end of the scheduled hour, we received an apologetic phone call from his secretary. She said that Jack was terribly embarrassed, but he was in a nearby city scouting a prospective player when he suddenly realized that he had totally forgotten us. At his next appointment, he was profusely apologetic. He felt embarrassed but admitted that forgetting had become a problem for him the past year. He was relying heavily on his wife and assistant coaches to make sure he didn't "drop the ball." Nonetheless, he still missed appointments and left on recruiting trips without taking along necessary paperwork. Worse, on one occasion, he even forgot to pick up Michael from school. We assured him that we were not offended. Rather, we saw his forgetting our appointment as further evidence that he was reacting to the terror of the plane crash. We explained that emotionally traumatic events often take away conscious control of attention and memory as the mind seeks to avoid pain and turmoil. Unfortunately, more than painful traumatic memories are forgotten in this process.

Jack had mixed feelings about our labeling his forgetting as a symptom rather than as a character weakness. He told us that he was raised to believe people should "pull themselves up by their boot-straps." He knew that his reaction to the plane crash was a problem, but he thought that the solution was to "get back on the horse" by forcing himself to fly. We agreed that getting back on an airplane was important, but pointed out that doing so had not eliminated his symptoms. Although he was able to fly by force of will, battling through fear was only part of the problem. His "get back on the horse" analogy went only so far because what he feared was not a single thing, but a series of "triggers" that were stimuli related to the accident. Jack paused, obviously reviewing his experiences in his mind. Slowly he began to nod in agreement. He told us that a number of objects and situations concerning flying bothered him. We suggested that these were all "horses" he would have to "ride," but in a more systematic and conscious way than he had been attempting to do.

Turning to a second part of our treatment plan, we told Jack that people can't fully conquer something they don't understand. He was initially puzzled by this statement. When we likened it to the challenge his new players faced when they tried to learn his system of football, he grasped our meaning. He said that, during their first practice session, players experienced his system as a jumble of instructions, diagrams, and rules, and only as their careers progressed did these parts become connected. When his players saw the big picture, they could command the system instead of having it command them.

For the past year, Jack's experiences in the plane crash had stayed in his mind as an undigested jumble of thoughts, feelings, experiences, and memories, without a context. This is why, in addition to helping him systematically overcome his fears, the other part of the plan consisted of our helping him put the pieces in proper sequence. To do this, we would ask Jack to recount his experience of the crash as many times and with as much detail as possible. Like his system of football for his players, his trauma would then become an integrated whole that he could command and draw strength from. We counseled him that both tasks, the systematic overcoming of fears and the remembering and reintegrating of his experience, would require him to tolerate a great deal of fear, turmoil, and other intense feelings. If this were not the case, he would have been able to resolve his trauma without psychological help.

We also informed Jack that there is a biological component to trauma. Had he not originally come to us through the medical emergency room when his pulse and blood pressure were raised and he was sweating and his heart was pounding? We pointed out that insomnia, although partially explained by his nightmares, also was a biological event. We told him that, as we worked with him behaviorally and psychologically, it might be a good idea at times to attack the biological side of the problem with medications. His initial response was to reject our offer on the grounds that he didn't believe in "mind-altering" medications. We pointed out that he was already treating himself with a drug, alcohol. We suggested that he curtail his drinking, which he subsequently did.

In the following sessions, the two sides of his treatment began to reinforce each other. As Jack recalled more details of the crash, he began to identify triggers that were particularly fear provoking. For instance, he noticed that now when he was flying, he would experience onset of anxiety when the crew asked passengers to prepare for landing. As the plane approached the ground, he would watch anxiously for the runway hash marks that indicate the proper landing area. The sound of the landing gear and reverse thrusters after touchdown brought back vivid recollections of his horror and helplessness during the crash. We encouraged him to think of other anxiety-provoking experiences that he associated with the crash. He quickly named the preflight safety instructions. Pressed for details, he became aware that the sight of the dangling oxygen mask during the flight attendant's demonstration brought back the sight of all the oxygen masks dropping from the ceiling of the plane during the crash.

Then Jack looked puzzled. He said that, although it made no sense, he had insisted all year long on being seated on the right side of the cabin. He then realized that his left side avoidance extended beyond airplanes. He recalled taking Michael on a roller coaster shortly after the accident. The sudden drops of the ride did not cause him any distress. However, when the coaster entered a hairpin turn to the right, his anxiety became overwhelming. Similarly, when he was driving and had to make a sharp right-hand turn, he involuntarily slowed his car to the point that other cars honked at him. Now he could see that both situations put pressure on the left side of his body, which reminded him of how it felt to have powerful centrifugal force pressing his left side against the bulkhead during the crash. Even minor left-sided pressures such as people pushing against him produced anxiety. Jack did not need any introduction from us to the concept of "muscle memory." Nevertheless, he was dismayed to realize that traumatic memories could reside in his body as well as in his mind and significantly influence his behavior and preferences.

We asked Jack to "scout" for other triggering sights, sounds, or situations. He added to his list the gate through which the passengers had been herded into the terminal after the crash and where he had called Lenore. He also recognized that the curbside pickup area where he had encountered the intrusive questions and microphones of television news crews now caused him to feel anxious, but less so than being in an airplane. These and other observations allowed us to set up a hierarchy of fears, ranging from least to most anxiety provoking. We suggested that he begin with the curbside, proceed to the terminal, and then go to right-hand car turns. We told him to put himself in each situation and, most importantly, to remain there until he felt minimal anxiety before proceeding to the next situation. We assured him that, contrary to people's fantasies, forcing himself to remain in these situations would not result in an ever-increasing crescendo of anxiety. Instead, his fear would eventually subside or dissipate entirely.

At the same time, we gave Jack some tools for controlling the physical side of his anxiety. We taught him to control his breathing and avoid hyperventilating. We also taught him some progressive muscle relaxation techniques to use while exposing himself to the triggers. As we expected, once Jack had a clear direction, he attacked the problem aggressively. He set a goal for himself, which was to be completely comfortable with the airport by the next session.

Two days later, Jack's emergency room doctor called to tell us that he was back in the emergency room after suffering a panic attack at the airport. We spoke briefly with Jack on the phone. He clearly didn't want to talk then, but he agreed to an emergency appointment the next day. He arrived irate. He said we had promised him that using our techniques would make his anxiety go away. Instead, the techniques had put him back in the emergency room. We agreed that we hadn't expected this to happen and must have missed something. We encouraged him to give a detailed account of his experiences at the airport leading up to this panic attack. He described progressing from the curbside, where he felt fairly calm, to the gate, where he was not aware of experiencing more than moderate anxiety, even when seeing skid marks on the runway that were reminiscent of the accident.

Suddenly, then, Jack's narrative broke off. Words seemed caught in his throat. Finally, he forced out, "Michael." Puzzled, we asked "What about your son?" He whispered, "Not my son, my older brother." This was new to us. We had previously taken a comprehensive life history and were told he had a sister. We asked why he never mentioned having a brother. He replied that, when we asked about siblings, he thought we meant living ones. His brother Michael had died in childhood. Setting aside for the moment the question of why he hadn't mentioned Michael, we asked Jack what his brother had to do with his panic attack. He said that just now, as he was reviewing the moments before the attack, he remembered that it was raining. As he stood looking at the skid marks, a lightning bolt hit the runway. He said that Michael had been killed by lightning while they were outside playing together.

Jack went on to relate that, after Michael's death at age 12, his parents removed all reminders of him from the home, and he was seldom spoken of again. Jack had just assumed that Michael's death and even reminders of his existence were too upsetting for his parents to talk about. In the intervening years, he seldom thought of him. He even found it difficult to recall whether he had consciously chosen to name his son after his brother. However, he did know that an intense dislike of thunderstorms was one of the reasons he had chosen his current job, which was located in a southwestern part of the country where thunderstorms are infrequent.

Discussion

Sometimes the treatment of a single traumatic event goes smoothly. The combination of reviewing the event repeatedly and in detail, combined with gradual reexposure to fear-inducing stimuli, proves sufficient to enable the person to overcome the trauma. Typically, the course of such treatment requires no more than 12 to 20 sessions spread over a few months. However, as in Jack's case, unexpected complexities can arise because of trauma-induced forgetting. Whether this is called dissociation, avoidance, denial, or repression, it is a common posttraumatic reaction. The traumatized person first tries not to think about what happened because it is painful. Forgetting soon becomes automatic. People with PTSD not only forget what upset them, but they forget that they have forgotten. By the time they appear in the clinic, even though they are disturbed by posttraumatic symptoms, they no longer connect the symptoms to something that actually happened. Jack probably would have had less difficulty confronting his present fears had it not been for the trauma of his brother Michael's death and his family's silence about it. He soon discovered that he could not overcome the trauma of the plane crash without fully exploring his grief and horror at Michael's death. This also was a wound that time alone did not heal.

Even highly functional people may be secretly struggling to avoid thinking about a past tragedy. Despite obvious personality strengths, they may find that they cannot overcome a horrifying event in their present while continuing to avoid their past. When Jack connected the terror of his current trauma and his fear of thunderstorms to his feelings of horror and loss when Michael was killed, he could no longer avoid grieving for his brother and facing secret fears that he had carried with him since witnessing his death. All along in his life, there had been a cost to avoiding these feelings. Most importantly, as Jack worked through his grief, he discovered that he had always been limited in the depths of his feeling and commitment to his loved ones because of his fears of losing them. As his treatment progressed, he and Lenore felt the closeness between them deepening. It took additional months for Jack to "connect the dots," as he put it, between his feelings about Michael's death and his current traumatic symptoms. Once he did, however, dealing with his airplane fears went quickly. Within a year, we agreed that further treatment was no longer necessary.

We began by telling you that PTSD is unique among recognized psychological conditions, in that its very name implies knowing its cause, a traumatizing external event. Something horrible happens that threatens life, something so overwhelming and uncontrollable that we cannot believe it is real, even though we know it is. In fact, studies have shown that people who experience a strong sense of unreality during a traumatic event are more likely to develop PTSD than those who do not.

To understand how most people are able to overcome a traumatic event, think for a moment about your response to the terrorist destruction of the World Trade Center. We all had a dose of trauma then. After a period of disbelief and a sense of unreality about what had occurred, people could not stop thinking, talking, and even dreaming about it. We were drawn to look again and again at hundreds of televised and printed pictures and descriptions of the event as we attempted to grasp its enormity. In doing this, we worked to master our feelings and take some meaning from an event that caused such intolerable horror, pain, loss, and confusion. This is not so different from how people normally deal with any significant event, even if it is not traumatic. We find ourselves compelled to tell and retell, think and rethink, until what happened becomes integrated with our overall sense of the world and ourselves. Not surprisingly, then, research shows that the best natural therapy for dealing with trauma is talking about it with friends and family over and over. In doing so, we gradually gain perspective on our trauma, learn from it, and give it a proper place in our lives.

Jack attempted to deal with his trauma in this way when he agreed to talk to reporters. During and immediately after the plane crash, he put his feelings away to act bravely, logically, and helpfully at a time of extreme danger, fear, and chaos. But just hours later, when he tried to reconnect these strong hidden feelings with the intellectual side of his trauma story, he became overwhelmed. He quickly found that reliving the event was too disturbing for him to continue. In fact, he felt as if the reporters were torturing him. At that point, his natural recovery process stopped, and he began avoiding memories of the event in every way he could.

Jack still looked strong to outside observers because they mistook his growing emotional numbness for stoicism and calm. They could not see the battle that raged within him. His intrusive and insistent memories were sometimes so vivid that he felt he wasn't really remembering moments of the plane crash but was right there again, reliving them. These are the kinds of experiences known as *flashbacks*. In addition, by working very hard to forget events surrounding the crash, Jack unintentionally sacrificed control over his memory. As a result, internal cues, such as his feelings of fear, and external cues, particularly during flights, triggered more flashbacks. Traumatic associations intruded into his sleep in the form of disturbing nightmares and into his waking life in the form of anxiety attacks that mimicked his thoughts and physical reactions at the time of the crash. He began to use alcohol as a way of controlling his hyperaroused state.

As disturbing as these anxieties were, even more destructive to Jack's life were the numbing and withdrawal caused by his efforts to avoid and control his anxiety. He was occasionally able to make connections between his anxiety attacks and the crash, which contributed to his recognizing the need for treatment. What he did not realize, however, was that shutting down his negative emotions also shut down his capacity for positive excitement, his feelings for other people, and his ability to care about anything. As a consequence, traumatic avoidance symptoms are especially destructive to relationships.

Even stable marriages can be destroyed as a side effect of untreated trauma, particularly if the trauma has involved sexual assault.

In some ways, Jack's airplane crash was a simple trauma to treat. He was a high-functioning person before the event. He had an excellent social support system, and the fact of his trauma was socially validated. The plane crash was investigated, blame was assigned, and Jack was seen as a hero. By contrast, the complexity of the effects of trauma increases when conditions are less favorable than in Jack's case. Soldiers traumatized in Vietnam returned home to find no validation for their sacrifices and no sympathetic forum for recounting their horrifying experiences. The frequency and severity of PTSD among these war veterans were consequently substantial. Children who are traumatized, especially if their trauma occurs at the hands of people they trust or on whom they depend, can suffer considerable damage to their developing personalities. Serious psychological damage is particularly likely if they must remain silent about the trauma.

To some extent, such silence was true for Jack. He came to believe that his parents could not talk about his brother's death and that he would hurt them if he brought it up. Without realizing it, he was angry that his family's code of silence prevented him from expressing his feelings about the tragedy and the loss it represented for him. During treatment, he was able to work through his anger over having to suppress his fears, guilt, and grief. He recognized that he became furious with the reporters because, after years of holding in his feelings about Michael, he was now being urged by them to "spill my guts." In our last session, he told us, "I no longer feel angry and guilty about my brother Michael's death. I only feel bad that until now I didn't fully appreciate being alive and having Lenore and my son Michael in my life."

Recommended Readings

Cardena, E., Butler, L. D., & Spiegel, D. (2003). Stress disorders. In G. Stricker & T. A. Widiger (Eds.), *Clinical psychology* (pp. 229–249). Vol. 8 in I. B. Weiner (Editor-in-Chief), *Handbook of psychology.* Hoboken, NJ: Wiley.

Duggal, S., & Sroufe, L. A. (1998). Recovered memory of childhood sexual trauma: A documented case from a longitudinal study. *Journal of Traumatic Stress, 11,* 301–321.

Foa, E. B., Keane, T. M., & Friedman, M. J. (2000). Guidelines for treatment of PTSD. *Journal of Traumatic Stress, 13,* 539–588.

Shay, J. (1994). *Achilles in Vietnam.* New York: Atheneum.

van der Kolk, B. A., McFarlane, A. C., & Weisaeth, L. (Eds.). (1996). *Traumatic stress.* New York: Guilford Press.

Widom, C. S. (1999). Posttraumatic stress disorders in abused and neglected children grown up. *American Journal of Psychiatry, 156,* 1223–1229.

CHAPTER 11

Generalized Anxiety Disorder

IRVING B. WEINER

Mr. Valdez was the second of two sons born into a working-class Hispanic family in a large Midwestern city. His father was a steadily employed factory worker, and the family lived modestly in a relatively peaceful neighborhood. Mr. Valdez' father had little interest in family affairs, but his mother was a devoted homemaker whose first priority was the safety and welfare of her husband and children. She was a nervous and fretful woman, however, given to constant worry about possible threats to her family's security. She kept the house heavily locked while inside, although theirs was not a high-crime neighborhood, and she avoided going out of the house as much as possible for fear of having an accident on the street. She worried about her sons' health, became excessively alarmed if they showed the slightest symptom of illness, and limited their activities to protect them from harm.

Overprotected by his mother while growing up, Mr. Valdez had little opportunity to develop good social skills or confidence in his ability to fend for himself. He was a shy and insecure boy who, like his mother, became a worrier, especially when he was in school. At least a few days each week, from the fifth grade on, he would walk into the school building with his pulse racing and a sinking feeling in the pit of his stomach, as he worried about what kind of embarrassment he might confront that day or dreaded repetition of some awkward situation he had been unable to manage adequately the day before.

Mr. Valdez, nevertheless, did above-average academic work, attended a local college, and graduated with a major in science and mathematics and a teaching certificate. He found a position as a high school science teacher, a job that proved disastrous for his peace of mind. He worried constantly and excessively about whether his lesson plans and classroom presentations were adequate, whether his students liked him, and whether his colleagues respected him. He experienced frequent episodes of distress in which he would feel hot all over and sweat profusely, his heart would pound rapidly, and he would have difficulty concentrating during the day and sleeping at night.

Mr. Valdez left his teaching position after the first year and took a job as a bookkeeper in a public agency. Working now with numbers rather than people and left largely on his own without close supervision, he felt fairly comfortable and performed capably. Although he continued to worry more than most people about routine aspects of daily life (e.g., that he would be late for work or fall behind in paying his bills, neither of which ever happened), he remained for a time free of major episodes of distress. Then he began dating a coworker at the agency and got married, and now he had something new to worry about—whether he would be able to satisfy his wife psychologically, financially, and sexually. As matters turned out, he could do none of these.

Mr. Valdez' wife was an assertive and domineering person who had been attracted to him because she envisioned him as a dependable and undemanding husband who could be counted on to do things her way. In time, however, she found him too passive and insecure for her tastes, and she became highly critical of how he looked and dressed, his modest income and lack of ambition, and his performance as a lover. In response to this criticism, Mr. Valdez' episodes of palpitation and hot flashes returned in full force, again accompanied by concentration difficulty and sleep disturbance. He worried almost constantly about what he could do to improve his marital situation, while feeling helpless to find any solution to his problems.

His wife solved Mr. Valdez' marital problems for him, in a manner of speaking, by leaving him for another man with whom she had become romantically involved. He felt humiliated by this turn of events and vowed never again to expose himself to being psychologically abused in this way. Aside from continuing to do his job, he withdrew into an almost solitary existence. For many years, he lived alone with a pet dog, rarely left the house except to go to work and take care of necessities (e.g., buying groceries), and did not pursue any relationships with women or become involved in any friendships. Although he continued to be relentless in finding things to worry about, his self-imposed seclusion allowed him for many years to avoid major sources of stress and the recurrent episodes of dysfunction they would have been likely to cause.

Then there came a time when Mr. Valdez was assigned to a new supervisor at work who was harshly critical of his performance in ways he had not experienced before—and the supervisor was a woman. Attacks of acute distress reemerged, interfered with the quality of his work, and made him feel apprehensive about even going to the agency, especially on days when he anticipated having some contact with his supervisor. Receiving unfavorable reports about him from the supervisor and concerned about his psychological health and future work potential, his agency arranged for him to have a fitness-for-duty evaluation. Thus, it happened that Mr. Valdez, now age 54 and having experienced emotional problems since childhood, came for the first time to the attention of a mental health professional.

Formulation

Mr. Valdez' case illustrates a condition codified as Generalized Anxiety Disorder (GAD) in the American Psychiatric Association (2000) *Diagnostic and Statistical Manual of Mental Disorders* (*DSM-IV-TR*). The chief characteristic of GAD is excessive and pervasive worry or anxiety about a multitude of situations or events. Unlike the anxieties that most people experience from time to time, GAD anxiety is excessive in the sense of being out of proportion to the physical danger or psychological threat actually posed by the events that are causing the person to worry. GAD anxiety is pervasive by virtue of extending to many different spheres of a person's life and encompassing matters large and small—including, but not limited to, personal, social, financial, occupational and political matters and ranging from worrying about world peace and life-threatening illness to fretting about whether a light has been left on in the closet.

Like Mr. Valdez, moreover, persons with GAD often show many types of concerns that are characteristic of other anxiety disorders. These may include avoidance of people (social phobia), reluctance to leave home (agoraphobia), stress reactions, obsessive preoccupations, and episodes of panic. What distinguishes GAD from other anxiety disorders is the co-occurrence or alternation of these various symptom patterns, rather than the exclusive or primary presence of any one of them.

A second main characteristic of GAD is a sense of powerlessness to control the constant worrying that defines this condition. Persons with GAD find it difficult, if not impossible, to push their worries out of their mind or to convince themselves that they are being more anxious than they need to be. It was typical of Mr. Valdez to feel that he had limited control over his destiny, and this sense of helplessness extended to his attitude toward his attacks of anxiety.

Finally, of note, the story of Mr. Valdez illustrates the typical longitudinal course of GAD and the role of experiential factors in causing it. As in his case, the symptoms of this disorder commonly begin to appear in childhood and, unless treated, can lead to recurrent episodes of acute and sometimes incapacitating distress during the adult years. Despite its usually early onset, GAD may not be diagnosed and treated until the advent of mid-life crises, as happened with Mr. Valdez. As for experiential factors, there seems little doubt that this man learned to be an anxious and fearful person while growing up with a distant father and a fretful mother, who set a worrying model for him to follow and, by overprotecting him, left him vulnerable to experiencing inadequacy in the real world.

Recommended Readings

Barlow, D. H., Pincus, D. B., Heinrichs, N., & Choate, M. L. (2003). Anxiety disorders. In G. Stricker & T. A. Widiger (Eds.), *Clinical psychology* (pp. 119–148). Vol. 8 in I. B. Weiner (Editor-in-Chief), *Handbook of psychology.* Hoboken, NJ: Wiley.

Brown, T. A. (1999). Generalized anxiety disorder and obsessive-compulsive disorder. In T. Millon, P. H. Blaney, & R. D. Davis

(Eds.), *Oxford textbook of psychopathology* (pp. 114–143). New York: Oxford University Press.

Stanley, M. A., & Beck, J. G. (2000). Anxiety disorders. *Clinical Psychology Review, 20,* 731–754.

Reference

American Psychiatric Association. (2000). *Diagnostic and statistical manual of mental disorders* (4th ed., text rev.). Washington, DC: Author.

CHAPTER 12

Pain Disorder

JEFFREY M. LACKNER

Maria is a 42-year-old, Caucasian female who sat quietly in a chair at the SUNY Buffalo Behavioral Medicine Clinic, gripping her right shoulder with her left hand. She wore a slightly oversized T-shirt that read, "My daughter is a Smallwood High School Honors student," a pleasant smile, blue nylon running shorts, and well-worn Nikes. With her hair pinned back into a tight ponytail, she could have passed as the older sister of soccer star Mia Hamm.

Christmas Eve, 2000: The Accident

Maria's story began on December 24, 2000. She had been out the whole day, doing last-minute errands for her family's annual Christmas party. The party, whose location rotated among her cousins, was hers to host. As she approached the red light, she settled into the seat, catching her breath for what seemed like the first time since leaving home in the morning. She felt content: The presents were bought and wrapped, the dinner prepared, her relatives had arrived safely from Pittsburgh—all she had to do was pick up her daughter at ballet class, drop off a gift certificate for the paper boy, and enjoy the holiday.

Her car came to a stop light at a busy intersection where she took in the sights and sounds of Christmas: The snowflakes that conspired to paralyze Buffalo this time last year seemed to be on their best behavior today as they tiptoed onto the hood of her SUV and evaporated under its warmth. The car speakers cranked out the obligatory Christmas carols that sounded surprisingly warm and quaint. She glanced through the passenger's window toward a cluster of well-bundled youngsters shrieking as they threw snowballs at one another.

Preparation of this chapter was supported in part by National Institutes of Health Grant DK-54211.

As she turned her head, her eyes caught the glare of two headlights in the rear view mirror. The lights grew bigger and bigger before she realized that the driver—a teenage girl putting on her makeup—was set to plow into her. "I'm going to get hit," she whispered to herself. Tightening her hands around the steering wheel, closing her eyes, clenching her jaw, and squishing her face into what looked like a walnut, Maria braced herself to absorb the crash as her right foot slammed on the brakes. The impact of the car zapped her body of strength, transforming her into a rag doll. Her shoulders were propelled forward, while her neck dropped and tilted slightly down toward the steering wheel. The sudden stop then threw her head and neck backward against the headrest. She had never been in a car accident before so did not know what to expect. Maria recalled that, for such a horrific incident, its sounds were rather mundane, recalling an auditory stew of fallen bowling pins, the crunching of dried tree leaves, the crashing of a tray of plates and glasses. The sound was the last thing she remembered until the ambulance arrived to transport her to the local trauma hospital. Strapped in a gurney, she said to herself "This cannot be happening. This must be a dream. All I have to do is open my eyes and I'll realize it's a nightmare."

But when she opened her eyes, she was greeted not by the familiar surroundings of her bedroom but by the face of a paramedic who was patting her arm in an effort to sooth her obvious discomfort. Realizing that she was not dreaming, Maria grew shaken. Her breathing quickened, her heartbeat pulsed faster, her fingers numb and tingly as if they were "asleep." She scanned her body and felt a tight sensation in her chest as if someone was standing on it. As the ambulance whizzed to the hospital with its siren blaring, her neck began to throb. Her biceps were burning as though they were on fire, while her head felt as though a "2,000-pound weight was pushing down on my head." At the hospital, she underwent x-rays, which were negative, and was diagnosed with whiplash, a neck injury also called a neck sprain or neck strain. Maria was subsequently prescribed a nonsteroidal anti-inflammatory medication to reduce inflammation, a muscle relaxant, and a soft cervical collar by an emergency room physician. The physician's striking physical resemblance to the television character Doogie Howzer—curly blond hair, cherubic face—did little to bolster her confidence in his recommendations. Worse, his Santa Claus tie served more to accentuate her own discomfort and unease than to impart any festive holiday cheer.

She returned home, confident that her pain would dissipate within a couple of days and permit her to get on with her life. Her optimism eroded when she woke three days later with additional pain in her right jaw, lower back, and between her shoulder blades. At times, it felt as if a toothache filled her whole body. Her back "burned like hell" and "felt like somebody was taking a hot poker and sticking it in the small of my back." Her neck droned with a constant stiffness and soreness. The worst pain felt like an electrical shock that was shooting from her right jaw to her chest. Her forehead pulsed with a throbbing sensation that reminded her of the steady drumbeat of some tribal death ritual. Maria had given birth to twin girls and was a former amateur athlete, so she was no stranger to pain. She had even experienced occasional periods of backaches that flared up when she did too much lifting around the house. These pain episodes hurt but they came and went. She was easily able to chalk these up to a combination of overexertion and advancing middle age. But the pain she had experienced since the accident was different. It was not only more physically uncomfortable but also constant.

Seeking a Cure, Finding Frustration

Two weeks after the accident, Maria's pain had not subsided. She decided to schedule an appointment with her primary care physician. She was looking forward to and was almost excited about this appointment. She could get to the bottom of this pain and get on with her life. Since the accident, she had found herself muttering, "I'm too busy for this pain . . . I've got a life to lead, children to take care of, a home, a job to do." Her physician explained that a diagnosis of whiplash is termed a soft tissue injury because it affects body structures such as disks,

muscles, and ligaments, which are soft tissues. He explained that while
the neck is a very flexible structure, it could be injured during motor
vehicle accidents, after a fall, or diving into a pool that is too shallow,
when the weight of the head exceeds the neck's ability to control its motion. The actual cause of the symptoms is unclear. It can be caused by a
stretch or tear of the ligament (strain/sprain), a muscle stretch or tear,
or a pinching of the nerves caused by the bending that occurs during
sudden extension and flexion of the neck. Her physician assured her that
soft tissue injuries are benign and that her prognosis was good. "Most patients recover within three months max after the injury," he said. Maria
did not know what *benign* meant, but she felt satisfied with the assur-
ance that she would be back to normal within a few weeks or months at
the most.

But days passed into weeks and weeks into months. Before long, six
months had passed since the date of her accident. Although her memory of the details of the accident diminished with time, this did little
to stem the waves of pain that flooded what seemed like every muscle
in her body. If anything, in fact, her pain had not only persisted but
worsened since then. Putting on a pair of jeans felt like coarse sand-
paper was rubbing against a fresh scab. When she awoke in the morning, she felt as though her whole body was in a giant steel vise. There
was never a period of time when she did not experience pain. She grew
increasingly frustrated not only at the persistence of her pain and limitations, but at what she perceived as the indifference of her physicians, who were as reluctant to order diagnostic tests as they were quick
to administer pain medications. Antidepressants, muscle relaxants,
anti-inflammatories, narcotics—her doctors prescribed them all. At
one point, she was taking eight different medications a day. Some of
these medications caused such bad side effects—including confusion,
stomach distress, fatigue, and loss of concentration—that she was
forced to discontinue them. Other drugs relieved the pain briefly before it returned full force.

Exasperated, Maria scheduled another appointment with her primary care physician. At the appointment, she pleaded with him to "do
something . . . order a CAT scan, an MRI." He ordered an MRI scan of

the neck, the results of which were negative. She felt a weird combination of relief and disappointment. On the positive side, she was relieved that her condition was not as serious as she feared. Yet, the lack of physical findings made her feel uncomfortable. She wanted some answers to what was causing her pain, which she believed was no longer confined to her head and neck but was spreading to her legs. The results did little to fill in the blanks. What could be causing the pain? A broken back? A dislocation of the spine? Damaged nerves, a torn muscle? The results were not really results; they just made her more eager to get to the bottom of the pain puzzle.

Maria returned to her primary care physician and asked whether he thought further medical tests would be helpful. "I doubt it but, quite frankly, Maria, it does not matter what I think." Maria was taken back by his comments and left his office feeling angry, dejected, and a hypochondriac. She switched to a new physician, who diagnosed her with fibromyalgia, a muscle disorder characterized by widespread musculoskeletal pain, fatigue, and multiple tender points (i.e., tenderness concentrated in precise, localized areas, particularly in the neck, spine, shoulders, and hips). She was prescribed the antidepressant Prozac and was sent to physical therapy. There, she underwent traction, massage, heat, ice, and ultrasound. These treatments helped for a while, but their relief wore off by the time she returned home, where she needed relief the most. Her physical therapy exercises were so uncomfortable and draining that she stopped treatment within three weeks.

Suffering with Pain

Pain soon became a part of everyday life for Maria. She likened her pain to a tattoo: It accompanied her wherever she went—to the bathroom, the mall, her job, church, the garden; it even pierced the intimate quarters that she shared with her loving husband. Unlike a tattoo, however, her pain was invisible to the naked eye. In fact, she looked normal. There were no tangible observable signs of the pain and suffering that accompany most illnesses. The skier who breaks her leg has a cast, the cancer patient with a brain tumor who undergoes radiation loses her hair, the AIDS patient loses weight—but there was nothing to signify Maria's condition save for her words of pain and suffering, which she was reluctant to express because others were, she feared, tired of hearing them.

Maria's pain was private, lurking deep under her skin, close to the bone. Before her injury, she had never thought pain could be so complex. Pain was pain, right? Wrong. It had its own language—not made up of words, signals, or letters. Its lexicon was expressed though different sensations and emotions. At times, pain was expressed through sensations that were felt alternatively as gnawing, throbbing, shooting, stabbing, cramping, pulling, burning, tingling, or aching. Her pain also elicited strong emotions of misery, fear, frustration, and exhaustion. Worse, her pain would not quit. Its stubborn resilience was like annoying dinner guests who stay long past the end of the party and are immune to suggestions that their departure is long past due.

As her pain persisted, Maria found that it took a toll on many aspects of her life. She was not experiencing simply a pain disorder. It was a whole body disorder attacking her body, soul, and mind. Pain was, as she said, an "equal opportunity offender." Early on in her illness, she was able to cope with pain by telling herself to be brave and to carry on and that she could overcome the pain. Just grin and bear it. These tools had helped her get through seven hours of natural childbirth, two cavities, countless blood draws, and an arthroscopy of her knee following a soccer injury in high school. These pains, although severe, were finite. They were like a book with a beginning and an end. But the persistence of her pain was more like an endless loop audiotape that played on and on and on.

With time, Maria's outlook darkened. She began to focus on how terrible her pain was and how it was never going to get any better. She feared that the pain would get worse. Her confidence in her ability to manage her pain gave way to discouragement, isolation, frustration, and feelings of helplessness. Her increasingly negative thoughts reminded her of a fourth grade science experiment where her teacher placed a drop of black ink into a beaker of clear water to demonstrate the phenomenon of dispersion. The small drop of ink clouds the water before the water takes on a dreary, charcoal grey color. Her mind had become like the water in that beaker—once crystal clear, now dreary and muddied with darkness.

Maria also noticed changes in her personality. She had always been a bit of a worrywart; but the pain, the uncertainty over her future, and her physical limitations heightened her anxieties about her health, her family, and her future. She found herself more anxious, keyed up, irritable, and tense. The pain had shortened her fuse to the point that any little thing—her children bickering over the remote control, traffic jams, a long line at the supermarket, losing her keys—set her off. She began to feel uncomfortable in her own skin. Much of her anxiety focused on the pain and the fear of further injury. Its presence served to heighten her worries about whether her condition might deteriorate. She anxiously wanted the pain to go away so that she could return to her life as she had known it before the accident. "Why can't I just go back to how life was before that idiot rear-ended me?"

But the pain would not leave. Maria worried that the pain would worsen and render her a cripple unable to work, love, and laugh. For years, she had performed household chores—vacuuming, washing dishes, carrying groceries—as reflexively as breathing or swallowing. These activities did not call for any conscious thought. Following the accident, doing physically demanding daily activities became a source of fear ("What if I hurt myself?"). She now carried out routine activities with the careful deliberation and apprehension she had observed in the residents of a nursing home where her mother once lived.

Maria's fears led to significant changes in her lifestyle. She tried to function in her roles as wife and mother, but her inability to perform physical tasks without pain and her fear of injury sidelined her from previously enjoyable family activities—skiing, touch football, playing board games, carpooling. Her children pitched in to do laundry, take out the trash, and mow the lawn. Part of her felt grateful that she had nurtured a family who would rally around her to ease her load. Another part of her felt guilty and ashamed that she was unable to carry out tasks she "should do" as a mother and wife. She would watch her husband, fresh from a 12-hour workday, put in another three hours of work doing chores that she used to perform. He never complained, but as she saw him working, Maria could not help thinking that this was not the life he envisioned when they married 15 years earlier. This saddened her. Over time, she began to feel like a spectator in her home—like a "goldfish in a fishbowl." Because she was apprehensive of further pain, Maria began withdrawing from other relationships. Friends would call and ask her to go out to a movie, get a cup of coffee, or go shopping, but she would quickly offer an excuse: What if she had a spasm while at the mall? What if she got too tired? No, it was just easier to pass.

Before long, the telephone stopped ringing, and, although she was relieved that she did not have to offer excuses to explain her fears of pain and injury, she longed for the companionship of her friends. Maria also found it increasingly hard to concentrate and remember simple things. Stepping out of the grocery store, she found herself struggling to find the location of her car. She felt like she was in a fog. At Back to School Night, she tried to introduce a friend to her husband but was embarrassed to find that the friend's name had disappeared from her memory bank. Just when Maria thought her situation could not get worse, it did. The no-fault insurance company that had been paying her medical bills notified her that they had scheduled her for an independent medical examination (IME).

An IME is often requested by insurance companies to assess the extent of claimants' disability, the type of treatment they need, if any, and their likelihood of permanent disability or loss of earning capacity. The insured person is required to give a medical history and go through a physical exam conducted by one or more doctors chosen by the insurance company. The physician who conducted Maria's IME concluded that her pain complaints were unrelated to the accident and recommended termination of payment for her medical care. This outcome of the IME had a devastating effect on Maria's health, finances, and mood. Because the insurance company refused to pay for ongoing treatment, she was forced to pay for it out of pocket. This was a source of financial pressure and psychological distress that overwhelmed her already-precarious mental state.

To make matters worse, her pain forced Maria to give up a part-time job she had as a bookkeeper for a local restaurant. She hoped she would still be able to continue her full-time job. Without her income, the prospect of sending her children to college on her husband's income alone was questionable. Yet, she doubted how much longer she could keep up with the physical demands of her job. As it was, her days were robotically scripted: Wake up, go to work, work, return home, feel exhausted, make dinner, wash the dishes, do laundry, sleep, wake up. She thought she would be able to carry on in this way for the next six months—maybe. But realizing their dream of a better life for their children would require sustaining this pattern of activity for another 10 years. This seemed to her a painful, grueling, uphill battle that her weak, tired, pitiful body was ill equipped to win. Worse, a sense of vulnerability that had dogged her since she was a little girl was reignited.

Background Information

Important influences on Maria's life began shortly before she was born. It is safe to say that these influences began in the winter of 1960, when her mother, Elizabeth, fell in love with a man named Jack. At the time they met, Elizabeth was working as a waitress at the Highland Park diner the kind of place that is a frequent pit stop for locals looking for an energizing cup of coffee on their way to work. What began as an exchange of chitchat gave way to an intense and passionate relationship between Elizabeth and Jack. In January 1961, Elizabeth discovered she was pregnant. Because she was a Roman Catholic living in a predominantly Catholic, conservative, blue-collar community and Jack was married, she had no choice but to carry the child on her own. Young, poor, and mostly uneducated, Elizabeth entered the Father Barker Home for Unwed Mothers, where she delivered Maria in the early morning hours of December 4, 1961. When Maria was approximately 6 months old, she was placed in the first of a series of foster homes located in rural western New York. At age 3, her care was transferred to a maternal aunt, whom Maria recalls as an affectionate, playful, and compassionate individual who gave Maria her first taste of family, love, and affection. When Maria turned 7 years old, her aunt died.

Maria subsequently returned to live with her mother, who by this time had married a local steelworker and given birth to three children. Maria never felt at home in this house. The love that was a part of her aunt's family was fleeting, if not missing altogether, in her new home. She felt like a fifth wheel. To her stepfather, who had been raised in an observant Roman Catholic family, Maria was—and always would be—a bastard child whose very being symbolized moral lapse and sin. To her mother, Maria was a symbol of her own personal inadequacies. Both Maria's mother and her stepfather played out their negative feelings first through the withdrawal of love and then the administration of punishment, brutality, and abuse. "As a toddler, I lived in the home for unwed mothers; as a child, I lived in a home for unwanted children," Maria said. She recalled that her being physically abused lasted for more than 10 years and was as unpredictable as it was an enduring part of her home life. What made beatings painful was that they were triggered by her parents' frustrations with the stress and strain of daily life. Maria's stepfather was particularly abusive after drinking alcohol. If an unexpected bill arrived in the mail, it was Maria's fault and warranted a good "ass kicking." If he were laid off temporarily from the steel mill, he would take his frustration out on Maria. If her brothers played hooky, it was Maria's fault for not telling her parents. She came to see hairbrushes, hangers, belts, even a dinner fork, not as mundane objects of daily life, but as weapons that her parents would use to vent their frustrations and hostility.

Surprisingly, the dark, dreary cloud that hovered over Maria's home life did not extend to her school, where she distinguished herself as a pleasant, hardworking, and bright student. She was easy to like, even though she had a difficult time opening up to other people. When Maria turned 17 years old, she moved into an apartment. Two years later, she graduated from high school and entered the State University of New York (SUNY) at Buffalo. There, Maria earned a BA in business administration. Shortly after graduating from college, she took a job as a bookkeeper for a doctor's office. In 1990, she married her high school boyfriend. The couple had twin girls in 1995 and settled into a comfortable, easy life in suburban Buffalo.

Nature and Treatment of Chronic Pain

One year after Maria's injury, her best friend, an occupational health nurse, told her about a clinical-research program at the University of Buffalo Medical School designed for treating patients with persistent pain disorders. Unlike a modality-oriented clinic that features a single type of pain treatment (e.g., injections, acupuncture, biofeedback), the SUNY Buffalo pain center had a multidisciplinary focus staffed by doctors of multiple disciplines who specialize in the management of patients with different chronic pain syndromes, including headache, musculoskeletal pain, irritable bowel syndrome, pelvic pain, and nerve pain. The rationale of the program is based on the biopsychosocial model of health. This model holds that individual biology (e.g., genetic predisposition, physiology), behavior, and higher order cognitive processes (coping, illness beliefs) influence persistently painful medical disorders through their interaction with each other, with early life factors (e.g., trauma, modeling), and with the individual's social and physical environments (e.g., reinforcement contingencies).

Although psychological factors do not cause pain, they play a significant role in its course. Research based on the biopsychosocial model has identified three main pathways through which psychological factors influence pain. The first of these pathways is directly through physiological systems. Psychological factors (e.g., stress, negative mood states, and cognitive processes) can increase physiological arousal (e.g., muscle tension), which can increase pain. The second pathway is through the adoption of illness behaviors that can exacerbate pain, prolong recovery following diagnosis, obscure symptom profile, and compromise functioning. Health behaviors are strongly influenced by psychosocial factors. Patients with chronic pain disorders show higher levels of psychological distress and higher rates of concurrent emotional disorders than non-treatment-seeking patients. The third pathway by which psychological factors (e.g., early abuse, interpersonal stressors, family reinforcement of illness behaviors) influence pain is by increasing the risk for the onset of chronic pain. For example, a significant number of patients with a history of abuse, particularly sexual abuse, develop chronic pain disorders, although the mechanism underlying the relationship between abuse and chronic pain is not clearly understood.

To the extent that psychological factors influence the expression, course, and outcome of chronic pain disorders, it is believed that they can be most effectively managed by addressing both the psychological processes that maintain the condition and any physical influences that are causing it. By targeting at least one of the pathways linking psychological factors to chronic pain, psychological treatments are designed to improve symptoms and improve as well the person's functioning, health care use, and quality of life. Among various psychological treatments, cognitive-behavioral methods are probably the most extensively studied and empirically validated. The rationale of these treatment methods is based on the assumption that, as pain disorder persists, patients learn maladaptive behaviors that contribute to continuing pain and related problems. From a treatment perspective, these same learning processes are used in behavioral interventions to reduce self-defeating behaviors associated with chronic pain and disability. In other words, pain-aggravating behaviors can be unlearned and replaced with more adaptive behaviors through formal skills-based training that helps patients reduce pain, distress, and disability. This training includes the following components:

- *Patient education and corrective information about the nature, myths, and components of chronic pain.* Particular attention is paid to educating the patient about the difference between acute and chronic pain. Maria learned that acute pain generally comes on suddenly, for example, after an accident or surgery. Maria's therapists told her that acute pain is considered good pain, because it serves a useful purpose. For example, an ankle that hurts helps the jogger recognize the possibility of a sprain and the need to apply ice to reduce inflammation. Acute pain typically lasts between a few seconds (stubbed toe) and three to six months (broken leg), and it usually has an identifiable physical cause. Maria was taught that pain lasting longer than six months is typically called *chronic pain*. While chronic and acute pain may feel similar, chronic pain is not simply a sign of physical injury. Nor is chronic pain an acute pain that lasts a long time. Instead, chronic pain is often aggravated by a range of physical, environmental, and psychological factors. These factors keep pain signals firing in the nervous system long after an injury has healed.

- *Cognitive therapy exercises aimed at modifying or eliminating distorted, negative beliefs contributing to symptoms.* The rationale for this component comes from research showing that patients who develop chronic pain disorders appraise and interpret pain stimuli differently from normal controls. They attend selectively to pain cues, mislabel bodily sensations, inaccurately predict the probability of painful events, and have distorted memories for pain episodes. Through cognitive restructuring exercises, Maria learned to recognize how she created tension in her life by the way she interpreted situations, such as overestimating the risk of negative events (i.e., thinking the worst, jumping to conclusions) and blowing things out of proportion (i.e., catastrophizing). The goal of cognitive therapy exercises was to challenge inaccurate beliefs and replace them with more constructive and/or accurate self-statements. For example, Maria's thought, "I can't understand why the tests are negative. I feel the pain; it is probably something really unusual that I have that my doctors missed" was challenged and replaced with the thought that "The pain is real, but I've been checked out physically, and I have had all the relevant tests. Many triggers can cause my pain."

- *Structured muscle relaxation exercises designed to help achieve a sense of mastery or self-control over symptoms.* By learning to relax (which is a physiological response incompatible with tension), Maria acquired the ability to reduce the intensity of pain episodes aggravated by physical tension. Maria's ability to relax was strengthened with electromyelographic (EMG) biofeedback. *Biofeedback* refers to a physiological monitoring technique that can give people better control over body function indicators such as blood pressure, heart rate, temperature, and muscle tension that generally function outside an individual's awareness. In EMG biofeedback, special sensors attached to a patient's face, neck, or shoulders transmit the level of muscle tension to a computerized monitor. As the patient applies specific relaxation skills to reduce muscle tension, the monitor provides real-time feedback, either by showing the level of muscle tension on a gauge or by emitting a sound or beep that decreases as the tension is reduced. With home practice, Maria learned to use biofeedback to achieve voluntary control of physical tension that aggravated pain and related distress.

- *Formal problem-solving training to help patients cope more effectively with distress and realistic stressors that accompany pain experience.* Approaches to problem solving included identifying pain-related problems, generating or brainstorming possible solutions and choosing one, planning and implementing the chosen alternative, and evaluating the outcome of this effort in terms of changes in behavior.

- *Activity/rest pacing to increase the patient's activity level and reduce the tendency toward pain cycling and activity intolerance.* Activity pacing skills were designed in particular to reduce Maria's predilection for periods of overexertion that led in turn to recurrent experiences of tissue strain, fatigue, pain, and failure. By increasing her understanding of physical activities that exceeded her personal tolerances and learning the importance of taking short, strategically spaced rest breaks (e.g., five-minute "micro breaks" every 20 to 30 minutes or when fatigued) to promote muscle recovery, Maria learned to minimize biomechanical stress and increase physical performance.

- *Contingency management interventions based on the premise that behaviors associated with chronic pain are partly an acquired (learned) conditioned response to environmental cues that can be changed (or unlearned) though a system of rewards and costs (reinforcement delivery).* These rewards and costs serve as incentives for increasing "well" behaviors (e.g., activity level, self-care skills) and reducing pain or "illness" behaviors (e.g., attention from physicians or family members, medication level, financial incentives for disability, avoidance of work). In Maria's case, a relatively simple form of verbal reinforcement, which consisted of reinforcing self-statements such as "I am making progress" and "It was much easier than I thought it would be" following specific increases in activity level, was used effectively to increase the frequency of healthy (i.e., nonpain) behaviors.

Outcome

The goal of behavioral self-management interventions is to reduce pain, decrease distress, and strengthen self-confidence and coping skills. Because chronic pain is a complex problem that does not often respond to a single approach, Maria's behavioral self-management interventions were combined with pain medication and rehabilitative treatments to enhance her functioning and pain control. As she learned to improve her self-care skills, she worked closely with a pain medicine specialist, who prescribed her an antidepressant (Norpramin) to improve her pain control and quality of sleep. Within three weeks of beginning treatment at the pain center, Maria experienced a lessening in the severity of her pain. Once her pain diminished, she became able to undertake a physical conditioning program that emphasized graded mobility exercises, strength training, and aerobic conditioning. Although treatment did not cure Maria of her pain, it did teach her a set of concrete, practical skills for coping with and taking control of her illness, while, in the process, improving her overall level of functioning. At the conclusion of treatment, the intensity of her pain had decreased by approximately 40% from pretreatment levels. Behavioral treatment also decreased her anxiety, tensions, and worry to the point that she found her worries significantly less uncontrollable and excessive than they had been. As the emotional unpleasantness of her pain decreased, her tolerance for pain improved. Although her condition had not been restored to its preaccident level, she was able to resume many physical activities she found it necessary to avoid following her accident.

Recommended Readings

Barsky, A. J., & Borus, J. F. (1999). Functional somatic syndromes. *Annals of Internal Medicine, 130,* 910–921.

Gatchel, R., & Turk., D. (Ed.). (1999). *Psychosocial factors in pain.* New York: Guilford Press.

Mayou, R., Bass, C., & Shapre, M. (Eds.). (1995). *Treatment of functional somatic symptoms.* Oxford, England: Oxford University Press.

Melzack, R. (1996). *The challenge of pain.* London: Penguin Books.

Speckens, A. E., van Hemert, A. M., Spinhoven, P., Hawton, K. E., Bolk, J. H., & Rooijmans, H. G. (1995). Cognitive behavioral therapy for medically unexplained physical symptoms: a randomised controlled trial. *British Medical Journal, 311*(7016), 1328–1332.

Williams, A. C., Pither, C. E., Richardson, P. H., Nicholas, M. K., Justins, D. M., Morley, S., et al. (1996). The effects of cognitive-behavioral therapy in chronic pain. *Pain, 65*(2/3), 282–284.

PART FOUR

Identity Disorders

CHAPTER 13

Dissociative Identity Disorder

PAUL M. LERNER

In this chapter, I present a case of possible Dissociative Identity Disorder. The fourth edition of the *Diagnostic and Statistical Manual of Mental Disorders* (*DSM-IV-TR*) of the American Psychiatric Association (2000) used this term to replace an earlier and more familiar diagnosis of Multiple Personality Disorder. As in the case of its predecessor, the essential feature of Dissociative Identity Disorder is the presence of two or more distinct identities or personality states. Individuals who present with this disorder typically report struggles in daily functioning, an inability to recall events from the previous day, and major gaps in memory for significant periods of their history. They also report severe physical and sexual abuse during childhood; however, such reports are often so vague as to leave listeners questioning their authenticity.

I use the word *possible* for several reasons. First, as evident in this case, the so-called different identities do not emerge as clear, distinct personalities but instead as vague illusionary states that seemingly can be called forth at the individual's whim. Second, and more generally, as an experienced diagnostician, I am skeptical of diagnostic labels. I regard a diagnosis as a working hypothesis that is neither absolute nor concrete. Third, as a therapist, I continually diagnose and rediagnose my patients, recognizing that the original diagnosis is tentative or possible. Finally, because patients with Dissociative Identity Disorder typically present material that is sketchy, confusing, and contradictory, I believe that it is especially important to maintain an openness as to diagnosis.

Background Information

The patient is a 42-year-old, highly talented but incapacitated writer, who was referred to me by a therapist who had seen her for six months. This therapist indicated to me that she herself had recently been diagnosed with chronic fatigue syndrome and was closing her practice.

The patient's immediate family consisted of two children, ages 15 and 11, and two men, each of whom had fathered one of the children. One of the men, a 39-year-old college graduate, worked full time as an electrician. He supported the family financially. The patient described him as shy, reclusive, aloof, shut off from his feelings, a borderline alcoholic, and totally absorbed in sports and television. The other man, age 41 and also a college graduate, worked sparingly as a music teacher. His time was spent studying and writing a history of fiddle playing in Appalachia. She described him as warm, sensitive, supportive, and singularly cherishing of her. Both children attended public schools and, from all accounts, were excelling, academically and relationally.

The oldest of four children, the patient had a very unusual family of origin. Her father, who was raised on a small farm in rural Alabama, spent his lifetime in search of his own identity and place in the world. In his mid-30s, after attempting and then failing as a carpenter, printer, poet, and storyteller, he arrived in New York City and obtained work at a Quaker-sponsored soup kitchen. It was there he met his future wife. Born in New England of German immigrants, she was working in the soup kitchen to help pay for her college education. She was completing a degree in early childhood education. He was 17 years her senior.

After she completed her degree and following a brief courtship, and over the protests of her parents, they married. They decided to live in a small Quaker community in New Jersey. It was into this community the patient was born. When the patient was 4 years old, her father became dissatisfied with the community and began searching for a different one. He decided on a highly fundamentalist religious group. After joining this new group, together with several other families, he and his wife agreed to participate in a newly established religious community in the forests of Brazil. Thus, at age 4, the patient, her parents, and a younger brother, age 2, emigrated to Brazil.

The new community was like a kibbutz. All the adults worked, children were cared for in a communal day care center and spent limited time with their parents, and life consisted of hardship, simplicity, and sacrifice for the common good. The ruling body was referred to as *elders,* and order and discipline were maintained through the practice of shunning or group exclusion. For example, the shunned individual was excluded from group meetings, had to eat meals alone, and was rarely spoken to.

After an initial sense of having found Shangri-La, her father, in his characteristic way, became disenchanted with the elder's authority and attempted to reorganize the community. His efforts were met with increased shunning. Feeling increasingly alienated, the family returned to the United States when the patient was 8 years old. By this time, two additional siblings, a boy and a girl, had been born.

On their return to the United States, the parents separated. The mother, together with the four children, moved to Vermont to stay with her parents. The father drifted through South Carolina and Florida searching for work. After six months of their living apart, the father obtained work, and the mother, again over her parents' protest, joined him. Not surprisingly, within several months, he lost his job. The family then moved to a rural Quaker area in western North Carolina. The mother opened a gift shop, selling her own pottery with her husband occasionally assisting. The shop sustained the family.

The remainder of the patient's history is long, confusing, and complicated. I met twice with her mother during the assessment period. Her father had died seven years earlier. I found her mother remarkably unhelpful and uninformative. I experienced her as vague, amorphous, indifferent, and extremely committed to denying that anything bad had ever happened in her life.

As for the patient, she reported that, from ages 14 to 16, she had been sexually involved with her next younger brother and several of his friends. This sexual activity consisted of intercourse with her brother, usually at night when her parents were away, and mutual masturbation with his friends in a group setting. She described herself as complying passively with these activities rather than being actively engaged or initiating them. She continued to be sexually active from ages 16 to 18, but during this period her involvement was with men older than herself, including two men who were acquaintances of her father, not with her brother and his contemporaries.

In high school, she impressed her teachers as a model student. She did her assignments in a responsible way, was always prepared for tests, and each year was an honor student. Rather than participate in extracurricular activities, she spent nonschool time working at her mother's gift shop. Although not especially social, she did have several close girlfriends.

To the casual observer, all was well. However, when we look more closely, we see that the patient was leading two separate and very different lives. She was the model student, the good friend, and the dutiful daughter. On the other hand, she was involved in numerous secretive, clandestine sexual affairs with much older men.

On graduating from high school, the patient was accepted at a college and awarded a full scholarship. Instead of attending, she impulsively and without reason left home to visit a friend in Los Angeles and remained there for two years. While there, she worked in a massage parlor, got heavily into drugs and alcohol, and lived an extremely chaotic existence. She then began hitchhiking across the country and, for the next two years, stayed with relatives, friends, or barely known acquaintances. Throughout this period, she was raped several times and almost killed twice. The rapes, to which she passively acquiesced, occurred while she was hitchhiking, involved total strangers, and were never reported to the police or mentioned to family or friends. This four-year period of drifting and endangerment came to an end when she became pregnant. She convinced the young man who had impregnated her to return with her to western North Carolina, which she had left six years earlier. They rented a house close to her parents, and she began working at her mother's shop.

During the summers, she, her daughter, and the daughter's father worked picking apples in New England. There she met someone who was to become the second man in her life. To the relief of the first live-in man, she spent considerable time with this second man, eventually slept with him, and became pregnant by him. After returning to North Carolina, she learned of her pregnancy and contacted the prospective father, who agreed to join them. This arrangement has endured for 12 years.

Assessment Period

I first met the patient in my waiting room. She was lying down on a sofa with her head resting on a man's lap. When I asked her to come into my office, the man virtually had to carry her in. Her long, unkempt, straggly hair covered an attractive face. She was wearing a loose-fitting housedress, had not shaved her legs, and was carrying a cloth doll in each arm. Despite her somewhat bizarre appearance, I did not regard her as having lost touch with reality. Instead, I thought of her as a mountain Orphan Annie, who was attempting to impress me with her helplessness, unattractiveness, and illness.

During that first session, she spoke of being bewildered, confused, perplexed, and lost. I, too, felt confused and could make little sense of what she was telling me. She spoke in a low, monotone voice, which served to dampen my interest rather than engage it. Although she complained of being immobilized by anxiety and referred to instances of being in despair, my overall sense of her was of someone who was remarkably shut down.

Throughout the assessment period, the patient described various sensations and experiences that I considered dissociative. Life and existence seemed to have little sense of continuity for her. She did not know how she might feel or act from one moment to the next. Days of the week blurred into one another, as did nights and days. She had little memory of experiences from the previous 24 hours, and members of her family could not count on her for anything.

Her manner of describing her sexual assault experiences gave the sense that they happened not to her but to a different self. She was outside and above her body, observing the rape and attempting to put herself into the mind of the rapist to experience what he was thinking and feeling. The patient continued to feel estranged from her body. She did not respond to experiences with bodily feelings, and she did not feel her body as being part of her.

The patient also complained of memory loss and of being unable to trust the reality of the memories she did have. What she did have in her conscious awareness were bits and pieces of information without affect and without any context for them. She had scraps of recollections of experiences, but these were mere fragments, and she had little idea of where and when, if at all, these experiences had actually occurred. Nevertheless, as the assessment deepened, I also recognized her as being a bright, warm, exquisitely sensitive, uniquely perceptive, and exceptionally literate human being.

Tentative Formulations

Following the assessment period, I developed several tentative and general hypotheses about this patient. Because of the vague, sketchy, and sometimes incoherent nature of the material she presented, these hypotheses were general in the sense of being applicable to most patients with dissociative disorder and not as specific to this particular individual as I would have liked.

There seemed little question the patient was dissociative. She used dissociation as her principal way of protecting herself from awareness of both internal and external dangers. This defense helped her avoid becoming even more disorganized internally, and it served to remove her from the immediacy of external situations and thereby avoid being overwhelmed by the affect they would generate. Thus, she used dissociation to disconnect herself from experiences, both at the time of their occurrence and in her remembering of them. It was in the context of dissociation used as a defense that I thought about various aspects of her presentation, including the discontinuity of her experience, the unreality of her memories, and her sense of self as shattered and fragmented.

Based on substantial clinical and empirical evidence, I consider dissociation and its associated symptoms, including memory loss and disturbances in identity, as a basic reaction to trauma. As a psychoanalyst, however, I also recognize that each individual processes external events in ways that give him or her unique internal meaning and mental representation. There is no simple cause and effect relationship between a traumatic event or series of events and the formation of symptoms.

It is also my experience, and that of other clinicians, that trauma does not occur in isolation. We need to pay attention to the intrafamilial relationship matrix that permits trauma to occur and the nature of the parent-child relationship. Trauma commonly evolves from a pathological parent-child relationship that is abusive, in the sense of being assaultive, intrusive, and both overgratifying and depriving. Such disturbed relationships often center on issues of power and involve sadomasochistic interactions. Based on this proposition about the role of the family and the nature of the child-parent relationship that are implicated in trauma, two concepts that I felt would be helpful in beginning to understand this patient from a dynamic perspective were masochism and externalization by parents.

Masochism, a form of behavior that has confused and baffled psychiatrists and psychologists, consists of the active pursuit of physical pain (suffering) or psychic pain (humiliation). Historically, observers have linked this type of irrational behavior to sexual gratification. More recently, however, theorists have turned their attention to other factors involved in masochism. Novick and Novick (1991), for instance, based on extensive clinical work and research with troubled children of all ages, suggest that children resort to masochistic behavior as a way of having their normal developmental needs met. More specifically, Novick and Novick have found that children who are not responded to empathically and who are continually disappointed give up on their own natural capacities for interacting with their caretakers and turn instead to pain. For these children, pain becomes their way of securing parental involvement as well as of managing their own feelings of helplessness and rage.

There was sufficient evidence in this patient's presentation and history to indicate that masochism was an important element in her intrapsychic life. As described previously, I took her rather bizarre appearance as an attempt to convey to me her investment in being a pathetic, suffering, and helpless person. She struggled walking into my office by herself, requiring the physical assistance of her companion. Significantly, when finding herself on the verge of separating from home and attending college with a full scholarship, she abandoned her own hard-won reality achievements and entered a life of debasement and endangerment.

As just indicated, full understanding of why children resort to the active pursuit of pain requires looking closely at the behavior of their parents. Novick and Novick (1994) found that, in addition to continually failing and disappointing their children, such parents make use of a particular defense referred to as *externalization by parents.* Externalization by parents refers to a process in which parents attribute unwanted and unacceptable aspects of themselves (personality characteristics, attitudes, feelings) to their children. Children who are the recipients of parental externalization, who have attributed characteristics and feelings placed onto them and into them, suffer a variety of disturbances in functioning, including low self-esteem and a confused sense of self.

Treatment Plan

Various treatment models have been proposed for treating patients with Dissociative Identity Disorder. Several of these call for a direct approach tailored specifically to the type of trauma people have experienced and the nature of their posttraumatic symptomatology. Classen, Koopman, and Spiegel (1993), for example, suggested an active treatment that involves a variety of techniques, including cognitive restructuring, the active mobilization of relationships, and hypnosis. Although gaining insight into the nature and origins of the disorder is a desired goal of their approach, they maintained that the type of insight being pursued differs from the insight sought in traditional psychotherapy. Instead of helping the patient to assume greater responsibility for life problems, they suggested directing insight toward assisting the "trauma survivor" to assume less responsibility for the trauma. Finally, in marked contrast to the traditional psychodynamic emphasis on therapeutic neutrality, they maintained that the therapist should take "a moral position that what had happened is unfair, the survivor did not deserve to have it happen, and that the therapist is an ally" (p. 191).

Given my theoretical orientation, which calls for attuning to structural and dynamic features of personality that extend well beyond a patient's diagnosis and presenting symptoms, I elected to see this woman in a traditional form of psychotherapy based on mainstream psychoanalytic beliefs and practices. I was concerned that introducing specific techniques would complicate the treatment relationship, which I saw as my major vehicle of understanding in this case. I also believed that departing from neutrality would put me in a position of meeting her needs, both legitimate ones and less legitimate ones, rather than understanding them. In retrospect, I can see now that, in holding onto traditional practices, I was also protecting my own identity from the anxiety engendered by a patient whose identity was fractured and jumbled.

Ideally, I would have wished to see the patient twice weekly for two 50-minute sessions. Because with more disturbed patients, the treatment situation itself serves as a container to help manage their fears and anxieties, I felt that a lesser frequency would not allow for this treatment function to occur. On the other hand, I anticipated that a greater frequency of sessions presented the risk of stirring feelings that the patient would experience as overwhelming. Were this to happen, ironically, the treatment might have the unintended effect of retraumatizing the patient.

Unfortunately, the ideal and the possible do not always match. Because of the distance involved in her traveling to my office, we decided to meet once weekly for a double session lasting 90 minutes. Maintaining this treatment arrangement proved relatively problem free. She was reliable and punctual in attending sessions, informed me of planned absences to allow appointments to be rescheduled, paid for each session at its conclusion, and rarely called me on the telephone.

Course of Treatment

For much of the first year of the patient's treatment, actually beginning with her initial call, the major issue was trust. Putting herself in my hands, in the arms of a caretaker, was fraught with intense apprehension and dread for her. She insisted on knowing my training and credentials; my experience with victimized patients; my awareness of the literature on the multiple personality; my orientation and philosophy toward treatment; and, most important, my attitude about the multiple personality diagnosis. I answered several of her questions and declined to answer others, but in every instance, I focused on her feelings about entrusting herself to me and my care.

The patient attended several conferences on the multiple personality, read all of the literature she could get her hands on, subscribed to a periodical called *Survivorship,* and brought all the fruits of her labor to me to read. There were volumes. I accepted and read the material to demonstrate to her that I valued her efforts and that I was interested in anything that would help me understand her as a unique individual.

At times, the treatment resembled and felt like play therapy. She spent entire sessions reading to me, singing for me, drawing for me, and even napping in my presence. Aside from the meanings of this childish activity, I felt myself being tested—my limits and tolerance, my willingness to accept all facets of her, and my capacity to maintain our therapeutic focus on seeking understanding.

Increasingly, as is evident in these interactions, I became aware of an effort by the patient to change our respective roles. I experienced her as attempting to redefine our relationship into one in which I was the student and she was my teacher and supervisor. This aspect of our relationship, coupled with new material she was bringing into our sessions, ushered in a second phase of our treatment, which I thought of as a reversal of roles. In her family, the patient had been coerced into a variety of roles and functions other than being a daughter. As a container of her mother's feelings, as one who imposed her own judgments over those of her mother, and as a caretaker for her mother during the mother's recurrent injuries and mishaps, she appeared to have mothered her mother, instead of having been mothered by her. At the same time, she performed many "wifely" functions for her father. She nursed his low self-esteem, soothed his bruised feelings, and patiently listened to his philosophical diatribes.

The patient referred to all of this as ". . . why I was made." That is, she believed that her parents had conceived her for the sole purpose of fulfilling these caregiving functions. I agreed with her that she had never been acknowledged and valued for herself, separate from being a person who met her parents' needs. However, I also called to her attention the absence of any anger and resentment on her part related to this sense of having been exploited.

In the midst of this discussion, the patient offered a new piece of information, which had to do with human sacrifice and a vague sense that the elders in Brazil had engaged in the practice of sacrificing newborn babies. Not trusting the reality of this recollection, she asked me if I would hypnotize her and then speak to her child alters (i.e., other personalities) about such possible events. This reference to her child alters reminded me of how, earlier in treatment, I had experienced several of our sessions as resembling play therapy. In any case, I refused her request. I told her that I did not feel hypnosis would be helpful; that, in time, we would come to know if the experience was real or whether instead its meaning was metaphorical; that we were sure of her sense of having been sacrificed in her family; and that perhaps, as in the rapes, she would be offering herself as a sacrifice to me.

This theme of sacrifice led into a closer look at her relationship with her father. She felt she had been made (i.e., conceived) to serve her father as her mother should have but did not. In time, her father emerged for us as a highly self-centered, brilliant, mercurial individual whose talents and potentials were never realized. He promised much but delivered little. From the time the patient was a young teenager, he was progressively incapacitated with Parkinson's disease. We examined her intensely ambivalent feelings toward him, her unquestioning devotion and loyalty to him, her melancholic reaction to his death, and her sexual relationships with his contemporaries.

She then introduced a second piece of information. Like the earlier piece, it was also a vague remembrance of questionable reality. She had the vague, emotionless impression that, when she was age 4 and living in New Jersey, her father had sexual intercourse with her. Again, she asked me to hypnotize her to speak with two child alters, a girl named Inanna and a boy named Virgil. I again declined but offered that I would like to learn more about Inanna and Virgil. She characterized Inanna as a coy, precocious, and highly seductive girl who sought control and power over men through her seductiveness. Virgil, by contrast, was described as an ethereal, naive, intellectual, and artistic boy who was constantly in pursuit of philosophical truths.

Increasingly, we discussed her father's sexuality, more particularly his "twisted sexuality" and likely bisexuality. In commenting to me about the movie, *The Crying Game,* she insistently pointed out that Dil, one of the major characters, was not homosexual, but instead was a woman in a man's body. The movie became an entry point for exploring further not only her father's "twisted sexuality," but also her bisexuality, her identification with her father, and her sense of estrangement from her body.

As we continued to discuss her father, she added specific details that she had previously omitted. With greater clarity and certainty, she described being awed and inspired by his genius and creativity, only to be let down by his unreliability and inability to follow through. She brought several of his poems and short stories to treatment to share with me. In addition to wanting to impress me with his talents and sensitivities, she also seemed bent on trying to understand him and how his mind worked.

From this material, it became evident that she was initially seduced and drawn in by his creativity, imaginativeness, and readiness to accord her a position of being special but then felt shoved back, cast aside, and stripped of specialness by his depressive withdrawal, frequent bouts of rage, and repeated and blatant sexual escapades. As a young-ster, she saw him as larger than life, and he apparently needed to be seen that way.

In the here and now of treatment, she was reenacting with her ther-apist the sexually toned, boundary-violating, push-pull interaction she had experienced with her father. However, in turning passive to active, she was doing with and to her therapist what she experienced her fa-ther had done with and to her. As the therapist, I used my inner reac-tions as a vantage point from which to empathize with her experience of her father.

Her father's rage and her reactions to it increasingly came to the fore. She recalled from childhood her feelings of terror, occasional numbness, and virtual paralysis. She remembered the glazed look in his eyes and her feeling that he was really mad. In describing her father's look, she recalled a similar look in the eyes of one of the men who had sexually assaulted her and threatened to kill her. I reminded her that during that rape she had placed herself outside her body, observed the incident from above, and then attempted to put herself into the mind of the rapist to understand his thoughts and feelings. I wondered with her if she had reacted in a similar way, earlier, to her father's rages. I also wondered if perhaps she was still dealing with his rage by trying to penetrate his mind through his writings.

As her father's rage continued to occupy center stage, we began to explore her unrelenting stance of hypervigilance and heightened sensi-tivity. We began to understand how she used her hypervigilance defen-sively, much like radar, to anticipate and orient herself to his moods, especially his anger. For the patient, heightened sensitivity was a mode of survival, a means of navigating through the minefields of her father's rages. Accompanying her hypervigilance was a marked tendency to-ward compliance. Her hypervigilance, then, not only alerted her to dan-gers, but also enabled her to tune into the expectations of others, to which she then accommodated. This left her feeling not only like a chameleon, but also as lacking a true sense of self.

As her compliance and the extent to which she had been terrorized and controlled by her father's rage came into therapeutic relief, changes began to appear in our relationship. Having been reasonably punctual in attending sessions, she now began to arrive late. She would then respond with irritation when I ended the session at the scheduled time. She insisted on changing appointment times, often for trivial reasons. Overall, she was becoming more assertive, demanding, and controlling in the treatment relationship. These changes were a prelude to a major struggle that would soon develop between her and me.

With a growing sense of urgency, the patient began to discuss the future plans of her daughter, an academically gifted high school senior. The patient insisted that her daughter attend college and choose one away from home. Recognizing that finances constituted a major obstacle, and with a previously unseen level of determination and competence, she assisted her daughter in obtaining scholarships and completing loan applications. She also began to complain of her already-lowered treatment fee. With mounting indignation, she presented me with an ultimatum. I would either agree to treat her free of charge, or I would find her another therapist who was a Medicaid provider. Acknowledging the legitimacy of her aspirations for her daughter and pointing out that treatment had helped bring her to a point where she could advocate effectively on her daughter's behalf had no impact on her demands.

Faced with this ultimatum, I took the position that I was unwilling to forego the fee, but that if she accepted part-time work, which she had been offered, I would assist her with work-related difficulties. She reacted with feelings of fury, betrayal, and being put upon. All at once, I became the embodiment of her abusing father, her abandoning mother, her ungrateful siblings, and her shiftless mates. Accompanying these reactions was a profound sense of entitlement. Given all the injustices and indignities she had suffered, she felt entitled to be regarded as special. As applied to treatment, this meant free therapy. It was owed to her.

Following a stormy period that included missed sessions, numerous phone calls, and instances of shutting down and not talking, the patient agreed to delay acting on her ultimatum. In an effort to budge me from my stance, she used leaving therapy as ransom. She also elaborated on her attitude of entitlement. For her, special treatment represented a genuine acknowledgment by other people of the validity and full extent of her suffering. Anything less meant that she was not being taken seriously and was experienced by her as a personal affront. Involved in her entitlement was also the issue of restitution. She looked to her therapist to make up for all the hardships and privations she had experienced. He was appointed the ideal parent she once needed but never had. He was to provide perfect empathic attunement, unconditional love, and unlimited generosity.

With an impasse looming, the patient came to a session and announced that she had found another therapist, one who accepted Medicaid. She wanted this to be her final session. This was said without rancor, reproach, or regret. At the end of the session, she dutifully acknowledged the benefits of her treatment, thanked me for my help, and left. One week later, I received a letter from one of the patient's live-in mates. He expressed his appreciation and gratitude and his concerns about the patient's decision.

Discussion

Overtly, the patient presented several of the complaints, symptoms, and observable characteristics associated with Dissociative Identity Disorder. Her sense of not knowing how she might feel moment to moment and her tenuous sense of time are reflective of a discontinuity of experience commonly seen in this condition. The vagueness, incompleteness, and sense of unreality of her memories are also characteristic of persons with this disorder. The lack of coherence and consistency in her presentation, her functioning, and her history all point to the lack of a coherent sense of self, a self that is fractured and fragmented, typically observed in these patients.

As in the case of this woman, and depending on the severity of their Dissociative Identify Disorder, these patients often appear as shut down. Their pervasive vagueness and confusion typically stir similar feelings in the clinician. Because they have only bits and pieces of memories of past experiences, the therapist is looked to as someone to verify the realness of these experiences. If the therapist declines to do so, they react with anger and disappointment and threaten to leave the treatment. Choosing instead to confirm their experiences runs the risk of going way out on a shaky limb.

If clinicians assume that dissociation used as a defense is a basic reaction to prolonged trauma and that it is necessary to understand both the intrafamilial relational matrix that allowed the trauma to occur and the impact of the trauma on the personality structure, they are in a position to move beyond what is observable and begin to see and appreciate the dissociated person in his or her depth, complexity, and individuality. Clinicians then recognize that they are treating not a diagnosis, but an individual who is struggling with life, is in considerable pain, and needs help.

Most compelling in this patient's family of origin and what I came to understand as the crux of her trauma was the parental exploitation. The extent and degree to which she had been used by her parents were profoundly expressed in her reference to her conception of "why I was made." Shengold (1989) evoked the powerful phrase *soul murder* to emphasize, at an individual level, the extent to which parental exploitation and abuse kills the human spirit. For Shengold, soul murder is not a diagnosis or a condition. Instead, it is a dramatic term to describe circumstances in which, wittingly or unwittingly, one person eradicates or compromises the separate identity of another person. The victims of soul murder remain in large part possessed by another, their souls in bondage to someone else.

In the case presented, the parents abdicated their function of protecting their child by using her as an object of their own needs and externalizations. They treated her as someone she was not. The traumas that the patient experienced, including overstimulation, deprivation, incest, and perhaps sexual assault by her father, took place against the backdrop of earlier and long-standing abuse in the form of her mother's abandonment and externalizations.

Consequent to the parental abuse and exploitation and as evident by the themes that emerged in this woman's treatment, she had difficulty trusting and entrusting her self to another person. Her assuming the role of teacher and supervisor in her therapy with me indicated more than simply a readiness to reverse roles. It also reflected her readiness to assume the parental role, her tendency to transcend boundaries, and her not knowing her place.

The patient's interpersonal relationships had a marked victim-victimizer quality, including a propensity for sacrificing herself. Beneath her willingness to be a victim, however, was intense anger and rage. Just before treatment came to an end, she was beginning to experience rage toward her father. Under the sway of this rage, the content of her treatment session swiftly and chaotically switched to attitudes toward her mother. This suggested to me that the anger she felt with her father was, in part, a displacement of deeper feelings of anger she felt toward her mother and her mother's inadequacies. She described her father as "promising much but delivering little." The real and more basic promise, however, is a mother's promise to provide caretaking functions. And, more pointedly, it was her mother who did not deliver. To paraphrase the patient, that is why mothers are made.

It was at a point in treatment that she was about to experience not only the rage toward her mother, but also the pain and disappointment with her, that entitlement emerged as a defense and as a formidable resistance to the continuation of treatment. Her feeling entitled to free treatment was defensive in that it served to shield her from accepting responsibility for her own sadism and extractivness. The claim to free treatment was driven by her own pain and victimization but also justified by her relationship with her daughter. By turning passive into active, she looked to her therapist as an object for meeting her needs, much as she, as a child, had been viewed by her parents.

The decision to treat the patient in a psychoanalytic psychotherapy was based on several assumptions and led to several later decisions. Because the information that identity-disordered patients provide is typically vague, sketchy, and of questionable reliability, therapists need to find special ways of coming to know and understand them. For me, this way is through the treatment relationship. Abundant clinical evidence indicates that careful and sensitive attunement to the nature of the interactions between patient and therapist in the here and now provides a royal road to comprehending and reconstructing the there and then. At the same time, like a light tower, the treatment relationship serves to organize and guide the therapy. As a constant and reliable frame of reference, the treatment relationship enabled me to think coherently about this case and bring to it a semblance of order and understanding.

Implicit in therapeutic use of the treatment relationship is the assumption that the therapist is a relatively neutral person who has done little to provoke whatever reactions a patient has toward the therapist. When therapists depart from their customary way of treating a patient—for example, by introducing some technique different from the methods they have been using—this change inevitably alters the therapeutic milieu. In addition to altering the nature of the patient-therapist interaction, a change in method also affects the stimulus value of the therapist, who now, whether by intent or accident, becomes provocative. With these considerations in mind and having chosen to use the treatment relationship as my beacon, I did not want to alter my approach by introducing a nonrelationship technique such as hypnosis. Recognizing that the patient's request for hypnosis probably reflected some underlying needs to reprise her childhood role as a passive victim, I chose instead to regard the request as a multilayered issue to be explored and understood.

By external and observable standards, the three-year treatment was of considerable benefit to the patient. In contrast to her initial presentation, she was no longer shut down, she presented herself appropriately instead of as a pathetic waif, and only rarely did she lapse into altered states of consciousness. She was more assertive, direct, reliable, and responsible than before. She was increasingly doing for herself many things that she had earlier looked to others to do for her. Her initial preoccupation with the reality of certain memories, such as the possibility of child sacrifice when the family lived in Brazil, was no longer in evidence.

From an internal perspective, with respect to the treatment goals and her inner life, her premature termination left several issues unexplored and unresolved. At termination, for example, we were just about to approach the anger and resentment she felt toward her mother. Left unresolved, then, was not only her rage toward her mother, but also the feelings of pain, depression, and disappointment she experienced about the maternal care she had missed in her life.

Also awaiting exploration but never brought into therapeutic focus were the patient's sense of entitlement and her accompanying feelings of omnipotence. Viewed narrowly, entitlement involves a current claim for reparation for past mistreatments. As applied to this patient, however, I found Coen's (1992) understanding of entitlement more accurate, which he expressed as follows: "The most malignant forms of entitlement occur in the context of patients' feeling that they have been misused and exploited by a parent(s); as a result they now feel free to take what they want from others, who deserve their exploitation. Chronic vengefulness and exploitation involves a wished-for, but reversed, exploitive parent-child relationship" (p. 55).

As for her feelings of omnipotence—which is an aspect of Dissociative Identity Disorder that is probably more common than is recognized—she was almost delusional. Generally, the process of dissociation allows patients to live out and believe in their fantasies. The patient presented here believed in the omnipotent fantasies that her past traumas had not happened to her, that she had triumphed over her mother, that she could magically remove herself (i.e., dissociate) from any unpleasant situation, that she could have two quasi husbands with little asked of her, and that she was entitled to free treatment. In her mind, in other words, the normal rules that govern other people did not apply to her. Because her angry and resentful feelings toward her mother, her sense of entitlement, and her delusions of omnipotence remained unresolved, she had not yet matured to a point where she could experience genuine gratitude for anything anyone did for her.

Summary

I have described the treatment of a woman who was diagnosed as having a Dissociative Identity Disorder, as defined in the *DSM-IV-TR*. As noted in introducing this case presentation, the key criteria for this disorder are the presence of two or more distinct identities or personality states and a marked inability to recall important personal information. In this patient's case, her two childhood alters (Inanna and Virgil) and the significant gaps in her memory met these criteria. In addition, her reports of being outside her body during traumatic experiences of being raped, her recurrently vague and incomplete accounts of events, and the nature of her daily difficulties in living bore witness to her defensive use of dissociation. Of further note, individuals who exhibit Dissociative Identity Disorder commonly report having been physically or sexually abused as children. Although my patient's report of sexual abuse by her father was especially vague and incomplete, her recollections and reflections as treatment evolved made it seem likely that he had in fact been sexually abusive to her.

Electing to treat this woman in a traditional psychodynamic fashion allowed me to see beyond her symptoms and gain a clearer understanding of her underlying conflicts and concerns than would otherwise have been possible. The nature and severity of her disturbance influenced my planning with respect to the frequency of sessions, but not how the sessions were conducted. For me, each treatment case seems to take on a life of its own. Basing my approach on psychoanalytic principles, I used the treatment relationship as my means for coming to know, understand, and think about this woman. It was by attuning to interactions in the here and now that I was able to understand her there and then and to provide empathic and interpretive interventions that were helpful to her.

Recommended Readings

Allen, J. G. (1993). Dissociative processes: Theoretical underpinnings of a working model for clinician and patient. *Bulletin of the Menninger Clinic, 57,* 287–303.

MacGregor, M. W. (1996). Multiple personality disorder: Etiology, treatment, and treatment techniques from a psychodynamic perspective. *Psychoanalytic Psychology, 13,* 389–402.

Putnam, F. W. (1997). *Dissociation in children and adolescents.* New York: Guilford Press.

Ross, C. A. (1989). *Multiple personality disorder.* New York: Wiley.

Scroppo, J. C., Drob, S. L., Weinberger, J. L., & Eagle, P. (1998). Identifying dissociative identity disorder: A self-report and projective study. *Journal of Abnormal Psychology, 107,* 272–284.

References

American Psychiatric Association. (2000). *Diagnostic and statistical manual of mental disorders* (4th ed., text rev.). Washington, DC: Author.

Classen, C., Koopman, C., & Spiegel, D. (1993). Trauma and dissociation. *Bulletin of the Menninger Clinic, 57,* 178–194.

Coen, S. (1992). *The misuse of persons: Analyzing pathological dependency.* Hillsdale, NJ: Analytic Press.

Novick, J., & Novick, K. (1991). Some comments on masochism and the delusion of omnipotence from a developmental perspective. *Journal of the American Psychoanalytic Association, 39,* 307–328.

Novick, J., & Novick, K. (1994). Externalization as a pathological form of relating: The dynamic underpinnings of abuse. In A. Sugarman (Ed.), *Victims of abuse* (pp. 45–68). Madison, CT: International Universities Press.

Shengold, L. (1989). *Soul murder: The effect of childhood abuse and deprivation.* New Haven, CT: Yale University Press.

CHAPTER 14

Gender Identity Disorder

KENNETH J. ZUCKER

Sandy is a 26-year-old biological male. At the time of referral, Sandy was unemployed, living in a large city, and sharing an apartment with several gay men, who were also in their 20s. Because of Sandy's poor financial situation, but also because of discord with his room-mates, he was about to move back home to live with his parents and a younger brother, where he had lived until age 24. For reasons to be noted, Sandy had dropped out of high school in the tenth grade. Both of his parents had a high school education and were from a lower mid-dle-class background.

Presenting Problem

Sandy's referral for psychological help was initiated by his mother. She had contacted me because I had initially assessed Sandy at the age of 7 in relation to concerns about his gender identity development. Before the current referral, I had last seen Sandy and his family when he was 14 years old. His mother reported now that Sandy was "trans-gender [sic] or transsexual" and, with a sense of urgency and desper-ation, said that Sandy was "having a lot of problems."* She said that he was displaying intense mood swings, and she feared that he was "a manic depressant" [sic]. She described him as being "extremely ver-bally abusive one minute, and then the next minute he is fine." She said that his sleep patterns were erratic and that his short-term memory "was gone." She reported further that, since first moving out of the family home, Sandy would periodically move back and then leave again. She then told me that he had been "living as a woman" for the

---

* Throughout this case report, I vary in using male or female pronouns, depending on the context. For example, Sandy's mother consistently referred to Sandy using male pronouns. When discussing Sandy's childhood, I use male pronouns but shift to female pronouns when discussing her current presentation.

past two years. Although "it" was prevalent beforehand, she said he did not show "it" before moving out two years previously.

Sandy's mother then commented, "He always looked like a female." She reported that Sandy was sexually attracted to "straight [heterosexual] men" because gay men were too "girly" for him. Because of his mood swings and unpredictable behavior, Sandy's mother said her husband no longer wanted him to live with the family. She then remarked that Sandy has "always liked you" and was "moved" on hearing my voice when I telephoned to set up this appointment. Sandy's mother also volunteered the information that she herself had had a "nervous breakdown" at the age of 12 and then a second breakdown when she was 21: "I was extremely hyper and moody." Hence, she said, "I feel like I understand what he is going through."

At present, Sandy's mother was extremely concerned that he was suicidal, and it was for this reason that she had contacted me. She noted that, over the past few years, Sandy had refused professional help and that she had called me as a last resort. Indeed, while Sandy was on a short waiting list to be seen, he had overdosed on "some pills." He was treated on this occasion only by his roommate, a paramedic, who had helped him induce vomiting.

History of the Problem

Sandy was seen initially for an assessment, which consisted of several interviews and some psychological testing. With respect to Sandy's physical appearance, she presented as a moderately overweight individual about 5'10" tall. She had curly, brownish-auburn hair fashioned in a feminine style. She was dressed casually, wearing running shoes, blue jeans, and a pink T-shirt with "SEXY" written on the front. She wore a white necklace and had a silver ring on her middle finger. She had obvious facial hair that was partially concealed by heavy makeup. Sandy had rather prominent "breasts," which she created by placing silicone pads in a brassiere. A naïve observer would have been likely to perceive her as a woman, although her facial stubble would probably have aroused suspicion. The hair on her arms and legs was shaved. She spoke in a high-pitched voice that had an exaggerated hyper-feminine quality. When I had first spoken to Sandy over the telephone, before knowing that she was living as a woman, I had in fact felt as if I were speaking with a woman. Sandy retained her gender-neutral name after her transition to living as a female.

Sandy was diligent about keeping her appointments and was a forthcoming and interesting person with whom to talk. I got the impression that she could have spoken freely with anyone who was willing to listen to her. She was, nevertheless, a challenging person to interview because it was difficult for her to keep her attention focused on one topic at a time. Moreover, because the assessment occurred over several weeks, it was possible to observe that Sandy did not seem to retain any coherent narrative of what had previously been talked about. It was as if each interview was starting from scratch.

When asked in the first assessment interview to tell me about her current life situation, Sandy began by referring to her mother: "She tends to think I'm chemically imbalanced . . . that I'm unstable at times . . . I can be moody." Because of my prior involvement with Sandy, I asked her to tell me about her life since I had last seen her at age 14. Although at that time neither Sandy nor her parents had reported any evidence of gender dysphoria—that is, severe discontent with being a male—she now remembered things differently: "Back then, my mom knew I was gender dysphoric. My dad was uncomfortable with it. I totally knew what was going on. I was not comfortable [with being a male] but I said otherwise . . . my girlfriends knew."

Sandy recalled that entering high school had been very difficult for her and that she had tried to commit suicide. This attempt occurred 11 months after my last previous contact with Sandy, when she was age 15½, and hospital records confirmed that she had taken an overdose. The hospital records attributed her taking the overdose to a learning disability and associated academic difficulty she was having, but Sandy recalled her problems at the time differently: "People would ask if I was a boy or a girl. I was dressing androgynous." Sandy stated that she did not disclose to anyone how she was really feeling at the time.

After this overdose, she began to see a psychiatrist, who placed her on Prozac, an antidepressant medication, and said that they would talk together about her "transgendered feelings." Unfortunately, this psychiatrist was no longer practicing, and records of Sandy's treatment were not available. As Sandy recalled, however, she was having "fits of violent rages" at the time, and the psychiatrist identified her relationship with her father "as a big part of the problem." Beyond this recollection, she said, the year or two following the suicide attempt was for the most part "a blur," and she had few memories of her life during this period. It was at this point that she dropped out of high school.

When asked about her sexual feelings, Sandy stated that she became sexually active at the age of 10 with an adolescent boy, and she commented, "I remember you asking me questions about getting aroused." When I had seen Sandy at age 14, he reported not having had any sexual experiences. Now, however, Sandy described herself as "a sexually driven person—my mom tells me that." Indeed, on a self-report questionnaire, Sandy indicated that, since the age of 13, she had had sexual experiences with two to five females, including penile-vaginal intercourse, and sexual experiences with 36 or more males (this being the highest response option on the scale), including anal intercourse. She described the first boy with whom she had sex (while living as a male) as "heteroflexible."

Sandy also recalled that, in his mid-adolescence, his mother and his girlfriends would say to him, "You'd make a much better girl; biologically you're a man, but mentally you're not." Sandy then remarked that she never went through a "gay man period," but instead "transitioned to living as a girl as young as 14." It is interesting that this recollection, at least on the surface, was not consistent with my own records or with the hospital records at the time of the overdose incident. Sandy later modified this statement by reporting that she began to go out publicly dressed as a woman at the age of 20 or 21 and, for a brief time, ingested feminizing hormones that she obtained from a "transsexual person." At the time of the current evaluation, Sandy indicated that she was not taking feminizing hormones, although she was interested in doing so.

Sandy had a difficult time describing her adolescent years: "To be honest . . . I was dealing with so many things . . . I had an emotional breakdown. . . . I became a hermit for a while." Sandy felt that she had been very depressed and that her emotions had been exceedingly turbulent when she was a teenager: "If you looked at me cross-eyed, I'd flip out." There were times when Sandy believed her parents were afraid of her, and there were days on end when she refused to get out of bed.

As the interview proceeded, Sandy began talking about her present life circumstances, noting that "I'm not very good with stress." She attributed her recent overdose to problems with her roommates, her parents, her ex-boyfriend (whom she also referred to as "hetero-flexible"), and her current boyfriend. Sandy remarked, "My mother thinks I'm a drug addict and a prostitute." Appearing hurt, she added, "Sometimes my mom says things that are so cold that I want to kill her." She recalled that her mother once referred to her as a "hooker," and she claimed that, had she been in the same room with her mother at the time, "I would have bludgeoned her to death."

When asked about sex for money, Sandy acknowledged having "tried it" on one occasion and being paid $300 but feeling uncomfortable about the whole thing. She then talked about being able to understand how difficult it is for her father to accept her as a female, but, she added, "He's had a lot of time to adjust, and he does say I'm an attractive girl." All things considered, Sandy acknowledged, she was extremely irritable with her parents and easily annoyed by them, even over little things such as being asked to do a chore.

Sandy spoke further about her current sexual partners. She remarked that her ex-boyfriend, whom she had dated for seven months, liked to perform oral sex on her. When asked what it was like for her penis to be fellated, Sandy said that "It was weird at first. . . . Men who date girls like us like it that we have both parts or the illusion of both . . ." When asked what it was like for her to experience penile erection, Sandy answered, "It's arousing . . . but different." She then seemed to display some sadness, stating "I realize I'll never be as real as I want to be," which was a reference to her desire to be a woman. She recalled telling her ex-boyfriend, "You like to suck cock more than I do."

Sandy was currently dating a man whom she met in a bar. She said that it took him a couple of weeks to find out that she was a transsexual, but once he did, he remained interested in her. She commented, "I'm the girl next door, but I'm not the real girl." She characterized this man as "a really sweet guy" who has not been too pushy in terms of sexual activity. Again, in a somewhat sad tone, Sandy remarked, "Sometimes I feel really real, but other times I feel so self-conscious. . . . You always have doubts." Sandy expressed regret that, at the age of 26, she had not progressed further in terms of physical treatments, including feminizing hormones, penectomy, castration, and vaginoplasty.

Before moving out of her parents' home, Sandy believed that her mother had always known about her transgendered feelings: "I was allowed to wear make-up in the house, but no dresses." Sandy then stated that she had not had any gay friends until the age of 21: "Gay people help you confront things . . . your abnormalities." Sandy talked about how she always knew that she was different but that her friends "knew I was going to get a sex change before I did." She then talked about her various efforts to keep a job as a model, as a phone sex operator, and in retail sales. She indicated that her mood states and poor reaction to criticism often led to conflicts with her employers. She showed impaired judgment, however, in denying having difficulty keeping a job, even though she talked about how she was let go on one occasion because "I was having a breakdown . . . a meltdown." She acknowledged that, over the years, her parents had supported her financially and had always bailed her out of difficult financial situations. Indeed, in one of my telephone conversations with Sandy's mother, she said that she could not help herself when it came to paying Sandy's bills: "He's my baby."

Sandy then abruptly switched to talking about her parents' "surreal relationship." She reported that she had caught her dad cheating on her mom and that was why she had moved out of the house. In Sandy's words, "I told him I'd kill him. I probably would. When I get upset, the consequences aren't there. The other day I thought I'd bash my cat's head in." Sandy claimed that her mother told her that the marital relationship was none of her business. Sandy then talked about feeling nervous all of the time and frequently vomiting due to anxiety. When her mother asks her to do something, she said, she is prone to giving an aggressive retort, such as "Stick your . . . thoughts up your ass."

When asked about her use of recreational drugs, Sandy reported frequent use of Ecstasy and occasional use of cocaine, "crystal," "K" (Ketamine), marijuana, and LSD. She acknowledged getting high as frequently as once a day. She also talked about using "G," which she claimed was a male sex hormone that made her "super-aggressive and I want to fight someone." Sandy talked about being vaguely suicidal, not eating for days on end, and experiencing fluctuations in her weight. She also talked about not sleeping for two to three days at a time. The first interview ended with Sandy commenting, in a wistful manner, "Sometimes I wish I was a real girl . . . I'll never be happy until I'm internally happy." At this point, Sandy telephoned her mother from the office, and they had a 15-minute conversation characterized by screaming and intense hostility. She screamed to me, "If she was here right now, I'd kill her."

At the next interview, I asked Sandy if she could articulate what she felt were her most prominent problems at the present time. She said that this was a hard question to answer, after which she stated that she wonders why she has not made a greater effort to obtain feminizing hormones: "If I'm not on hormones, what's the point?" she asked rhetorically. She wondered if something were holding her back: "I think part of it is being scared." Sandy indicated that she had spoken with her parents over the weekend about having a sex-change operation. She said that she did not like being touched "down there," but also that it "felt good . . . but it doesn't feel like me." Sandy remarked that "technically I have a penis . . . but mentally I'm not a male." She claimed that some of her female friends even "forget I'm transsexual . . . sometimes I forget." Sandy then stated that she knows that she has a "chemical imbalance. . . . I almost smashed my cat's head in."

Sandy then talked further about feeling criticized by her mother: "I wanted to pick up the computer and throw it at her." Sandy agreed that she was depressed and added that her preferred method of dealing with depression was to sleep. Her brother had called her a "freak" over the weekend, she reported, and "I thought I was going to kill him." I remarked to Sandy that her life appeared to be drifting, that she was having obvious problems in coping, and that I thought that she required a great deal of help. Sandy replied that she knew this was the case and that, if she did not get help, "I'm gonna end up killing myself one of these days."

As part of the assessment, Sandy participated in psychological testing. Four subtests from the Wechsler Adult Intelligence Scale-III (Wechsler, 1997) indicated average intellectual functioning with an estimated IQ in the 95 to 100 range. On the Symptom Checklist-90-Revised (Derogatis, 1983), Sandy had markedly elevated scores on all of the scales related to symptoms of disorder and global maladjustment. On the Diagnostic Interview Schedule (Robins, Helzer, Croughan, & Ratcliff, 1981), a structured interview that covers a range of disorders codified in the *Diagnostic and Statistical Manual of Mental Disorders* (*DSM-IV-TR*; American Psychiatric Association, 2000), Sandy endorsed a wide range of symptoms. She met diagnostic criteria for four *DSM* disorders: Bipolar Disorder, Major Depressive Episode, Alcohol Abuse, and Bulimia. In addition, Sandy met criteria for four other disorders that, because of the broad range of symptoms she was showing, would not be diagnosed separately: Dysthymic Disorder, Obsessive Compulsive Disorder, Panic Disorder with Agoraphobia, and Generalized Anxiety Disorder. She was also close to meeting diagnostic criteria for Drug Abuse and Drug Dependence. On self-report questionnaires pertaining to gender identity and sexual orientation, Sandy reported substantial gender dysphoria and a predominant homosexual orientation, as defined by sexual attraction to biological males.

Family Background and Developmental History

An unusual aspect of this case is my having seen Sandy as a child, which meant that actual documentation as well as recall was available. At age 7, Sandy was first referred to me at the suggestion of his second grade teacher, who observed that he always drew pictures of himself looking like a girl. The teacher and his parents both reported that Sandy preferred to play with girls, liked to dress up in women's clothing, emulated females in fantasy role play, played with stereotypical girls' toys (e.g., Barbie dolls), displayed effeminate mannerisms, was much closer to female relatives than to male relatives, and had recently told his mother that he had had a dream in which he was a girl named Suzie. The dream aside, however, Sandy's parents stated that he never verbalized a wish to be a girl or discomfort about his sexual anatomy. Sandy did not particularly like rough-and-tumble play and avoided group sports. During the previous year or two, he had been subject to a great deal of social ostracism by other boys because of his cross-gender behavior, including being called "Shirley Temple."

Apart from the gender identity issue, Sandy was noted to be a sensitive child who was easily bothered by parental quarrels, parental mood states, and losses, such as the death of the family dog. He often misinterpreted playful quibbling between his parents as real arguments. In the first grade, he was diagnosed by a psychoeducational consultant as having a reading disability. When interviewed by this consultant, Sandy was thought to be anxious, to have difficulty answering questions directly, and to give answers that seemed unrelated to what was being asked.

Sandy was very pretty as a young child, his parents reported, and was often mistaken for a girl. When asked how they had reacted to Sandy's initial displays of cross-gender behavior, which began during the preschool years, the parents indicated that they had been inconsistent. They would try to discourage it on some occasions, but at other times his mother, in particular, would "back off," in her words, because she was concerned that Sandy was a "moody" child who easily became depressed.

Before delivering Sandy, his mother had had a miscarriage. When interviewed jointly with her husband, she stated that she had wanted a girl while she was pregnant with Sandy, but that "his being a boy didn't matter." In a subsequent individual interview, however, she reported feeling sad that she never had a girl. Sandy was full term at birth, but for his first three days, he required phototherapy for jaundice. He then remained in the hospital for an additional two weeks until he became able to digest formula properly. Once home, he was colicky for the next three months. He was described as an active infant who seldom napped. As an infant and toddler, he reportedly did not display any anxiety or distress when separated from his mother. At 18 months, his sleep became irregular, and he was given Phenergan until the age of 4. He also developed several food allergies as a young child. Two years before his being assessed at age 7, a maternal aunt and her son moved in with Sandy's family, after this woman left her alcoholic and physically abusive husband. Sandy's cousin was a very aggressive boy, who often teased him for his cross-gender behavior and apparently orchestrated such teasing by other boys in the school setting.

As for the earlier history of Sandy's parents, his mother described having had her own problems with affect regulation in late childhood and early adolescence, including periods in which she would become violent, both verbally and physically. Her previously mentioned "nervous breakdowns" at the ages of 12 and 21 were primarily depressive episodes, and in the second instance, she was treated with antidepressant medication. She was conceived before her parents' marriage, she said, when her mother was age 17. Both of her parents came from poor families with many children. She described her father as having a violent temper and stated that, as a child, he had almost killed one of his brothers with an axe. Following this incident, she reported, he had vowed never to lose his temper again and had become "a passive person."

Sandy's mother described her own mother as having been "a nurturing person" until she had a "nervous breakdown" when she was age 11. One of her main caregivers both before and after her mother's breakdown was her maternal grandmother, whom she also described as a nurturing person. According to Sandy's mother, one of her paternal uncles had a homosexual orientation, and she recalled once overhearing her father talking about his brother being interested in a sex-change operation. To her knowledge, however, this operation never occurred.

In an individual interview, Sandy's mother described her courtship with Sandy's father. She met him shortly after ending a several year relationship with another man whom she felt was too dependent on her and caused her to feel "claustrophobic." Sandy's father had been married previously, and this marriage had ended precipitously and left him feeling despondent. After knowing Sandy's mother for only two weeks, he asked her to marry him, and she thought he was joking. She declined his offer of marriage but agreed to live with him, and they lived together for three years before getting married. Sandy's mother reported a "general dissatisfaction" with her marriage at the moment. She felt that her husband was no longer "open and loving" and had become "obsessed" with his work. He no longer was interested in talking with her about sensitive topics, and he wanted to have intercourse with her several times a night. She did not share his level of sexual interest, she said, and stated that, for the past few years, her husband had been going on periodic drinking binges, perhaps twice a year. She reported missing her sisters, who lived in a different city, and said that Sandy, being the "emotional barometer of the family," recognized her unmet emotional needs. She gave the impression of being under a considerable amount of stress and indeed reported getting migraine headaches that she attributed to stress.

As for Sandy's father, he reported that his parents separated when he was age 7. He described his father as an alcoholic man who was abusive to him and to his mother. He was close to his sister, who was several years his senior and said that he was upset when she married and moved away. As an adult, Sandy's father worked long hours, and there were periods in which he was away from the family because of his job. He was unemployed for a year during Sandy's infancy and served at that time as his primary caregiver while Sandy's mother worked. He was then able to find another job and, for several years thereafter, he was rarely at home during the week and able to return home only for the weekends. Hence, in his early years, Sandy had little contact with his father.

Sandy met most of the *DSM* criteria applicable at that time for Gender Identity Disorder of Childhood. However, because he did not strongly and persistently state a desire to be a girl, he was given the residual diagnosis of Atypical Gender Identity Disorder. His high level of anxiety was noted at the time, but he was not given the formal childhood diagnosis of Overanxious Disorder. After this assessment, the family was referred to a child psychiatrist, who was asked to provide Sandy's parents with counseling as to his cross-gender behavior, issues pertaining to parenting, and their marital difficulties, and to work with Sandy on helping him to feel more confident as a boy.

At a one-year follow-up when Sandy was age 8, his parents indicated that their family situation had improved for the most part. They had moved to a better neighborhood, and they felt that Sandy related more easily to the children in their new area than to his peers in the former neighborhood. In their opinion, Sandy had settled down emotionally and was becoming increasingly self-confident. Although Sandy's father could not recall the name of their therapist, he referred to him as a "super guy." However, Sandy continued to have academic difficulties over the past year, the parents reported, and there still seemed to be considerable confusion about how to help him with his learning disability.

As to Sandy's gender identity development, the parents reported that he had made some gains. He was playing with both boys and girls, they said, instead of only girls. He was less aggressive by nature than his younger brother, but he had become more assertive in his peer group. Although Sandy enjoyed playing organized games, such as soccer, with other boys and engaging in unstructured activities such as bike riding, catching animals, and "getting dirty," he refused to participate on a sport's team because "I am not very good at it." The parents reported a reduction in certain cross-gender behaviors, such as female doll play, but noted that he continued to enjoy "doing hair." He had ceased cross-dressing, although he would occasionally role-play as Superman or use a robe and pretend to be in Saudi Arabia. The parents felt that his effeminate mannerisms had mostly disappeared. He had not made any remarks about wanting to be a girl or indicated a dislike of his sexual anatomy. His mother observed, however, that Sandy seemed "fascinated by the female form" and liked seeing females in the nude.

When interviewed individually, Sandy was talkative but characteristically had difficulty remaining focused on a topic and, at times, answered questions with unrelated comments. He indicated that he now liked being a boy, although he acknowledged that he still liked to play with girls and that his best friend was a girl. Sandy reported a diminution of his cross-gender identification and interests, but it was also apparent that he continued to be interested in emulating females. He talked about how he and his mother often screamed at each other, apparently in relation to his school difficulties. In a task I set for him, he created a story with various toys, in which there was a rather marked preoccupation with animals having babies and the female animals being very pretty. The farm animals were being attacked by other animals, and the father, who had previously been away, returned home and made everything all right.

Nine months after this follow-up, I was contacted by the psychoeducational consultant at Sandy's school, who reported that he was doing poorly, particularly in his writing skills. He was also having great difficulty in spelling, although his reading was apparently adequate. Socially, it was reported that Sandy had reverted to playing mainly with the girls and that he was now being teased for cross-gender behavior. In an interview with Sandy's mother at this time, she reported that he was becoming increasingly volatile and that she was concerned about being unable to control him any longer. During one argument with her, he had blurted out that they had originally taken him to the hospital because he was "a crazy lunatic." He demanded that his mother let him play with female dolls and, in his anger, called her a "fucking bitch." Sandy's aunt told his mother that he was acting just the way she did as a young child.

With respect to Sandy's gender development at this time, his mother reported that she had bought him a female Cabbage Patch doll for his birthday because he wanted one to go along with his male Cabbage Patch doll. She then remarked that both Sandy and his brother want to have a "real sister," which was perhaps a reflection of her own conscious desire to have a daughter. She agreed with the psychoeducational consultant that Sandy had reverted to playing mainly with girls and added that he had lost the friendships he had previously developed with some boys. In drawings he was making, he was creating dresses, although he also drew male figures and talked about wanting to be a rock star. When asked how she thought Sandy was feeling as a boy, his mother replied "I think he feels okay."

When asked how she was feeling, Sandy's mother said, "I'm going crazy." She described having anxiety attacks and reported that she currently was not working and was home alone all day. She was experiencing anxiety feelings in her stomach, she said, and was smoking two packs of cigarettes a day. She provided the further information that her husband was now attending a clinic for alcohol abuse after experiencing some blackouts. He had sought treatment after a fire in their apartment building, during which he could barely be aroused to help get the family out of the building and for which he had no recollection the following morning. She went on to state that her husband's mother, father, and stepfather were also alcoholics.

At a two-year follow-up when Sandy was age 9, his parents reported that he was continuing to have learning difficulties at school, for which he was receiving special education assistance. His father expressed considerable anger at the school authorities for Sandy's difficulties, which seemed inappropriate. The psychoeducational consultant at the school reported that Sandy was not considered to be severely learning disabled and that his learning was progressing at an adequate pace. A new piece of information that emerged during this follow-up assessment concerned the father's employment history. Apparently, there had been several occasions when, after achieving some success in his work, he had found ways to sabotage his own performance and undo his accomplishments.

As to Sandy's gender development, his parents reported that he was playing with both boys and girls and was not showing any preference. His toy and activity interests were varied, and he was not role-playing as a female. He continued to dislike competitive sports, but he had not made any remarks about wanting to be a girl. In an individual interview, Sandy did not appear effeminate in his mannerisms or voice quality, and he was more focused and organized than in the previous two assessments. He also seemed calmer and less anxious than before.

He was worried mainly about his father's drinking and temper and their impact on the family.

At a three-year follow-up when Sandy was almost 11, his parents reported that the special education he was receiving had improved and included more one-to-one teaching than before. Despite still having learning difficulties, Sandy reported that he "loved" school. According to his parents, he had gone to his first school dance, and he was socializing with both boys and girls in the neighborhood. His best friend continued to be a girl, but Sandy reported that he liked playing with boys and girls equally, including a game of "kissing tag." The parents did not report grossly feminine interests although Sandy continued to show a strong aversion to sports, including an explicit hatred of hockey.

In an individual interview, Sandy was calm and coherent, as he had been the previous year. He did not have the look of a particularly masculine youngster, and now, like his parents, he was somewhat overweight. During this interview, I explored with Sandy his recollection of why his parents had brought him to see me when he was 7. He talked about how, when he was very young, there were some older girls who took care of him and, in his words, "It was confusing, because they would dress me up in doll clothes." He then talked about not wanting to be a girl and was emphatic in asserting that he liked being a boy. He, nevertheless, indicated that he felt comfortable playing with both boys and girls and enjoyed diverse kinds of activities. He talked about being on the boy's team during games of "kissing tag" and stated that it was nice sometimes to kiss girls, but "sometimes they're really not nice or polite and really rude . . . when you kiss them they burp . . . gross."

Because sexuality was not a taboo topic in his family, I talked with Sandy about early sexual feelings. Asked the meaning of a "crush," he said, "It means you love them a lot." He reported having a crush on a particular girl for the past year and said that "every time I get near her, I get all nervous and everything." He was able to acknowledge that penile erection "sort of" happened and then added, "all the time when I get near Amy." Sandy believed that it was a "little normal" to have such feelings. He denied any crushes on boys and said that he would feel weird if a boy had a crush on him "because guys don't, are not supposed to like other guys, like in a brotherly way but not in that way." He said he has always known this to be so. He indicated that he was too young to have sex but that he hoped to marry Amy when he was older.

Before the current assessment when Sandy was age 26, he had been seen last when he was 14, at which time he was asked to participate in a research follow-up study. By telephone, his mother reported that Sandy had become more "mouthy" as of late, although he was said to be well behaved outside the house. She said that most of his current friends were girls, whom she sexualized as "some really good-looking ones." She noted that he was very interested in clothing and occasionally designed clothes for his female friends. Sandy had had a difficult year academically in the seventh grade but was doing better this year in the eighth grade, she said. She also noted that there were periods when Sandy avoided social contact and seemed depressed. When I spoke with Sandy, the quality of his voice and his bodily movements initially struck me as being very effeminate. These features of his presentation became less pronounced as the interview progressed and he became more relaxed. He reported no gender dysphoria, reported minimal sexual feelings other than crushes on a few girls, and denied masturbation.

Diagnostic Impression and Formulation of Problem

By virtue of her strong and persistent cross-gender identification and discomfort with being a male, Sandy as an adult met *DSM* criteria for Gender Identity Disorder, which included a homosexual orientation in relation to her biological sex. She saw herself as a transsexual woman, who was attracted to putatively heterosexual men. Sandy also met criteria for both mood and anxiety disorders and, following a diagnostic consultation with the Mood and Anxiety Disorders Clinic in the hospital where my Gender Identity Clinic is located, she was given a diagnosis of Dysthymic Disorder. The possibility of her having a Bipolar Disorder was also considered but rejected on the basis of Sandy's never having had any full-blown manic episodes. As a further diagnostic consideration in this complex case, I believed that Sandy also met criteria for Borderline Personality Disorder.

Turning to the emergence of Sandy's disorder, he showed considerable cross-gender behavior and a strong cross-gender identification as a child. Nonetheless, it was never entirely clear that Sandy wanted to be a girl at this time. Although he had the dream in which he was a girl, Sandy never verbalized a desire to be a girl, according to his parents' report. By contrast, the majority of children who are referred for gender identity issues do directly express a wish to be of the opposite sex. Sandy's childhood was also notable for his academic struggles, diagnosed learning disability, and special class education. In addition, his behavior at home was intermittently problematic and difficult for his parents to manage, primarily because of his poor affect regulation as shown in his moodiness, irritability, and volatility.

Prospective studies of boys with Gender Identity Disorder indicate that most do not persist in their desire to be a girl. Instead, the majority develop a homosexual orientation, without associated gender dysphoria. When Sandy was seen for follow-up assessments in late childhood and early adolescence, there were no clear signs of gender dysphoria, and he gave the impression that he was becoming comfortable with being a boy. It is obvious in retrospect, however, that either this impression was incorrect at the time or there had subsequently been a change, with Sandy becoming increasingly gender dysphoric and eventually making a transition to living as a woman in young adulthood. In addition, Sandy as a young adult showed other more general adjustment difficulties, including substance abuse, poor affect regulation, substantial problems in close interpersonal relationships and occupational functioning, and probable Borderline Personality Disorder. In formulating Sandy's current psychological problems, then, it is necessary to understand why her gender identity difficulties either persisted or resurfaced and the origin of her more general difficulties in psychosocial functioning.

As to Sandy's gender identity development, it may be that, for whatever reasons, the clinical impression of improvement by early adolescence was incorrect. Perhaps the wrong questions were asked.

Perhaps the available data were interpreted incorrectly. Perhaps Sandy and her parents did not fully acknowledge issues that were present at the time. Alternatively, it may be that new difficulties arising for Sandy in his mid-adolescence acted as stressors that reactivated and intensified his earlier gender identity issues. Thinking along the lines of this alternative possibility, I propose the following formulation.

When Sandy entered high school, he was subjected to renewed teasing and social ostracism, perhaps because he appeared effeminate and unmasculine. In addition, he was probably experiencing homoerotic feelings that were ego-dystonic, that is, not acceptable to him, not considered by him to be a natural part of himself, and anxiety-provoking. These anxiety-provoking feelings, coupled with renewed academic difficulties and a biological predisposition to mood disorder, severely compromised Sandy's functioning and led to his overdose at age 15.

As Sandy withdrew socially and then dropped out of high school, he began to develop the fantasy that being a girl and later a woman would solve all of his problems. As mentioned previously, Sandy as a young adult talked about this period as a time in which his girlfriends all "knew" that he was really a woman, as did his mother. Hence, Sandy may have received either subtle or not so subtle reinforcement from these significant others in his life for beginning to act on his fantasies. As his mother remarked in a rather unusual way, "Well, my father said that the family doesn't have a granddaughter, and we always wanted one." Living life as a woman would also solve any internalized feelings of homophobia (aversion to homosexual involvements) because being a woman would "normalize" his sexual attraction to males. The data from the present assessment at age 26 appear to show that Sandy's transition to living as a woman has been a gradual process, building slowly over the years on her childhood femininity and lack of a strongly grounded male gender identity.

Although Sandy had behavioral and learning problems as a child, his general psychosocial functioning was not nearly as impaired as later in adolescence and young adulthood. Sandy has been having severe problems in mastering young adult developmental tasks, including being unable to form stable romantic attachments and a firm occupational identity. Her mood disorder and substance abuse have contributed to these impairments, and her personality disorder is also playing a significant role in undermining her adjustment. Sandy has a very hostile relationship with her father and a highly ambivalent relationship with her mother that vacillates between close enmeshment and distant antagonism. She seems to have become increasingly vulnerable to losing control of her affects and impulses. Her parents have become perplexed and torn as to how to deal with her. On one hand, they feel that she should be expelled from the family because her conduct is too difficult to manage; on the other hand, her mother in particular feels compelled to nurture and rescue her. Whatever the precise antecedents of Sandy's problems may be, there is little doubt that she has very poor coping capacities and is severely limited in her ability to manage her day-to-day psychosocial functioning in a comfortable and effective manner.

Treatment Recommendations, Prognosis, and Outcome

The prognosis for Sandy's being able to resolve her Gender Identity Disorder is poor, which is almost always the case when the condition is present in adulthood. At present, her disorder is ego-syntonic, that is, acceptable to her, considered by her to be a natural part of herself, and not anxiety-provoking. There were no indications that Sandy wanted to explore the factors that led her to choose living as a woman as the best route for her to take, as opposed to living life as a gay man. Feminizing hormones and a surgical sex change might result in improved adaptation for her. However, her general problems in psychosocial functioning make it unlikely that a sex change would solve all or even most of her psychological problems. In light of the range and severity of Sandy's problems, the treatment recommended for her consisted of antidepressant medication combined with supportive psychotherapy aimed at working with her on stabilizing her life, moderating her turbulent emotions, and increasing her level of self-esteem and capacity for self-control. Because of her chronic difficulties in delaying gratification, however, the prognosis was guarded for Sandy's being able to participate effectively in a treatment program and resolve her core problems, and she was considered at high risk for suicidal behavior.

Although Sandy was diligent in attending the assessment sessions, she has so far shown little motivation for treatment. In the beginning, Sandy claimed that her health insurance card had been stolen and that she had been unable to secure a replacement card. Without this card, she has not been able to complete the blood tests that should precede her beginning to take the recommended antidepressant medication. She has also failed to attend all but one of her psychotherapy appointments. Most of the time, she does not call to cancel these appointments. When she does call, she gives a variety of less than compelling reasons why she cannot attend (e.g., she has no money for public transportation, her parents will not drive her, she is too depressed, she is out looking for an apartment). At present, then, the outcome for Sandy remains very uncertain. As an alternative to the current effort to help her with outpatient treatment, perhaps Sandy would do better in a partial hospitalization program for young adults. A program of this kind might provide the necessary external structure to allow her to begin systematic exploration of strategies for the multiple problems that beset her.

Recommended Readings

Blanchard, R., & Steiner, B. W. (Eds.). (1990). *Clinical management of gender identity disorders in children and adults.* Washington, DC: American Psychiatric Press.

Green, R. (1987). *"The sissy boy syndrome" and the development of homosexuality.* New Haven, CT: Yale University Press.

Green, R., & Blanchard, R. (1995). Gender identity disorders. In H. I. Kaplan & B. J. Sadock (Eds.), *Comprehensive textbook of psychiatry* (6th ed., vol. 1, pp. 1347–1360). Baltimore: Williams & Wilkins.

Zucker, K. J., & Bradley, S. J. (1995). *Gender identity disorder and psychosexual problems in children and adolescents.* New York: Guilford Press.

References

American Psychiatric Association. (2000). *Diagnostic and statistical manual of mental disorders* (4th ed., text rev.). Washington, DC: Author.

Derogatis, L. (1983). *SCL-90: Administration, scoring and procedures manual for the revised version.* Baltimore: Clinical Psychometric Research.

Robins, L. N., Helzer, J. E., Croughan, J. L., & Ratcliff, K. S. (1981). National Institute of Health Diagnostic Interview Schedule. *Archives of General Psychiatry, 38,* 381–389.

Wechsler, D. (1997). *WAIS-III administration and scoring manual.* San Antonio, TX: Psychological Corporation.

PART FIVE

Habit Disorders

CHAPTER 15

Polysubstance Dependence

PETER E. NATHAN

The interview takes place at a local substance abuse treatment program. Two chairs stand at the front of a room. In one sits Abby, a young woman in her mid-20s, casually dressed in blue jeans and a rumpled blouse. She appears very agitated. An older man, wearing a conservative suit and looking like a professional of some sort, sits in the other chair. Ten young people in their early 20s, dressed casually, sit in chairs facing the two. The older man begins.

Dr. Norton: Hi, Abby. My name is Dr. Norton. Thanks very much for coming here today. Let me explain about our meeting. These folks are all students in the clinical psychology program at the university. One of the ways they learn how to be psychologists is by coming here to watch experienced psychologists like me talk to patients. I'm very grateful to you for your willingness to help teach these young psychologists. Let's begin by my asking you how you came to be here?

Abby: I came here after my mom got the judge to commit me here for treatment. I've been drinking a lot, close to a fifth of vodka a night, and most of the time I drink until I pass out. The other night, my mom couldn't wake me up, so she got scared and called the police. They said I had a BAC [blood alcohol content] of more than 0.40% [more than four times the legal limit].

Dr. Norton: Have you been drinking that heavily for very long?

Abby: Well, let me see. I guess I've been drinking that much for three or four years; before that, I wasn't exactly a social drinker, but I didn't drink nearly so much.

Dr. Norton: Did something happen three or four years ago that made you drink so much more?

Abby: That's about when my boyfriend made me have an abortion. I got pregnant and I thought he wanted to get married and have a family, but he said he'd leave me if I didn't have the abortion. So I had it and then he left me. And I got so depressed, I just pretty much gave up and drank all I could as often as I could.

Dr. Norton: Over the past few years, it sounds like drinking has become the focus of your life.

Abby: Absolutely. Even though I've been told I shouldn't drink because I have some stomach and digestion problems because of it, I drank. I stopped seeing friends and dating; all I did was drink.

Dr. Norton: Did you ever stop drinking during that time long enough to experience withdrawal?

Abby: Only when I ran out of money. And when that happened, I got very sick, threw up all the time, couldn't keep still, got even more depressed. This time, I thought I was going to have the dt's [reference to delirium tremens, a serious and, fortunately, rare consequence of alcohol withdrawal], but they gave me some medicine and I just had the usual symptoms.

Dr. Norton: Tell me about the depression after your boyfriend made you get the abortion.

Abby: Actually, that wasn't the first time I got depressed, even though it was the worst time. I've always been a kind of depressed person, at least since I was a kid. I always expected the worst and usually got it. But every once in a while, things would really get bad and I'd take to my bed. I'd stop eating and refuse to see anyone.

Dr. Norton: During those times, the world looked even worse for you?

Abby: I was convinced I was no good and that I had no future. Nothing made me happy, even my friends. When my mood improved, after a few weeks, I'd drink heavy again to make things better.

Dr. Norton: How often did you experience those really bad times?

Abby: Oh, I don't know. Maybe three or four times during junior high and high school, then a couple times a year since then, since my abortion. I still feel really bad about that.

Dr. Norton: I can well understand that. Let me ask you: Have you experimented with other drugs?

Abby: I've used marijuana since I was a kid. I usually smoke a joint or two when I'm drinking. I've tried other drugs but the only one I really like is meth [methamphetamine, a stimulant drug that has neurotoxic effects], but I'm scared of it. They say it scrambles your brain.

Abby meets *Diagnostic and Statistical Manual of Mental Disorders* (*DSM-IV-TR*; American Psychiatric Association, 2000) criteria for Alcohol Dependence. Specifically, she met one tolerance criterion (she drank increasing amounts of alcohol as her addiction deepened), two withdrawal criteria (she experienced symptoms of withdrawal on the rare occasions that she stopped drinking, and she kept drinking, at times, to avoid withdrawal symptoms), and three loss of control/compulsive use criteria (she spent a great deal of time drinking and recovering from the effects of drinking, she had given up most other activities because of her drinking, and she continued to drink even though she knew doing so had become dangerous to her health). Abby almost certainly meets *DSM* criteria for Marijuana Dependence as well and might also meet them for Methamphetamine Dependence. Hence, she meets standards for Polysubstance Dependence, which means that she is clinically dependent on more than one drug.

Abby also meets criteria for both Major Depressive Disorder and Dysthymic Disorder. Substance dependence is commonly comorbid with mood disorder, in part because many substance abusers, like Abby, become substance dependent in an effort to medicate themselves for depression. Because alcohol is a sedative, it can relieve depression and reduce anxiety during the time the person experiences alcohol intoxication. However, when alcohol is abused and tolerance develops, as happened in Abby's case, it loses its capacity to ease the emotional distress of depression and anxiety.

Recommended Readings

Grant, B. F., & Dawson, D. A. (1999). Alcohol and drug use, abuse, and dependence: Classification, prevalence, and comorbidity. In B. S. McCrady & E. E. Epstein (Eds.), *Addictions: A comprehensive guidebook* (pp. 9–29). New York: Oxford University Press.

McCrady, B. M., & Nathan, P. E. (in press). Impact of treatment factors on outcomes of treatment for substance abuse disorders. In L. E. Beutler & L. G. Castonguay (Eds.), *Integrating theories and relationships in psychotherapy.* New York: Oxford University Press.

Moak, D. H., & Anton, R. F. (1999). Alcohol. In B. S. McCrady & E. E. Epstein (Eds.), *Addictions: A comprehensive guidebook* (pp. 75–94). New York: Oxford University Press.

Nathan, P. E., Skinstad, A. H., & Dolan, S. L. (2001). Alcohol-related disorders: Psychopathology, diagnosis, etiology, and treatment. In P. B. Sutker & H. E. Adams (Eds.), *Comprehensive handbook of psychopathology* (3rd ed., pp. 595–622). New York: Kluwer Academic/Plenum Press.

Reference

American Psychiatric Association. (2000). *Diagnostic and statistical manual for mental disorders* (4th ed., text rev.). Washington, DC: Author.

CHAPTER 16

Bulimia Nervosa

P‌ETER S. H‌ENDRICKS AND J. K‌EVIN T‌HOMPSON

Therapy was, by her own admission, Carey's last resort. A 22-year-old woman of Cuban descent, she had never experienced a problem she couldn't handle on her own. Carey was resourceful and independent, and she enjoyed a diverse and active social life. Things had changed drastically for her in the previous year, however. The carefree days of her college life had passed, and each day felt like a burden. Despite her attempts to deal with her difficulties on her own, her problems only became worse as each day passed. It was clear to Carey that she needed help.

Carey was 6 feet tall and weighed 150 pounds. She was slender in appearance, with long black hair and brown eyes. She was well dressed, and although she wore no make-up, she had obviously paid meticulous attention to every aspect of her physical appearance. Her hair was all one length, just past her shoulders, and not a strand lay out of place. Her nails were shaped as if professionally manicured, and not the slightest trace of dry skin could be found on her hands. Her clothes were color-coordinated, and her shoes looked as though she had just taken them home from the store. She was, without a doubt, a striking individual.

Unfortunately, Carey did not share this sentiment. The only thing striking about her appearance, she believed, was the fact that she was clearly overweight. Her body disgusted her, and no aspect of it was free from scathing criticism: Her stomach was flabby and noticeably expanding, as far as she was concerned; her arms were undefined and entirely unattractive; her legs, the most hated aspects of her appearance, were grossly disproportionate to the rest of her body; her face was too full and round; and even her toes and fingers were undesirably pudgy. Carey was completely unhappy with her body, and thoughts of an increasingly obese physique consumed her. She avoided large mirrors at all cost, fearful that she might lay her eyes on her body. She had not been shopping for new clothes in almost a year because she was not willing to think about her size and certainly not willing to confront the idea that her size had become larger. Dressing herself each day had even become an unpleasant experience, as the slightest piece of snug-fitting clothing became a worrisome indication of weight gain. Carey brooded about her body all day and dreamed about it at night. It was as if she could think of nothing else.

Carey devised a plan to deal with the seemingly uncontrollable influx of negative thoughts flooding her mind. She decided that it would be easiest to suppress these thoughts when she knew she was doing everything within her power to solve the problem. For this reason, Carey put forth every effort to lose weight. In losing weight, Carey saw the return of her life to its previous contented state, with periods of unhappiness being few and far between. With tremendous motivation, she decided to do whatever was necessary to reach her goal. She approached each day with the discipline of a soldier, and she soon settled into a steady rhythm. In the early morning, before leaving for work, Carey would resist the urge to eat breakfast, instead waiting until lunchtime to eat a small snack consisting of a banana, a cup of yogurt, or a few crackers. She would eat nothing more at work, resisting her body's signals to eat and ignoring all pangs of hunger. It is interesting that this self-starvation actually made it easier for Carey to concentrate—an empty stomach reminded her that she was doing all she could to lose weight, and she had no further reason to worry about her unattractive figure. In the absence of ruminating about her body, Carey was efficient, clearheaded, and always on the ball.

On returning home from work, the first item on Carey's agenda was burning off as many calories as possible. She would run three to five miles, although she was not always able to make it that far. Often, she would have to settle for as far as her malnourished body would take her. At times, she could make it no farther than her front door, and her exercise for the day would consist of a few hundred sit-ups. Carey was not distraught by her lack of energy. On the contrary, Carey found it to be another encouraging reminder that she was forcing her body to use its fat as a source of energy—a source of energy that was insufficient to meet her strenuous demands.

Carey's biggest meal of the day was dinner, which she ate well before going to bed for the night. Dinner usually took the form of a bowl of wheat cereal and a small serving of cottage cheese, although there were many variations. Sometimes Carey ate a frozen dinner made specifically for dieters, while other times she ate a small piece of chicken breast. Sometimes, she ate only a small piece of fruit. Occasionally, she ate nothing, perfectly happy to fall asleep to the sounds of a growling stomach. It was not always easy for Carey to sleep without eating dinner, but an empty belly quelled her anxiety, and often it was easier for her to sleep when she was hungry.

Initially, Carey's plan worked well. Although her appearance was still a major concern, she no longer obsessed about it throughout the day. She was able to focus more of her attention on pleasant topics in her life, such as her career opportunities, her social life, or topics as trivial as her favorite television programs. Unfortunately, though, this solution lasted for only a brief time. Although she no longer ruminated endlessly about her body, within a few weeks, she became completely obsessed with her diet. She counted every calorie, careful to keep her intake under 750 calories per day. She fretted over every ounce of food she ate, fearful that she might go over her prescribed consumption limit. The truth was that Carey simply could not abide by her strict guidelines every day. She was bound to slip.

The first of Carey's slips occurred four months before she came to therapy. To the best of her recollection, she had not had a particularly good day. Although she had been dieting and exercising for weeks, she noticed no change in her body composition. She couldn't help but think that nothing could be done to alter her appearance. It was in her genes, she decided, to be a heavy woman, and it was just a matter of time before she became obese. Having pondered this dreary outlook throughout the day at work, Carey arrived home more upset than she could ever recall. To make matters worse, she was hungry to the point of starvation. Carey entered her apartment, which she shared with another young woman, and headed straight for the kitchen. She had adhered to her rigid diet for so long but could take no more. Carey scanned her roommate's assortment of junk foods, and grabbing a jar of peanut butter, she began to cry.

Suddenly and inexplicably, Carey had become a passive observer of her own actions. As if she were being controlled by an outside source, she finished the entire jar in minutes. Her appetite raged on. Opening the refrigerator door, Carey found a cheesecake. In the blink of an eye, it was gone, and she continued to sob. Her appetite satiated, Carey slowly came to a realization of what had just happened. In a few brief moments, she had put more calories in her body than she had during the entire previous week. Months of dieting, she thought, had been for naught. She was sure to gain weight because of her behavior—all of her hard work had been in vain. Carey began to panic. Eager to regain control of the situation, she ran to the bathroom. Standing over the toilet, she forced a finger down her throat. Crying more intensely than before, Carey vomited until her stomach was empty once again. Immediately, she began to feel better. She had handled the situation to the best of her ability. Strangely, she no longer felt the hopelessness that had gripped her throughout the day. For whatever reason, Carey felt better because of this episode. Her resolve renewed, she went to bed that night on an empty stomach.

It was not difficult for Carey to return to her previous pattern of behavior. In fact, after eating so much that one night, she was especially motivated to maintain her diet. Days passed, and Carey remained faithful to her strict regimen. Her mood, however, did not improve. She became increasingly dissatisfied with her physique, frustrated that she was yet to see any significant weight loss. This frustration made Carey only that much more certain of her lot in life. Without her constant attention, she thought, she would surely gain weight. She decided that, although she might not ever lose weight, she could certainly do her best to keep from getting fat. No longer was she attempting to lose weight; she was preventing weight gain.

The urge to eat was stronger than ever. She held on as long as she could, but the hunger, combined with her hopeless outlook, was too powerful. Two months after the first incident, Carey stuffed herself with a gallon of ice cream and threw it all back up shortly afterwards. As before, the vomiting seemed to relieve Carey of her negative feelings, at least to the point where they were tolerable. This is not to say that eating and vomiting were pleasant for Carey. On the contrary, the experience was very upsetting. Although she did feel better after throwing up, she also felt very confused, as well as ashamed and disgusted with herself. Doing her best to ignore these feelings and move on, Carey continued with the arduous task of what was, in her mind, weight maintenance.

This was not Carey's last episode of bingeing and purging. In fact, the episodes became more frequent, each under similar circumstances. After days of rigid dieting, a bingeing and purging episode would occur when her mood sank to an almost unbearable level. Afterwards, she would return to her routine until her sadness and frustration would again culminate in one of these unpleasant episodes.

The act of eating and vomiting was not the only outlet through which Carey would release her feelings. She particularly enjoyed going out on the weekends to unwind and have a good time. Along with her roommate, she would visit the various bars the city had to offer. In the beginning, these were pleasant outings. Carey would have a few drinks, enjoy live music, and occasionally, meet a few interesting men her age. However, coinciding with her eating difficulties, Carey's weekend behavior soon became troublesome. Entering whichever bar she and her roommate decided to attend that night, Carey would head straight to the bar. Having one drink after another, Carey would make no effort to socialize with any of the people around her. Instead, she would drink until she was well intoxicated (usually 10 to 12 drinks within three hours), becoming angrier with each beer, shot of tequila, or vodka tonic.

Carey didn't fully understand why she was angry, but she couldn't help but think that life had been unjust. Here she was, making every sacrifice to fight obesity, surrounded by people who had no idea how fortunate they were to be thin and beautiful. As the bar closed and people filed out, Carey would pick an unsuspecting bystander and mercilessly berate that individual. Firing every insult she could conjure, she would create a remarkable scene. People would stop and stare at this obviously drunken woman, yelling at the top of her lungs and barely able to pronounce the words leaving her mouth. Carey would continue until her victim had walked away, and finding her roommate, would head home for the night, fuming with animosity.

Carey's behavior frightened her. She had hoped she could get a handle on her problems, but they only seemed to be spiraling out of control. Her dissatisfaction with her body was dominating every aspect of her life. She entered therapy desperate for help.

Social History

Carey was raised in an affluent Cuban American community. In early childhood, along with an older brother, she thrived in a happy, close-knit family, free of any significant troubles. Although her family had lived in the United States for generations, they still held strong ties to their heritage. Holidays were particularly joyful times in which they engaged in the numerous customs of their culture and spent time with extended family. Unfortunately, these were the few good memories that Carey could remember. When she was 6, her father left the family to live with another woman. There were no goodbyes or explanations. From what Carey could recall, one day her father was simply gone. He would not have any contact with his family again.

With the absence of her father, the tight bonds that had once held the family together quickly dissolved. Her mother and brother became distant, increasingly involved in the details of their own lives. Holidays passed without celebration, and the family gradually lost touch with extended family and friends. Rarely did the family spend time together. Even meals were eaten on each family member's own time. Carey's mother provided the necessities for her daughter, but beyond that, the two had no meaningful relationship. At a very young age, Carey learned to depend on herself.

When Carey was 13, she left home to live with her grandmother on a permanent basis. According to Carey, her mother felt that she had fulfilled her duty as a parent. Having sacrificed enough of her life and happiness for her children, Carey's mother decided to start a new life as a woman free of obligations. From that point on, Carey saw her mother only occasionally and for brief periods of time. She once went as long as a year without seeing her mother, who at the time was traveling throughout the country with a boyfriend. Her grandmother, a kind and caring woman, was simply too old to be truly involved in her grandchildren's lives. Anything resembling a family had completely disappeared from Carey's life. Whereas before she had little interaction with her brother, the two now lived almost completely distinct lives, sharing only the roof over their heads.

In stark contrast to her home life, Carey had many meaningful relationships with her peers. Popular and well liked, she was often invited to spend time with friends after school and on the weekends. These relationships were particularly meaningful to Carey, and in the absence of intimacy at home, her friends became the only people she could count on for unwavering warmth. The one companion who meant more to Carey above all was Lisa, her best friend for as long as she could remember. Lisa was like a sister to Carey; their bond was unbreakable. Lisa's family embraced Carey as one of their own, welcoming her to share in their holiday celebrations, family outings, and other special occasions. Without them, Carey explained, she was not sure how she would have survived.

Carey was a gifted student. She excelled in every subject and won the admiration of her teachers, who encouraged her to continue on to college. Despite the knowledge that she would receive no financial support from her mother, Carey decided to continue her educational career. An impressive applicant, Carey received numerous offers from many highly reputable institutions throughout the country. Ultimately, she chose to attend a university close to home.

Carey continued her superior academic performance in college. Finding particular interest in chemical engineering, she attained excellent grades with little effort. Carey flirted with the idea of increasing her course load so that she could graduate in three years, but she loved college and had no desire to leave early. Academics were not the focus of Carey's efforts. Her true passion was her social life. Carey belonged to a tight circle of about eight close companions and had dozens of casual friends and more acquaintances than could be counted. She had a talent for making those around her laugh, and she was often the center of attention during parties and other social gatherings. She made new friends quickly and easily, and she had the ability to engage even the most reserved person in lively conversation.

Carey had no desire for romantic involvement with members of the opposite sex until her senior year of college. She recalled no particular reason for this, only that she was a late bloomer who had previously been perfectly happy without a boyfriend. When she made the decision to start dating, Carey expected to be as successful as she had in other aspects of her social life. Initially, she saw no reason to suggest otherwise. In a short amount of time, she was dating a fellow senior with whom she shared many common interests. They enjoyed fun and casual time with each other and rarely had any disagreements.

As this relationship grew in intensity, however, it became a cause of stress and anxiety in Carey's life. Her boyfriend began to criticize her about her figure, suggesting that she weighed too much or needed to tone certain parts of her body. He pressured Carey to change her eating habits, implying that she either ate too much or not the right kinds of foods. He encouraged her to exercise whenever she had the chance, and he became impatient with her when she did not heed his advice. For the first time in her life, Carey began to feel self-conscious about her body. She had given little consideration to her physique in the past, but now she felt fat and unattractive. As the relationship progressed, she became increasingly dissatisfied with her appearance and more uncomfortable around her boyfriend. Whenever the two were physically intimate, Carey insisted that the lights be left off. Ironically, her boyfriend brought an end to the relationship, explaining that she had too many issues concerning her self-image for the two of them to remain together.

After graduation, Carey moved to a major city far from her hometown to pursue a graduate degree in chemical engineering. She was sad to be leaving the friends with whom she had shared a wonderful experience, but eager about what the future held. Graduate school, she believed, would be the next exciting step in her life. Like college, it would be filled with fun times and new, engaging people. Unfortunately, her experiences were the opposite of what she had expected. Her free time was markedly diminished, and the few other students she knew were interested in little outside their studies. School, although not difficult, was tedious. Unhappy, Carey left school to work in a nearby city.

The move did little to change Carey's situation. Life outside college, she realized, was a big adjustment. Whereas before she had had countless hours of free time and endless opportunities to socialize, she now found herself punching a clock day in and day out, working as much as 60 hours per week. She had no friends in the new city and nothing to interest her outside her job. Luckily, just when things seemed like they couldn't get any worse, she met Eric. The two hit it off immediately. In Eric, Carey felt that she had found her first true love. He was considerate, attentive, and affectionate, and he shared Carey's desire to have fun. In her eyes, she had found the perfect match. Regardless, she couldn't keep from thinking that the relationship would eventually come to a painful end. Although anything could contribute to Eric's inevitable loss of interest, Carey believed that what was most likely to drive him away was her overweight appearance. Picking up where she had left off in her previous relationship, Carey avoided tight or revealing clothing and refused to let Eric see her even partially unclothed. Despite her efforts, Carey believed little could be done to prevent her from driving Eric away. She braced herself for the breakup.

After six months, Eric told Carey that he just wanted to be friends; her apparent inability to relax and excessive concern about her body was too much for him to handle. Although Carey had been preparing herself for this outcome, she could not avoid sinking into a deep depression. In one short year, her life had been turned upside down. She had lost the ability to control the direction of her life. There was one thing, though, that Carey felt she could still control: her appearance. If she handled her weight problem, Carey believed, all of the other problems in her life would fall away.

By her own account, when Carey first started dieting, she ate almost nothing. For years, her weight had held steady at 175 pounds, which, for a woman of her height, was a reasonable amount. Within four months, however, her weight had dropped to 135 pounds. Still entirely unhappy, Carey decided to move back to her hometown to have the comfort of familiar surroundings, and, importantly, to be closer to Lisa. She quickly found a job as a chemical engineer and moved into an apartment with one of Lisa's acquaintances. She increased her food intake, albeit very little, because she was still determined to lose weight. By the time she came to therapy, Carey weighed 150 pounds.

Case Conceptualization

Aspects of Carey's life can be examined for certain themes that may help understand how her past experiences contributed to her current eating disturbances. First, it was clear that Carey experienced a significant amount of anxiety in dealing with her intimate relationships. This might be due, at least partially, to the fact that her father had walked out of her life when she was young and her mother became a nonfactor in her life only a few years later.

Second, the negative comments about her body and pressures to lose weight that she received from her first boyfriend had a substantial impact on the way she viewed her body. Indeed, she was completely satisfied with her physique until he began to criticize her. Subsequently, Carey viewed her overweight appearance as a major obstacle to developing and maintaining romantic bonds with the opposite sex. Although it is unclear if Carey held herself responsible or even partially responsible for her father's disappearance, it is clear that she blamed herself for the failure of her romantic relationship. This belief resulted in a markedly heightened degree of unhappiness with her body and tremendous motivation to lose weight.

Third, leaving college was a difficult transition for her. Suddenly, Carey felt as though she had little control over the direction of her life. She focused her attention on her diet, the one aspect of her life she still felt she could control. Doing so, she believed, would cause everything to fall into place, and her life would soon return to the way it was before she left school. For Carey, as for many young women who develop an eating disorder, family dysfunction, adjustment to a new life situation (college), and negative feedback from others about her appearance (criticism, comments) contributed to the onset of restrictive eating and dieting, which led to the development of bulimic behaviors.

The cognitive-behavioral formulation of eating disorders, which focuses on traumatic experiences (e.g., criticism from others about appearance) and negative cognitions (e.g., extreme or erroneous beliefs about appearance), fits well with Carey's case. In addition, the interpersonal theory of eating disorders, which focuses on the important role of close interpersonal relationships, is relevant for understanding Carey's experiences with her father and close male friends. Perhaps losing her father created a fear that she would lose other important men in her life, a fear that was realized in her first important romantic relationship because (or so Carey believed) of her undesirable appearance.

Treatment

Carey was noticeably tense as she introduced herself to her therapist. She had never before shared the intimate details of her life with anyone, so the prospect of openly discussing her current difficulties with a stranger was anxiety provoking. Carey was ashamed and embarrassed that she had let her behavior get so out of hand. She was convinced that her therapist would look down on her as a weak and incompetent person, incapable of taking proper care of herself. At the same time, however, Carey was desperate for help with problems that were making her life miserable. It was with this ambivalence that she began to describe her situation. Although still somewhat guarded, she freely discussed the details of her life and quickly answered the therapist's questions.

It was plain to Carey's therapist that she was experiencing significant disturbances in her body image and eating behavior. For this reason, the first objective of therapy was to assess Carey's physical status to determine the need, if any, for emergency medical intervention. Fortunately, her body weight at the time was not in the anorexic range (i.e., at least 15% below ideal), and she otherwise exhibited all the features of a healthy, functioning woman. Additionally, her bingeing and purging about once a week was well below the daily or multiple times per day that constitute a dangerous threshold for such behavior.

The initial treatment plan was based on a cognitive-behavioral strategy. First, in an attempt to increase Carey's food intake, the therapist began by addressing her belief that, if she ate meals regularly, she would almost immediately gain weight. Using a technique called *cognitive restructuring,* the therapist asked Carey to discuss a time in the past when an increase in her diet resulted in rapid weight gain. She could remember no such time. Going a step further, the therapist asked Carey to recall an instance when substantial food intake resulted in an even small increase of weight. Again, she could give no example, and she admitted that there was no logical basis for her beliefs. Seizing the opportunity, Carey's therapist asked her if she would be willing to eat every three to four hours throughout the day on a consistent basis, explaining that such a change in her habits would likely elevate her energy level, improve her mood, and prevent future bingeing and purging episodes. Despite her acknowledgment that this plan made sense, Carey worried that such action would result in eventual weight gain. Her therapist decided to strike a deal. Carey would weigh herself at the beginning of every weekly therapy session. In the event of any significant weight gain, she could return to her old pattern of eating. Reluctantly, she agreed.

The therapist next addressed Carey's use of alcohol by asking if she had the desire to change her drinking behavior. She immediately expressed the desire to curb her excessive alcohol consumption. *Stimulus control* and *response cost* strategies were then instituted. Whenever she went to a bar, Carey would pace herself, drinking a large glass of water between each alcoholic beverage. If, at any point, she drank to intoxication, she would be required to donate $5 of her own money to an organization she despised, which, in this case, was a political party.

Carey's mood at the following session had improved dramatically. She was cheerful, energetic, and decidedly talkative. Smiling from ear to ear, she was barely able to contain her happiness. The change in her diet, she explained, had an amazing effect on her mood; she hadn't felt this good in almost a year. Her therapist congratulated Carey on her success and encouraged her to keep up the good work. At the same time, however, the therapist wanted to prepare her for a long road ahead that would have, along with its peaks, many valleys. Carey's problems were deep-rooted and, sadly, would not diminish so easily. With her therapist, she proceeded to explore the foundations of her negative body image.

A *psychoeducational* strategy was then employed that involved a discussion of the societal definitions of attractiveness, and this discussion was particularly eye-opening for Carey. Thumbing through a magazine, she saw numerous images of remarkably slender women. Pondering movies and television, she noted a pervasive theme in the portrayal of women. She had never really considered it before, but it angered Carey that the ideal woman was always, without exception, portrayed as unrealistically thin. Empowered by this revelation, Carey resolved to reduce her expectation that she meet these impossible standards and also to reduce her tendency to compare herself to these images.

This groundwork having been laid, Carey's therapist next enacted a *desensitization* strategy to help her feel more at ease with her body. Carey was instructed to spend time focusing on a particular body part in the mirror for a brief period every day. She would start with an area that made her feel only slightly uncomfortable. Over time, as she felt more at ease with the particular feature, she would move on to another that elicited a little more anxiety. Eventually, Carey would devote time to each body part until she felt less dissatisfied with her appearance.

Over the next few weeks, Carey continued to show promising improvement. She gradually increased her food consumption until she was eating at least 1,500 calories per day, and she rarely skipped a meal. Although it took some time for her to feel comfortable gazing at herself in the mirror, doing so eventually helped her feel much more positive about her figure. Moreover, she had not reported a bingeing and purging episode since the beginning of therapy. To say that therapy was going well was an understatement.

After two months, things took a sudden change for the worse. Taking a seat in the therapist's office, Carey's behavior was reminiscent of her first session. She avoided eye contact, shifting her eyes from the floor to the various pictures on the walls. She bounced her feet, cracked her knuckles, and stirred from side to side in her chair. Her eyes were red, and she looked on the verge of tears. Concerned, Carey's therapist asked why she seemed so unsettled. The past week, she explained, was miserable. A man she had been seeing failed to show up for a planned date, causing her to feel completely dejected. Overwhelmed with negative feelings, Carey ate half of a Key lime pie and then threw it all back up. The following day, she ate nothing. At night, she drove to the nearest bar and drank until she almost passed out. Driving home, she consumed an entire box of doughnuts, vomiting when she reached her apartment.

Since then, Carey had limited her food consumption to nothing more than a piece of fruit each day. Calming her, the therapist explained that such setbacks were not only normal but also expected. Carey was reminded of the exceptional job she had done to that point, and she was encouraged to maintain her determination. They then discussed *relapse prevention* strategies for preventing future incidents of this kind and developed a list of alternative behaviors for her to engage in whenever she felt like bingeing and purging. These behaviors included going on a run, calling a friend, or calling the therapist. Carey was instructed to write these activities on a small card to keep with her at all times. Whenever she felt an episode was imminent, she could access the card to be reminded of these behaviors.

This strategy did not prove entirely effective. Although Carey had stopped bingeing, she continued to purge whenever she felt especially sad. Sometimes, she would purge after eating as little as a banana; at other times, she would throw up after having not eaten for hours. She returned to restricting her diet, consuming fewer than 500 calories per day. Carey explained that, at the beginning of therapy, she had followed the instructions of her therapist because she was eager to please. With the passing of time, however, she had become increasingly despondent over the future of her intimate relationships. Convinced that she would never be in a loving, secure relationship, Carey had begun to deal with her problems the only way she knew how—by controlling her eating habits. She did not intend to manage her weight by doing so. In fact, she had reached a point of acceptance of her body. Purging, Carey explained, served another purpose altogether. It was her way of expelling the negative feelings related to her interpersonal life.

Carey's therapist instituted *cognitive restructuring* strategies to challenge her notion that she would never find herself in a long-term relationship by asking her to develop arguments that ran counter to her belief. Together, they practiced substituting her negative thoughts with more positive and evidence-based statements. In doing so, Carey thoughtfully asserted that her negative outlook was in large part a product of her painful experiences with her father and mother. Encouraged by this insight, the therapist began using some *interpersonal therapy* strategies. He asked Carey to discuss other meaningful relationships of her past. With carefully phrased questions, the therapist helped Carey see a pattern that she had not before considered. Specifically, Carey realized that excessive worry over the fate of her relationships inhibited her not only from having a good time, but also from forming close bonds. She further realized that her happiness was in large part dependent on whether she was dating anyone at the time and that she unfairly placed sole blame on herself for the end of any relationship. Armed with this new awareness, Carey aimed to change her pattern of thinking and behavior.

Next, the specific antecedents of Carey's purging behavior were examined. In every instance, it was discovered, she had vomited at her apartment in the evening. Furthermore, she had always done so while feeling hopeless about the future of her relationships. Carey was, therefore, instructed that she was allowed to contemplate this topic only during the day, all the while using the thought techniques she and her therapist had practiced. Finally, with the help of her therapist, Carey constructed a *reinforcement* strategy aimed at increasing her food intake. She decided to reward herself every two weeks with a professional massage if she ate at least 1,500 calories per day on a consistent basis. Furthermore, Carey would be allowed to watch her favorite television show every night only if she had eaten sufficiently throughout the day.

By limiting thoughts of her intimate relationships to daytime hours, Carey was able to reduce her purging behavior substantially over the next month. Occasionally, however, she would vomit at home whenever the idea that she would never find a romantic partner became particularly intrusive. Feeling much more at ease with her appearance, Carey maintained a dietary intake of at least 1,500 calories per day. It is interesting that she never seemed motivated by the external reward system she had set up with her therapist. In fact, much of the change observed in Carey's behavior was a product of intrinsic motivation. For a brief period of time, she saw a man on a casual basis, and although she tried hard to take a laid-back approach to the relationship, it elicited overwhelming feelings of anxiety in Carey. The therapist worked hard to ease Carey's worry and prevent purging episodes with some success but wished to see further improvement before concluding the treatment.

Conclusion

A review of this case reveals several aspects of the treatment that were especially effective and likely to be implemented by Carey in the future. First, the therapist's challenge of Carey's thoughts about food intake and its relationship to weight gain seemed successful in reducing her restrictive eating behavior. Second, viewing her body in the mirror on a consistent basis appeared to reduce Carey's dissatisfaction with her figure. Consistent with theory, the anxiety she felt about her body decreased as she became more accustomed to the nuances of her physical appearance. Third, discussion of the trends in Carey's interpersonal behavior provided her with an awareness she had not previously possessed concerning her fear of losing important men in her life. This consciousness enabled her to change, even if only in a subtle way, several maladaptive thoughts and behaviors related to men. Finally, although the system of rewards and relapse prevention strategy that Carey developed with her therapist was apparently unsuccessful in changing her habits, other behavioral aspects of the treatment proved effective. In particular, the implementation of guidelines concerning when she was allowed to think about the future of her romantic relationships resulted in a dramatic reduction in purging episodes.

Recommended Readings

Steiger, H., Bruce, K. R., & Israel, M. (2003). Eating disorders. In G. Stricker & T. A. Widiger (Eds.), *Clinical psychology* (pp. 173–194). Volume 8 in I. B. Weiner (Editor-in-Chief), *Handbook of psychology*. Hoboken, NJ: Wiley.

Thompson, J. K. (1996). *Body image, eating disorders and obesity: An integrative guide for assessment and treatment*. Washington, DC: American Psychological Association.

Thompson, J. K. (in press). *Handbook of eating disorders and obesity*. Hoboken, NJ: Wiley.

Thompson, J. K., Heinberg, L. J., Altabe, M., & Tantleff-Dunn, S. (1999). *Exacting beauty: Theory, assessment and treatment of body image disturbance*. Washington, DC: American Psychological Association.

Thompson J. K., & Smolak, L. (2001). *Body image, eating disorders and obesity in youth: Assessment, prevention and treatment*. Washington, DC: American Psychological Association.

PART SIX

Mood Disorders and Schizophrenia

CHAPTER 17

Depressive Disorder

NANCY A. HAMILTON AND RICK E. INGRAM

Frank was a 57-year-old Caucasian man, who was referred for therapy because of depression and suicidal ideation, including intent and plans to kill himself. When first seen, Frank received a very high score, in the severely depressed range, on the Beck Depression Inventory (BDI), a widely used 21-item self-report measure of the extent of currently experienced depressive symptoms (Beck, Steer, & Brown, 1987). Frank's symptoms were consistent with a diagnosis of Major Depressive Disorder, as defined in the American Psychiatric Association (2000) *Diagnostic and Statistical Manual of Mental Disorders (DSM-IV-TR)*. He was sad, felt overwhelmed, and was experiencing guilt and indecisiveness. Along with his sadness, which is the cardinal mood symptom of depression, Frank also expressed anger and resentment, as do many depressed individuals.

In particular, he perceived himself as being controlled by obligations to his wife and children, and he resented their demands on him. At the same time, however, Frank felt guilty and demoralized because health problems including chronic pain, hypertension, and heart disease were, along with his depression, impairing his ability to meet his obligations. When faced with typical demands of everyday living, Frank reported that he often became mentally frozen or "stuck," unable to think or make decisions. During these periods of feeling stuck, he said, his perceived uselessness and his anger at his family's demands on him would cause him to experience "black despair."

After a period of initial treatment, Frank no longer intended to commit suicide, but he continued to have thoughts about death and was unable to enjoy activities that usually interested him and made him happy. For example, although his hobby was translating church documents from Latin to English, he reported that doing so no longer gave him any pleasure, and he added that he could not remember how to have fun anymore. Frank was also showing some biological symptoms of depression, including a considerable weight gain (30 pounds), long hours of sleep without feeling rested, and fatigue. His fatigue may have been due in part to medications he was taking for his cardiovascular illness, but his weight gain and excessive sleeping appeared related to and reflective of his depressive disorder.

Frank's family of origin included an abusive father and an erratic and ineffective mother. Frank learned to avoid much of the physical abuse he might otherwise have received from his father by being "the good son." His father's abusiveness proved much less damaging to his psychological development than his mother's sometimes-bizarre behavior. For instance, when Frank was age 9, he bought a canary with money he had saved from his weekly allowance. The next day he found that his mother had let the canary out of its cage while she was cleaning, and it had flown away. She expressed no remorse for her carelessness on this occasion. On another occasion, Frank recalled having become ill on the day of his birthday party. Instead of canceling the party, his mother confined him to his room, where he watched through the window as his guests ate cake and played party games.

Despite these negative early childhood experiences, Frank stated that he had remained close to his mother, who was still living. As for his adult life, Frank had become a successful person. He was well educated, had been married for 35 years, was the father of three adult children, was active in his church, and had been employed full time as a high school teacher until he became too physically ill to work. He was placed on temporary disability two months before the onset of the depression that led to his referral for psychotherapy, and, during his treatment, he applied for and was granted permanent disability because of chronic pain.

From a cognitive perspective on understanding depression, Frank's early experiences with his father, and especially with his mother, led to a self-schema that was dominated by themes of being unlovable and unworthy. During times of stress, this schema would become activated, and he would interpret his experiences through a filter of self-criticism and unworthiness that interfered with his capacity to find solutions to problems. He thus came to blame himself for his problems. In his marriage, he had been unable to assert his needs in his relationship with his wife because he perceived himself as being undeserving of having legitimate needs.

Frank was treated with a cognitive approach to therapy that clarified further how dysfunctional ways of thinking contributed to his mood disorder. For example, he was asked to record the thoughts he was having just before experiencing feelings of anger, sadness, or demoralization. These feelings frequently arose in the context of apparently routine daily tasks, such as driving his wife to her appointments, reading e-mail, and completing disability claim forms. Frank's thoughts at these times were on the order of "I am not capable of meeting my wife's needs," "She should know that I am sick and exhausted and can't do everything," "I've caused these problems," and "Nobody cares about what I want."

Because of how his self-schema colored his view of his world, Frank's thinking interfered with effective problem solving and also turned experiences of normal stress-induced sadness into clinical depression. His ineffective functioning further impaired his relationships with the important people in his life and contributed to his deepening depression. Not believing that he was worthy of expressing his needs directly, he instead expressed anger and resentment indirectly in ways that further disrupted his relationships and added to his burden of stress.

Over a 10-month period of treatment, Frank was encouraged to confront his conviction of being unworthy with homework assignments designed to help him develop self-nurturing skills. In particular, he was helped to seek out activities that he found pleasurable and to set aside time just for himself and just for fun. Frank's maladaptive thoughts were also challenged, especially those that revolved around assertiveness and the legitimacy of his needs. Frank was seen on a weekly basis for the first eight months of his therapy and once every two weeks for the final two months, for a total of 40 sessions. Before each session, he completed the BDI. In contrast to his initially very high BDI score in the severely depressed range, his BDI scores at the time of his last several sessions were consistently in ranges indicating minimal or mild depression.

Recommended Readings

Beck, A. T. (1967). *Depression: Causes and treatment.* Philadelphia: University of Pennsylvania Press.

Coyne, J. C. (Ed.). (1985). *Essential papers on depression.* New York: New York University Press.

Gotlib, I. H., & Hammen, C. L. (Eds.). (2002). *Handbook of depression* (3rd ed.). New York: Guilford Press.

Hollon, S. D., Thase, M. E., & Markowitz, J. C. (2002). Treatment and prevention of depression. *Psychological Science in the Public Interest, 3,* 39–71.

Ingram, R. E., Miranda, J., & Segal, Z. (1998). *Cognitive vulnerability to depression.* New York: Guilford Press.

Joiner, T., & Coyne, J. C. (Eds.). (1999). *The interactional nature of depression.* Washington, DC: American Psychological Association.

References

American Psychiatric Association. (2000). *Diagnostic and statistical manual of mental disorders* (4th ed., text rev.). Washington, DC: Author.

Beck, A. T., Steer, R. A., & Brown, G. K. (1987). *Beck Depression Inventory manual* (2nd ed.). San Antonio, TX: Psychological Corporation.

CHAPTER 18

Bipolar Disorder

CORY F. NEWMAN

Mendy, a haggard gentleman, looking defeated and demoralized, entered the therapist's office and slumped in his chair, scarcely looking the therapist's way. Mendy's take-home questionnaires, returned to the therapist in advance by mail, indicated that he was 36 years old, divorced, unemployed, and on disability for a chronic psychiatric disorder. He had been an attorney but had lost his job a number of years ago amid scandal after the discovery that he had slept with two of the firm's clients. Mendy's marriage disintegrated shortly thereafter, and over time, he wound up having less and less contact with his son Cody. At the time of his first appointment with his therapist, Dr. N, Mendy had not seen his son in more than a year. He lamented this fact but had written on one of the questionnaires that there was nothing he could do about it. This was the first of many examples of Mendy's sense of hopelessness and helplessness, a state of mind that insidiously worsened his situation by preventing him from exercising problem-solving or damage control. As a result, Mendy's condition—in terms of his mental illness, as well as his life in general—continued to deteriorate.

Mendy lived alone in a small apartment in a rather hazardous section of town. He informed his therapist that his living space was a "living hell," in that he let dirty clothing, dishes, and newspapers pile up, feeling insufficient energy to do basic maintenance chores. Not surprisingly, Mendy also failed to keep up with paying his bills, returning phone calls, eating and sleeping properly, and taking the medications that had been prescribed by a psychiatrist he admitted not having contacted in months. Mendy reported having no friends, saying that he had "alienated everybody," and he scoffed when the therapist asked if he was involved in a romantic relationship: "I am fully prepared to go the rest of my life without a relationship, unless you count hookers as a relationship."

Ominously, Mendy added that "the rest of my life" probably wouldn't be very long anyway. This comment spoke volumes, alerting the therapist that suicide risk assessments would have to be done regularly. The therapist's first goal was to engage Mendy in a dialogue, give him some empathy and support, and form the beginnings of a therapeutic alliance. He hoped to build enough trust to talk about the more personal and weighty topics of loss, shame, and suicidality by the end of the first session.

Mendy stated flatly that he was living in "chronic misery, overwhelmed with wretched ruin." It was clear that Mendy was distraught, but he was articulate in describing his feelings. He lamented that he had no earned income, no home life, no love life, no direction, no friends, no self-respect, and no expectation that anything would ever improve. Mendy stated, with an edge in his voice, that he had "lost everything that matters," and he said that he often wondered, "What's the point of going on?" In response, the therapist asked explicitly about Mendy's intentions to kill himself, whereupon he dismissively said, "Don't get all excited—I'm too much of a coward to kill myself—I just wish I would wake up dead, that's all."

When the therapist inquired about Mendy's previous mental health care, including his medication regimen, Mendy retorted that he was "sick to death" of medications, which "just make things worse." When asked to expand on this statement, he explained that he had been on "every medication you can imagine" but had still experienced recurrent symptoms. These recurrences made him cynical about pharmacotherapy, he said, adding that he wasn't very keen on talk therapy either. Dr. N knew from the start that it was going to be very difficult to engage with Mendy, to establish a collaborative therapeutic plan, and to make progress. Still, working with challenging patients like Mendy is a measure of professionalism, and it represents an opportunity to make a positive difference in the life of someone who truly needs competent care from someone who is willing to provide it. Hence, the therapist decided to move ahead forthrightly, with optimism and good will, regardless of the patient's cynicism about treatment.

History of the Problem

Mendy reported that his problems had begun six years ago when he "got a little wild" and lost his job at the law firm. On questioning for earlier episodes of dysfunction, the therapist learned that Mendy had had significant behavior problems since childhood. In grade school, Mendy would periodically be disruptive in class, had difficulty sitting still and following instructions, often failed to do his homework, and had conflicts with the other boys. He was diagnosed with *minimal brain dysfunction,* a term often used in those days to describe children who showed signs of hyperactivity, distractibility, and conduct problems. He was put on the stimulant Ritalin and promptly got worse, an outcome that perplexed Mendy's pediatrician and vexed his parents. He was taken off the medication and continued to experience periodic episodes of undercontrolled behavior. Although he managed to do well enough in school to be put into accelerated classes by the time he was in junior high school, a pattern of dysfunction had been established.

As a college student, Mendy experimented with illicit drugs. His most adverse incident involved an evening of snorting cocaine, during which he expressed the belief that he could cure the world of all evil, that he was an irresistible lover, and that he no longer needed sleep for the rest of his life. Mendy's friends thought nothing of this because they had often felt similarly following the use of cocaine. However, even his drug-using friends grew concerned when Mendy's mood, ideation, and behavior remained this way for many days. The resident advisor of Mendy's dormitory arranged for Mendy to be hospitalized, where, for the first time, the observation of a manic episode led to the diagnosis of bipolar disorder and the prescription of lithium, a mood-stabilizing medication.

Mendy survived this harrowing episode without losing his academic standing but also without recognizing the seriousness of his condition. He silently attributed his symptoms to the cocaine binge, and he secretly believed that, by staying away from stimulants, he would never again have such problems. He, consequently, did not follow through on the hospital's recommendation for outpatient therapy, and he was only sporadically adherent in taking his lithium. Nonetheless, Mendy's condition stabilized, and he was largely functional all the way through law school, in spite of some times when he felt depressed for weeks on end.

Mendy's most severe episode of mania occurred when he was 30 years old. The results were devastating. Mendy was a junior partner at a prestigious law firm, was married to a well-liked and respected woman who worked as a nurse, and had a newborn baby. Perhaps partly because of the baby's crying throughout the night, Mendy's sleep-wake cycle was greatly disrupted for many weeks. Whereas his wife responded to this expected situation with the customary irritability and extreme fatigue, Mendy became manic, an all too frequent outcome for bipolar patients who become deprived of sufficient rest over a period of time.

Mendy's behavior became erratic. For example, he began to spend large sums of money for no apparent reason. Mendy's behavior at work came to the attention of coworkers and clients alike because of his off-color and bawdy language and because his judgment was showing signs of serious impairment. All the while, Mendy seemed to be having the time of his life. Just as the senior partners were planning to suggest that Mendy take a leave of absence to seek psychiatric care, a client phoned the firm in a rage, claiming that she had caught Mendy having sex with someone on his office couch. Then she added that she herself was having an affair with Mendy, and she now realized that she was not the only client with whom Mendy was involved. In her anger and sense of betrayal, she blew the whistle. Mendy was finished at the firm, and his life began to unravel.

Mendy's wife had noticed that Mendy was coming home later and later, and she had already suspected that he was being unfaithful. When he was fired, Mendy went on a drinking binge, during which he lashed out at his wife for a variety of imaginary offenses and admitted defiantly that he had been having sex with other women. His wife took the baby and fled to her parents' home, and soon thereafter she served Mendy with divorce papers. At this point, Mendy, who was not actively receiving treatment for his mania, attempted to represent himself in the divorce proceedings, and he wound up with an extremely unfavorable settlement. He ended up with no job, no marriage, no home, and very limited child visitation rights, with supervision. Friends implored Mendy to seek mental health care, but he refused to do so and lashed out at anyone who suggested he needed help. One by one, Mendy burned his bridges to everyone who otherwise would have been helpful to him.

For the next six years, Mendy's condition generally worsened as he lapsed into a deep depression, went on disability, and isolated himself from other people. Mendy's contact with his child, his sister, and his friends dwindled over time. He felt so ashamed and helpless that he did not take any action to help himself, even when his depression occasionally lifted. Although he experienced a great deal of suicidal ideation, he never actually harmed himself, although his poor self-care was a sign of long-term neglect of his well-being.

At the urging of his sister, Mendy finally went to see a psychiatrist, but he expressed no interest in talking about his problems and only minimal interest in taking medications. Mendy tried many different medications, including (in addition to the mood-stabilizing lithium that he had taken previously) antidepressant medications (Paxil and Zoloft), antipsychotic medications (Risperdal and Zyprexa), and anticonvulsant medications (Tegretol and Lamictal) used in treating bipolar disorder. Unfortunately, Mendy never took these medications regularly or systematically, which made it difficult to know what worked for him and what did not. For example, whenever Mendy would start to feel better, he would stop taking his medications, which is a regrettable mistake often made by persons with bipolar disorder. Following the predictable manic episode that would result from cessation of his medications, he would start taking them again, but only sporadically. Then, when he became depressed again, Mendy would conclude that the medications were worthless. A true test of the efficacy of his medications was never achieved. During all this time, his attendance at sessions with a series of psychiatrists was irregular at best, which served further to dilute the treatment he was receiving.

Mendy decided to come to cognitive therapy after reading an article online, in which he learned that some studies in Great Britain had held out promise for the effectiveness of combining medications and cognitive therapy in the treatment of bipolar disorder. He told his sister about these findings, and she urged him to get this kind of treatment. Mendy decided to make the effort and began to look for a cognitive therapist. Because he had been disappointed before, however, and his life was in ruins, Mendy was not quite ready to buy the idea that this treatment might help. Nevertheless, here he was.

Developmental History and Family Background

There was a substantial history of mental illness in Mendy's family. His maternal grandfather was a chronically depressed man, who tried to commit suicide on numerous occasions, mostly in highly dramatic ways (e.g., putting his head in the oven). Mendy's mother never complained of being depressed, but she was constantly plagued with psychosomatic ailments that she acknowledged were brought on and worsened by stress. Her two older brothers, Mendy's maternal uncles, both had problems with smoking, drinking, and gambling and died relatively young. Mendy's father was prone to outbursts of anger and was often absent from the family. In retrospect, Mendy speculated that his father had a girlfriend and had used the tyranny of his anger to keep everyone from confronting him. Mendy's older brother experienced repeated bouts of depression and, as an adult, "wrote off" the family, moving far away and remaining out of contact. Mendy stated that his sister Rhonda was "the only sane person in the family" and served as everyone's "Florence Nightingale." That was certainly the case now because Mendy's pursuit of treatment would not have occurred without Rhonda's urging and support.

The patient grew up in a suburban community near Baltimore. As a schoolboy, Mendy had little trouble making friends, but he had serious difficulties in keeping them. He often had a charismatic appeal as the class clown, getting into all sorts of mischief with his buddies. This made him famous with the other boys but notorious with his parents and teachers. Even his peers would shy away from him, however, when Mendy continued to disobey adult authority even after getting into trouble repeatedly. The parents of his classmates tended to discourage their children from associating with a troublemaker like Mendy. Throughout his formative years, Mendy pretended not to care if other people disliked him or avoided spending time with him; privately, however, he felt rejected, sad, and angry. Yet, whenever Mendy changed schools, he would quickly find a new group of friends, because his strong personality would attract peers who were similarly extroverted and rebellious.

Mendy's record as a student was strikingly inconsistent. He could win the praises of his teachers with his skills in speaking and writing, but he could also exasperate and mystify them with his failure to turn in assignments and his apparent laissez-faire attitude toward deadlines, grades, and classroom decorum. Nevertheless, he found a way to graduate from high school, ultimately did well enough on scholastic achievement tests to attend a state college, and then was able to get into law school and receive his law degree.

As previously mentioned, Mendy was treated briefly with Ritalin as a child, but this medication was discontinued when his behavior worsened. Mendy never received counseling, nor did anyone else who lived in his house while he was growing up. Later, when Mendy's brother went into therapy as an independent young adult, he broke away from the family entirely. The parents blamed the therapist for the brother's estrangement, whereas the teenage Mendy pretended not to care. When Mendy was in his early 20s, his father died suddenly of a myocardial infarction, and his mother succumbed shortly thereafter to ovarian cancer. Only he and Rhonda remained. At the time, Mendy acted publicly as if he were unfazed by the sudden loss of both of his parents and his brother.

Social, Academic, and Occupational History

In spite of Mendy's behavioral and social problems in school, he was sufficiently intelligent and charismatic to have a very active love life. He met Eileen while he was in college, the year following his cocaine experimentation and resultant manic episode. She was not aware of his psychological problems, nor did he ever tell her about his psychotropic medications and occasional therapy appointments. Eileen found Mendy to be exciting, handsome, and infectiously confident, while Mendy thought that Eileen was the most emotionally stable person he had ever known. In retrospect, Mendy noted, he had probably tried to sabotage the relationship numerous times by dating other women and by frequently hinting to Eileen that he planned to travel far away to go to law school. Nevertheless, he and Eileen managed to stay together, despite having some rocky times. They married after Mendy completed law school, and they remained living in the geographic area where Eileen was already employed as a nurse practitioner.

Initially, the couple had an apparently successful and satisfying life together. They postponed having a child for a few years while they accumulated a sizeable nest egg with which to buy a spacious house. Eileen tolerated Mendy's slovenly and disorganized ways, Mendy put up with Eileen's orderliness, and they functioned fairly well for a time.

Mendy and Eileen then experienced a crisis when Mendy went through a two-week period of depression during which he could barely get out of bed. Eileen was alarmed and insisted that he see a doctor. Mendy resisted, whereupon they got into a long, heated argument in which Mendy finally divulged that he had seen "a few shrinks now and then" and that he was "supposed to be taking some medications." Eileen was furious that Mendy had kept such important information a secret from her, and she made it clear that she was not going to stand around and watch him sink into an abyss. She gave Mendy an ultimatum—get back into active treatment or find a new wife. Mendy complied half-heartedly, while internally harboring resentment toward his wife, whose approach he found to be overcontrolling and lacking in caring. Mendy repeated his pattern of having one foot in and one foot out of his psychiatric treatment, including underutilizing his medications. In the meantime, he would display his pill bottles prominently in the couple's shared bathroom, as if to say to Eileen, "I'm getting help and here's the proof, so get off my back!"

Things settled down for a while as Mendy recovered from his depressive episode, and the couple decided that it would be a good time to have a child. Unfortunately, neither foresaw the potentially dire consequences of sleep deprivation on Mendy's bipolar illness. The birth of their son Cody signaled the beginning of Mendy's worst manic episode, in which he acted with reckless abandon, bedded at least two clients at his law firm, and lost both his career and his marriage. It might be expected that someone in Mendy's position would have gone to his wife and his boss and begged both of them to take him back, while promising to get into treatment in a serious way, but he chose not to do so. This was just another example of Mendy's habit of giving up rather than trying to solve problems. Later, this issue would become a major focal point in his cognitive therapy.

The next five to six years saw Mendy in steady decline, even when his mania was in remission. The prominent symptom episodes during this time centered on depression, avoidance, helplessness, and hopelessness. Mendy never went back to work, depleted his rather substantial funds within three years, moved to an apartment in an undesirable location, lost contact with his young son, and went on disability. Mendy was isolated, participating marginally in his pharmacotherapy, and highly pessimistic about his future when he entered cognitive therapy. This downward spiral could probably have been stopped early in the process, but Mendy simply did not take steps to help himself. Now he was convinced that it was too late to do anything. On the other hand, the article about the success of cognitive therapy and pharmacotherapy in outcome studies in Great Britain caught Mendy's attention, so there was obviously a glimmer of hope left in him. As the therapist would soon discover, it was but a faint glimmer.

At this point in his life, the 36-year-old Mendy had virtually no contact with family or friends except for his sister. He had no income of his own and was living from month to month on disability checks. Mendy spent most of his days sleeping and "slumming" around his cluttered, chaotic apartment and most of his nights on the Internet. He interacted with others in person as little as possible, although he often chatted with people online, and he rarely used the telephone. His health habits were poor, and he presented himself to the world as someone who lacked self-respect. Mendy felt stigmatized by his bipolar disorder, which accounted in part for his not seeing his psychiatrist as often as he should have. He rejected the idea of attending any support groups for persons with bipolar disorder.

Mendy viewed his life as having "gone down a vortex," and he believed that it would be nearly impossible for him ever to become healthy again. He had thoughts of suicide but had not been engaging in deliberate acts of self-harm or making overt threats about killing himself. Even so, he did not think his life was worth very much.

Interview Behavior and Diagnostic Impressions

When Mendy was initially seen by a cognitive therapist, his behavior was strongly suggestive of a person who would rather be someplace else. He looked unkempt and unshaven, made little eye contact, spoke in a low and gravelly voice, and made frequent oft-handed comments such as "I don't even know why I'm here" and "I'm probably a hopeless case anyway."

The therapist noted that Mendy had taken the trouble to initiate this session and to trek down to the therapist's office, and he wondered what Mendy hoped he might accomplish by taking these steps. Mendy commented on the aforementioned article, adding that, "This cognitive therapy thing is probably my last chance." Therapists often say "Uh-oh" to themselves whenever they hear a new patient utter such a desperate and pressure-inducing opening statement. Nevertheless, the comment is informative because it cues the therapist in to the patient's drama, suggests that the patient is feeling hopeless, and predicts that the patient may look to the therapist either to do all the work of therapy for him or to wave a magic wand to make things better. This is not how therapy works, which means that therapists in such situations need to educate patients like Mendy about the active role and responsibilities they must assume as a participant in psychotherapy.

Moreover, the notion of a "last chance" is entirely subjective. Although Mendy was making this determination for himself, he believed it as strongly as if an objective medical test had proved it. The therapist later would use Mendy's comments to point out how his thinking style got him into trouble time and time again. By the same token, changing his thinking style could potentially be very helpful but only if Mendy bought into this idea and only if he participated in implementing the therapeutic strategies. The therapist realized that he was going to have a difficult time convincing Mendy that there were things he could do himself to improve his lot; yet, he also knew that, without the patient's active collaboration, therapy would likely confirm a self-fulfilling prophecy of failure.

Before commencing with the treatment, the therapist engaged Mendy in several diagnostic procedures. The most important of these was the Structured Clinical Interview for the *DSM-IV* (SCID; First, Spitzer, Gibbon, & Williams, 1995), which involves asking the patient numerous questions about past and present symptoms associated with various mental disorders. On Axis I of the *Diagnostic and Statistical Manual of Mental Disorders* (*DSM-IV*; American Psychiatric Association, 1994), which codifies clinical syndromes, Mendy met criteria for Bipolar Disorder, with his most recent episode being depressed and severe. High scores on two brief self-report measures of depression, the Beck Depression Inventory and the Beck Hopelessness Scale (see Katz, Katz, & Shaw, 1999), confirmed his severely depressed state at the time of the interview. Because Mendy reported that he had not used drugs since his freshman year of college, no diagnosis of substance abuse disorder was given. Had his earlier use of psychoactive chemicals been more extensive, the therapist would have considered assigning him a diagnosis of Polysubstance Abuse, currently in a state of sustained full remission.

It also seemed likely that Mendy had qualified for a diagnosis of Attention-Deficit/Hyperactivity Disorder (ADHD) in childhood and adolescence. Thus, it was reasonable for him to have been prescribed the Ritalin that he was given as a schoolboy. However, because he was also in the early and undetected stages of Bipolar Disorder at that time, this medication was contraindicated. Like antidepressants, stimulants given to bipolar persons in the absence of concurrent mood-stabilizing medication have the potential to induce manic episodes. Mendy's behavior having worsened when he was treated with Ritalin was probably attributable to its adverse effect on his emerging Bipolar Disorder, which is a condition that often makes its first appearance during adolescence. When Mendy was taken off the Ritalin, no other treatments were tried in its place. As a result, he did not receive pharmacotherapy for either the ADHD or the Bipolar Disorder, and his behavior continued to be erratic throughout his adolescence, culminating in the cocaine-induced manic episode when he began college.

On Axis II of the *DSM-IV*, which codifies personality disorders, Mendy responded to the SCID by endorsing multiple problematic personality traits typically associated with Obsessive-Compulsive, Narcissistic, and Paranoid Personality disorders, without fully qualifying for a diagnosis of any one of these conditions. He accordingly met diagnostic criteria for Personality Disorder NOS (Not Otherwise Specified). An important factor in determining that Mendy did indeed have a personality disorder was that he reported showing these problematic traits before the onset of his full-blown bipolar episodes in adulthood.

Axis III of the *DSM-IV* identifies medical problems that may be pertinent to a patient's psychological dysfunction. Mendy did not report any of the types of neurological problems (e.g., multiple sclerosis, Parkinson's disease, seizure disorders, chronic pain disorders) or endocrine disorders (e.g., diabetes, hypothyroidism, Grave's disease) that often contribute to psychological distress. Mendy was moderately overweight and had a high cholesterol count, both of which were probably the result of his poor eating habits. This did not particularly bother him, although he alluded to the fact that his physical shape was "just a shadow" of what it once was.

On Axis IV of the *DSM-IV*, which lists psychosocial stressors, Mendy's problems were severe. He was chronically alone, unemployed with no prospects, and living in a poorly kept apartment in a seedy part of town. He was leading an empty life. On Axis V, which calls for rating a patient's overall adaptive functioning on a scale from 1 to 100, Mendy's therapist scored him at 35 at the time of their first meeting. At this level, the patient is demonstrating major impairment in several areas of life functioning, including judgment and mood state. Because

Mendy's condition had not changed much in the past two or three years, the therapist also rated Mendy at 35 as to his best level of functioning in the past year. In other words, Mendy's psychological skills in dealing with life and the world around him were consistently poor. This finding usually predicts that therapy will be long term, complicated, and difficult.

Formulation of the Problem

Mendy grew up in a household in which there was chronic unhappiness. His mother never felt well and let the family hear about it regularly; his father got into rages when he was at home, which wasn't very often. Death was a prominent topic, given his grandfather's chronic suicidality and his uncles' high-risk lifestyles and early demise. Later, Mendy's parents died in rapid succession, and his brother disassociated himself from the family altogether. A sense of loss pervaded Mendy's life.

As a child, he had serious difficulties in school and highly intense but fleeting friendships. Mendy learned that he could survive and that he had the smarts to do as he pleased and still get ahead. Nevertheless, he often felt the sting of rejection and the humiliation of being publicly chastised. Hence, Mendy always had a nagging sense that there was something fundamentally defective about him, although he overcompensated for this concern by being brash and bold—as in being a conspicuous jokester; pursuing many girls and, later, young women; and aiming toward a high-profile education and career. When Mendy became manic in college, his fears about being flawed were heightened, but to his credit, he pushed onward and continued to achieve. On the down side, however, Mendy's need to give the appearance of functioning well—indeed, to appear superior to most people—contributed to his recurrent withdrawal from psychiatric treatment. Mendy's reluctance to invest himself in treatment increased his vulnerability to the full-blown development and progression of his bipolar disorder, thus cruelly fulfilling the prophecy of his fears of being defective.

When Mendy's life crumbled at the age of 30, he could have taken steps to repair his mental health and to try to rebuild his life and recoup his losses. However, taking productive steps such as getting into treatment, finding a new job, and being cooperative, respectful, and apologetic toward his estranged wife required a positive mind-set that Mendy lacked. Instead of taking stock of himself objectively, realizing that he had a significant mental disorder requiring treatment, and appreciating the importance of being a father to his son, he lashed out in anger, desperation, and hopelessness. It was as if he subscribed to the belief that he was being mistreated by his boss and wife and should be forgiven without making amends, just as he had been in school. At the same time, a competing voice within Mendy told him that he was an utter failure and deserved to have his life go up in flames.

Compounding this intense internal conflict was Mendy's heightened sensitivity to loss. In a life filled with premature goodbyes, the loss of his career, reputation, family, and future plans was more than even a person as brash as Mendy could bear. He gave up and retreated into bitter isolation. His surrender and retreat just made matters worse, especially when he realized he was now even angrier and less available in his relationship with Cody than his own father had been with him. Mendy felt great shame, but he would not be caught dead revealing his shamefulness to others, even to a therapist.

Mendy's views of the field of mental health were jaded and mistrustful. He remembered well the time as a child when his already-undercontrolled behavior was worsened by Ritalin and the resultant angry responses of his parents. His hospitalization during his first manic episode when he was a college freshman further soured him against psychiatric treatment because he found the experience to be humiliating and depersonalizing. His subsequent contacts with psychiatrists left him underwhelmed because he never established a therapeutic relationship with any of them. He generally took his medications just enough to hate them for their side effects, but never long or regularly enough to benefit from them.

As a consequence, he continued to have breakthrough depressive episodes, like the one that caused early marital strife when he first revealed his bipolar disorder to Eileen. Mendy concluded that medications did not work, that the field of mental health care was filled with quacks, and that there was nothing a therapist could tell him that he didn't already know. Following his catastrophic manic episode at the age of 30 and his subsequent personal decline, Mendy generalized his anger and mistrust to the world at large. He had become a basically misanthropic and embittered person. During his early sessions with Dr. N, Mendy's attitude seemed to be, "You have to prove to me that you can help me, and then maybe I'll look you in the eye—maybe."

Treatment Recommendations and Prognosis

Mendy had proved that he was not able to manage his life on his own, but he was ashamed of this fact. He desperately needed to be in treatment, but he had a history of adverse reactions to medications and no instances of positive bonding with a therapist. Such patients are difficult to keep in treatment long enough to make some progress. Whoever would see Mendy, whether for medications or cognitive therapy, would have to work very hard in a concerted effort to establish some rapport with him, even in the face of marked unfriendliness on his part.

In Dr. N's opinion, Mendy needed to have everything *plus* the kitchen sink thrown at him, including a regular regimen of well-monitored medication(s), weekly cognitive therapy sessions (perhaps occasionally with the participation of his sister Rhonda), bibliotherapy consisting of self-help books concerning bipolar illness, and participation in support groups such as those sponsored by the National Depressive and Manic-Depressive Association and the National Alliance for the Mentally Ill. It was expected that Mendy would reject this sort of comprehensive approach. After all, it represented a radical departure from the ways in which he had previously handled his problems. It would expose him to the potential scrutiny of many people, would demand a good deal of commitment and investment of his time and energy, and would likely add to his feelings of stigmatization.

Dr. N was prepared to acknowledge the validity of Mendy's concerns, while at the same time trying to motivate him to give a full spectrum of treatment options the best chance he had ever given it.

Without aggressive, comprehensive mental health care, Mendy had virtually no chance of improving his life significantly. Advanced cases of bipolar disorder do not spontaneously remit, especially when the patient's life circumstances are so adverse and dire. Even with a full course of medications, cognitive therapy, and supplemental help, Mendy's prognosis was guarded at best. Simply put, the hole that his illness and his own defeatist behavior had dug for Mendy over the years would require a long, long climb for him to see the light of day once again.

Treatment Course and Outcome

At first, Mendy was disgruntled when his therapist told him that cognitive therapy alone would be insufficient to help him significantly over the long term. Dr. N made a strong case that cognitive therapy and pharmacotherapy worked best in tandem and that it wouldn't be a bad idea to add family sessions, bibliotherapy, and support group sessions to the mix. When Mendy responded by sighing heavily and clicking his tongue, Dr. N asked a quintessential question common to cognitive therapy and interpersonal forms of treatment: "What is going through your mind right now?" Mendy at first demurred but, with a little empathic encouragement, acknowledged that he did not relish the idea of investing himself so extensively in a treatment that he believed would ultimately fail anyway. Dr. N and Mendy discussed his concerns frankly, seriously, and at length. The argument that finally garnered Mendy's stated commitment to the treatment program went as follows:

> *Therapist:* Do you know why scientists run double-blind experiments? It's because they know that the experimenter's expectations can subtly bias the results of the study. Well, that's true

of life, too. You are running your own natural experiment in life. If you expect things to fail and fall apart, such as your treatment, you risk doing lots of little, almost imperceptible things to fulfill the prophecy of your expectations, which is to make things fail. Then you would be technically right, but it would be a Pyrrhic victory. Mendy, can I interest you in biasing the natural experiment of your life in the *positive* direction? Can you invest in doing everything you can to make the treatment *work*? Can you fulfill this more hopeful prophecy instead?

Mendy: (Long, long pause, then haltingly . . .) I think . . . I see your point, but . . . I don't think I can take another letdown. If I get my hopes up . . . isn't that a setup . . . you know . . . for being crushed again?

Therapist: It's a risk, no doubt. I understand that, Mendy, and that's why you would have my total support and respect if you boldly took the step of investing everything you had to give into your treatment. Besides that, what's your alternative? At this point, you have thoroughly convinced me that your life is a shambles and that you are suffering terribly. So what do you have to lose at this point by trying?

Mendy: How about my life?

Therapist: Are you saying that you might kill yourself?

Mendy: Maybe. (Long, long pause) Maybe not. . . . I don't know. Do I really want to stir up all this stuff again?

Therapist: You tell me. I'm on your side. If you say yes, I'm on your side all the way.

Mendy: I think you're expecting too much.

Therapist: Well, let's spell out what we expect. Let's establish some goals for therapy. How about that?

At this point, Mendy and the therapist spelled out a list of goals for treatment:

1. Adjusting Mendy's sleep-wake cycle, so that he would be more interactive with the world around him by day and better able to sleep at night.

2. Learning how to make peace with medications and take them religiously.

3. Getting back into good health habits, especially eating better and exercising.

4. Reconnecting with old friends, perhaps starting with e-mails.

5. Spending time doing old and new hobbies, including reading, playing chess at the local community center's chess club, and practicing the guitar.

6. Looking for gainful employment, getting off disability, and moving to a better apartment.

7. Modifying his negative core beliefs about himself and his life.

8. Improving his self-respect.

9. Restarting a social life (one not involving the sex industry).

10. Reestablishing contact—and perhaps ultimately a relationship—with his son Cody, law permitting.

On completion of this list, Mendy actually smiled and said, "Yes, like I said . . . you're expecting too much!" However, there was a glimmer of enthusiasm in his eyes and voice. Therapy was off and running.

The therapist facilitated Mendy's meeting with a psychiatrist for the purpose of updating his medications in light of his current condition and history of abortive pharmacotherapies. The approach was to keep things simple by putting him on no more than three medications at a time and to start with just two, a mood stabilizer and an antidepressant. The goal of this pharmacological treatment was to improve Mendy's depressed mood without switching it into mania.

A possible complication in this part of the treatment plan was posed by Mendy's having had so many haphazard fits and starts with medications that he was now vulnerable to the kindling effect, a hypothesized condition in which successive episodes of depression and/or mania occur with fewer and fewer environmental and/or biological provocations. Thus, even if Mendy were optimally adherent with his medications, there was a reasonable chance that he would have setbacks anyway. He was warned about this possibility but encouraged to stay the course. In the cognitive therapy part of his treatment, he was taught to spot early warning signs of symptom episodes and to execute a preplanned coping skills package to mute the effects of impending mood problems.

To enact this cognitive plan, Mendy was instructed in using a basic, effective self-help strategy known simply as *problem solving*. Unfortunately, apathy, fatigue, and hopelessness are the natural enemies of problem solving, and Mendy had these difficulties in spades. His history showed how often and tragically he had missed opportunities to engage in damage control, thus allowing his condition and his life situation to worsen progressively. The therapist spent a good deal of time trying to encourage and motivate Mendy to use his intelligence in the service of helping himself in ways he had rarely done before. For good measure, the therapist added the following comment: "Mendy, you said that this time in treatment was your 'last chance,' but it can be your *best* chance if you actually participate in it!"

In the initial sessions, Mendy and his therapist set some specific behavioral goals, including:

1. Going to sleep by midnight and waking up by 8:00 A.M.

2. Charting his activities and rating on a scale from 0 to 10 how much pleasure and sense of accomplishment he derived from each of them.

3. Starting a modest regimen of physical exercise, regular healthy meals, and reading.

4. Keeping track of his moods and his use of medications each day.

5. Sending out at least three friendly messages every day, either by telephone or e-mail.

The purpose of these behavioral prescriptions was to activate this lethargic and unhappy man, foster enjoyment in his life, and increase his sense of control over himself, his health, and his daily schedule. It was anticipated that Mendy would feel empowered by experiencing success in these endeavors, and this success could then be parlayed into more significant therapeutic accomplishments related to his attitudes toward himself, his family, his social life, and his future goals.

At first, Mendy was not enthusiastic about becoming actively engaged in his treatment program. Dr. N had expected this lukewarm involvement and did not respond to it by chastising Mendy or predicting treatment failure. Instead, he persisted doggedly in supporting and encouraging Mendy, appealing to his personal strengths as a way of inspiring confidence and promoting cooperation. For example, the therapist refused to believe that Mendy was a "loser" (as Mendy insisted), emphasizing to the contrary that Mendy had once had the skills to become a capable lawyer, build an impressive home, and win the love of a successful and well-respected woman. The therapist pointed out that these facts identified Mendy as having what is known as a "good premorbid history," meaning that he had been successful in life before his disorder took hold and could, therefore, succeed again. Mendy typically scoffed at such observations, but the therapist was undeterred. He continued to support his patient at every opportunity and indicated that he expected Mendy to remain true to the treatment plan.

As Mendy began to make improvements in the quality of his daily life, new issues arose to trouble him. These new issues included fears about getting off disability and looking for employment, ambivalence about becoming involved as a father again, and aversion to getting involved with a support group. Although seeming disparate on the surface, these issues all touched on similar vulnerabilities, particularly Mendy's core beliefs about being an incompetent, defective, and unlovable person. To encourage Mendy to continue to make progress, it was, therefore, necessary to address his self-doubts, self-hatred, regrets about past mistakes, and sense of stigma. One method that was used to counteract his negative self-attitudes consisted of asking ask him to read the compelling works of Kay Redfield Jamison (1995), who has written informative, eloquent, and spellbinding accounts of her own manic-depressive disorder and of the mental illnesses of major literary and artistic figures of the past. Reading Jamison's works helped Mendy feel less stigmatized and less inclined to condemn himself.

Within six months after beginning the treatment program, Mendy became determined to seek a job, to buy new clothes, to search for a new apartment, and to call a former legal colleague for help in pursuing court-approved visitation of his son Cody. Despite continuing reluctance, he began attending a support group, where he met a woman with whom he struck up a friendship and later began to date. Although Mendy was cautious about his commitment to this budding relationship, he acknowledged that he and his new woman friend seemed to be good for each other, in that they understood the horrors of bipolar disorder, encouraged each other to stick with their respective treatments, did not judge each other, and viewed their relationship as an example of the hopeful rebuilding of their lives.

Mendy was now taking his medications and attending cognitive therapy as if they were routine behaviors for him. He was showing no signs of mania, but he still experienced occasional periods of mild depression. Through therapy, Mendy had learned not to let such mini-setbacks convince him that all was lost or to abandon his productive activities. Instead, when Mendy felt depressed, he would consult with his psychiatrist to determine whether an adjustment of his medications was called for; he would structure his days for maximum attention to his most important responsibilities; he would spend more time with his new girlfriend, and he would attend additional sessions of support group and cognitive therapy.

It is not possible to comment definitively about the long-term outcome of Mendy's treatment because bipolar disorder is a lifetime condition. However, Mendy succeeded in rebuilding a significant part of his life, even though he had to make peace with losses that could not be recouped. He no longer had his house or his marriage, but he had a decent apartment and a supportive girlfriend. He no longer had his career as an attorney, but he was earning a regular salary via a clerical job and had reasons for living when he woke up in the morning. He no longer saw Cody every day, but he now had the right to have supervised monthly visits. Mendy had some follow-up booster sessions with Dr. N that were focused on maintaining his gains and remaining effective in his self-help skills. These follow-up meetings allowed Mendy an opportunity to share his grief over the difficult course his life had taken and his fears about the unknowns of the future. For added support, these sessions sometimes included Mendy's girlfriend or his sister Rhonda. Mendy had suffered many losses in his life, but he now appreciated the fact that he was not alone and that he could count on himself again.

Recommended Readings

Hammen, C. (2003). Mood disorders. In G. Stricker & T. A. Widiger (Eds.), *Clinical psychology* (pp. 93–118). Vol. 8 in I. B. Weiner (Editor-in-Chief), *Handbook of psychology*. Hoboken, NJ: Wiley.

Johnson, S. L., Winett, C., Meyer, B., Greenhouse, W., & Miller, I. (1999). Social support and the course of bipolar disorder. *Journal of Abnormal Psychology, 108,* 558–566.

Lam, D. H., Bright, J., Jones, S., Hayward, P., Schuck, N., Chisholm, D., et al. (2000). Cognitive therapy for bipolar disorder: A pilot study of relapse prevention. *Cognitive Therapy and Research, 24,* 503–520.

Newman, C. F., Leahy, R. L., Beck, A. T., Reilly-Harrington, N. A., & Gyulai, L. (2001). *Bipolar disorder: A cognitive therapy approach.* Washington, DC: American Psychological Association.

Scott, J., Stanton, B., Garland, A., & Ferrier, N. (2000). Cognitive vulnerability to bipolar disorder. *Psychological Medicine, 30,* 467–472.

References

American Psychiatric Association. (1994). *Diagnostic and statistical manual for mental disorders* (4th ed.). Washington, DC: Author.

First, M. B., Spitzer, R. L., Gibbon, M., & Williams, J. B. (1995). *Structured Clinical Interview for DSM-IV Axis I disorders.* New York: New York State Psychiatric Institute.

Jamison, K. R. (1995). *An unquiet mind: A memoir of moods and madness.* New York: Vintage Books.

Katz, R., Katz, J., & Shaw, B. F. (1999). Beck Depression Inventory and Hopelessness Scale. In M. E. Maruish (Ed.), *The use of psychological testing for treatment planning and outcomes assessment* (2nd ed., pp. 921–933). Mahwah, NJ: Erlbaum.

CHAPTER 19

Schizophrenia

MARTIN HARROW, KALMAN J. KAPLAN, AND SURINDER S. NAND

Larry R was a patient suffering from schizophrenia. He was hospitalized with his first psychotic break at age 19, while in the military. After receiving treatment, he experienced a five-year recovery period during which he married, had a daughter, and worked with partial success at several different factory jobs. Toward the end of this five-year period, however, he gradually developed a paranoid system that included delusional ideas concerning other workers at his job, his "manhood," and sexual relationships with women other than his wife. He quit his job, his psychotic symptoms worsened, and he was hospitalized once more. On this occasion, his paranoid ideation was not completely resolved, and he was subsequently rehospitalized numerous times. Larry never fully recovered, and his story ultimately had a tragic ending.

Developmental History

Larry was the middle of three children. He was born approximately one year following the birth of an older sister, and he was age 3 when a younger brother was born. The adult guidance and parenting Larry received during childhood was poor. Larry described his mother as a harsh and rejecting woman who died of a perforated ulcer when he was age 5. Larry, in retrospect, reported feeling some guilt with respect to her death. After losing his mother, Larry lived for a time with his maternal grandmother, who removed him from his father's home because of the father's drinking. His grandmother was outspokenly critical of his father. For reasons that are not entirely clear, however, she took only Larry to live with her, whereas Larry's sister and brother remained with their father.

Two years later, at the age of 7, Larry moved in with a maternal aunt and her husband because Larry's grandmother decided that, at her age, she no longer had sufficient stamina to look after him. Larry's father remarried at around this time, but Larry never considered moving back with him, mainly, he said, because of his father's negative attitudes toward his grandmother. In describing his relationship with his grandmother and his aunt, Larry emphasized that he had not had a male figure with whom to identify during this period of his life. He apparently had very little to do with his uncle while he was living with his aunt, even though he described this uncle in very positive terms after this man died. He also seems to have had little relationship at this point with his father, whom he described as a "know it all," or with either his sister or brother.

Larry did not have much else to say about his childhood and school history, except for mentioning that he was elected president of his fifth-grade class. Larry was 10 years old at the time, and he stated that this was one of the high points of his life. His happiness was short-lived, however. Three years later, at age 13, Larry became aware of a change in his temperament. Whereas he had previously been happy, he now noticed that he was frowning a great deal. His already-limited relationship with his uncle seems to have deteriorated by this point. One night, Larry's uncle accused him of thinking only of himself and went on to make several other derogatory comments about him. The next morning, the uncle was killed in an automobile accident. Larry blamed himself for his uncle's death, speculating that his uncle may have been too sleepy to drive, after having been up all of the previous night worrying about him.

As another emerging problem, Larry developed a sexual fixation on his aunt during his adolescence, about which he felt very guilty. This fixation began at age 15 after he saw (or perhaps dreamt that he saw) his aunt with her breasts exposed. Larry described his aunt as a "well-built woman" and said that fantasies about her stimulated him to a pattern of chronic masturbation.

Larry provided only scant information about his experiences in high school, which he attended between the ages of 15 and 18. His limited recollection probably reflected the emotional impoverishment of these years in his life. According to his report, he was still living with his aunt at this time, was just an average student, and went on dates with only three girls during high school, only one time with each. Larry said that he regarded himself as a very ugly-looking person, so ugly that girls would groan as he passed by.

Larry graduated from high school at age 18. He then attended a community college but dropped out after two months and enlisted in the military. After basic training, he was stationed in Japan, where he worked as a medical aide in a pediatric service. Larry felt under a great deal of pressure in the service and did not get along well with other soldiers. He began drinking during this period and, at age 19, visited a prostitute for what was his first sexual experience with a woman. Larry's initial psychotic breakdown occurred soon after his encounter with the prostitute and appears to have been precipitated by it. Shortly thereafter, he began to hear voices, and these hallucinations were accompanied by the delusional belief that the other men were talking about him because they knew that he masturbated. He believed that they were discussing "ways to get rid of me," he said, because he was "not a real man." Larry remembered hearing a roommate who was 60 feet away from him saying, "I used to like him [Larry], but now I hate his guts."

Larry was admitted to a psychiatric unit at this time and remained there for 17 days. He was then transferred back to the United States, where he was hospitalized for an additional three months. At the end of these three months, he was given a medical discharge and advised to seek further outpatient psychotherapy. He did not follow through on this recommendation but instead continued to function as best he could without mental health care until he was age 25.

Adult History

After being discharged from the military and released from the hospital, Larry went back to live with his aunt and found a job in a factory. He did not remain with his aunt for very long, however. He began to attempt a rapprochement with his father, which angered the aunt and resulted in her asking him to leave her home. Now age 20, Larry moved into an apartment with his younger brother. During this period, he began a relationship with Joan, the woman he would subsequently marry, and impregnated her. According to his report, he forced her to have an illegal abortion, for which the abortionist was arrested and sent to jail. In later years, he felt guilty for having pressed his future wife to have this abortion.

At the age of 21, Larry impregnated Joan a second time and decided to marry her but only after learning that her father had said to several people, "If he doesn't marry her, he isn't much of a man." Even after agreeing to marry Joan, Larry postponed the wedding for five months, mainly because of fears of getting married and ignorance of how to go about making the wedding arrangements. After mustering his courage sufficiently to get married, he still left it to his future mother-in-law to arrange the ceremony. Joan was five months pregnant when they married, and Larry adjusted to fatherhood in a reasonably adaptive fashion when she gave birth to a daughter four months later.

About one year after Larry became a husband and father, when he was age 22, his sister died in an automobile accident. Aside from this event, the next few years were relatively uneventful for him until Larry began to develop paranoid concerns that led to his leaving his job at the factory. Some of this paranoid ideation, as previously mentioned, involved imaginary relationships with women he had met only briefly or did not know at all. He became particularly preoccupied with ideas and plans concerning another married couple with whom he and his wife were acquainted. Larry apparently felt emotionally involved with the woman, even though he had had little actual contact with her.

Other unrealistic ideas Larry was having caused him to feel uncomfortable at work. He became concerned that coworkers were hiding his tools, and he also started to feel self-conscious about having to change clothes in front of his coworkers. His stated reason for his self-consciousness was that his body was hairless, so from behind he looked like a girl. These delusional concerns influenced Larry to quit his job, which marked a significant turning point in his life. From this time on, for the remainder of his life, Larry experienced various delusional ideas and concerns, sometimes mild in intensity and at other times, severe.

Soon after leaving the factory, Larry was able to find a job working for an insurance company. Later he became aware that he had begun to do "goofy" things in this new place of employment. He dyed his hair light blonde and wore tight-fitting and unusual clothes because he believed, in his words, that "the look is the hook" for attracting other women, in addition to his wife. People laughed at him and said he looked queer. Larry began to wonder whether they were right. He sent a Valentine's Day card to a girl whom he had met briefly, and he wrote in the card that he wanted to take her out on a date. He was convinced that she had shown the card to her girlfriends and made a fool of him.

These events intensified Larry's belief that people disliked him, and he became so upset with himself and his life that he cut his wrists, although not severely. This wrist-cutting episode turned out to be the first of numerous self-destructive acts that were to follow. Larry began to hear voices again, this time accusing him of being responsible for his uncle's fatal accident years earlier. After seeing a girl he had dated in the past, he heard voices accusing him of being a name-dropper and a braggart. During this period, possibly in imitation of his uncle's death, Larry himself was involved in an automobile accident in which he was badly injured with a concussion and a hip fracture that required extended hospitalization and outpatient physical rehabilitation.

From this point on, Larry's mental health deteriorated to a functioning level, vacillating between periods of minimal improvement and episodes of severe incapacitation. Brief hospitalizations followed, first at a veteran's hospital and then at a state mental institution. After his release from the state institution, he was fired from his job at the insurance company. He then tried to asphyxiate himself with carbon monoxide and was hospitalized in the psychiatric ward of a general hospital.

During the course of these brief hospitalizations, Larry's financial situation as an unemployed person was eased by his starting to receive social security benefits and veterans disability compensation. At the same time, however, his relationship with his wife and daughter became increasingly strained. He stated that he feared he did not love Joan anymore. He became preoccupied with sex and then became confused about whether he was really experiencing sexual feelings toward a woman or instead was relating to a woman in the way a little boy would relate to his mother. He indicated that he desired closeness but was also afraid of it. He repeated that he was not a man because he had no body hair, but he wanted to be a man. He masturbated regularly and was intensely conflicted and concerned about doing so.

Larry was discharged from the hospital where he had been taken following his suicide attempt, but soon after that, because of his declining functioning and apparently psychotic state, he was admitted for an extended stay to a private psychiatric inpatient facility. It was in this facility that one of us came into contact with him. Along with a number of other patients, Larry consented to participate in a research program known as the Chicago Follow-up Study, in which patients were studied and assessed while in the hospital and then followed for 10 years with further assessments (see Harrow, Grossman, Herbener, & Davis, 2000; Harrow, Sands, Silverstein, & Goldberg, 1997).

Final Hospitalization

When admitted to the psychiatric inpatient unit for extended care, Larry initially exhibited some bizarre and impulsive behavior indicative of low frustration tolerance. For example, he poured hot coffee over his head, slammed a tissue box into a table, and attempted to knock a pitcher out of a nurse's hands. He continually expressed concern over his sexual identity and said that he wanted to cut off his genitals. He exhibited firmly held paranoid beliefs, including grandiose notions of being a very special and important person, a conviction that he was the Ugly American responsible for many of the world's troubles, and ideas of reference (i.e., that whatever people around him were saying or doing had to do with him in some way). He continued to express guilt about his wife's abortion, his uncle's death, and various other regrettable events that he attributed to his misdeeds. At the same time, Larry was very competitive with other patients in the facility, particularly with respect to receiving his share of attention, and he was concerned whether the staff's interest in him was genuine. These psychotic impairments of his sense of reality diminished somewhat over the course of his hospitalization, but they never disappeared completely.

While hospitalized, Larry developed a strong attachment to his psychotherapist and became very concerned that the therapist would be disappointed with him. When the therapist took his first vacation after beginning to work with Larry, Larry's condition worsened. The frequency of his paranoid delusions increased during the therapist's absence, and his self-depreciatory attitudes and guilt feelings became more intense. Such setbacks notwithstanding, however, Larry made some progress with his therapist in being able to explore his paranoid ideation and his concerns about masculinity, masturbation, and aggression. He also became better able to tolerate exposure to his underlying depression.

Despite the severity of his disorder, Larry was fully oriented with respect to who and where he was and the present point in time. On the other hand, psychodiagnostic testing confirmed the presence of disordered thinking involving circumstantial trains of loosely connected ideas and illogical reasoning about relationships between events. He also exhibited test signs of distorted perception of reality, consistent with his paranoid delusional behavior (e.g., watching out the window to guard against any plots against him) and unwarranted self-depreciation and guilt (e.g., feeling responsible for other people's problems). He was not hearing voices or showing any other hallucinatory behavior at this time, however. Measures of his intellectual functioning identified above-average intelligence with superior verbal abilities, even in the face of cognitive disruptions during this acute phase of his illness. His surprisingly good intellectual performance, even when he was acutely psychotic, indicated potential talent to succeed in many pursuits if his psychopathology were not interfering with his personal effectiveness.

Because Larry was part of the Chicago Follow-up Study, we were able to assess his intellectual functioning on a regular basis over a 10-year period after this hospitalization. His cognitive abilities during the posthospital period remained at a relatively high level and did not show any decline. Significantly, this finding resembled the results we obtained with most of the schizophrenia patients in our long-term study and is consistent with other research indicating that schizophrenia patients do not necessarily show greater than normal cognitive declines over the years (see Zorilla et al., 2000). Larry was unusual in this regard, however, because he started out and remained at a relatively high level of intellectual functioning, whereas most (though not all) of our schizophrenia patients began and remained at a lower than normal level of cognitive performance.

Larry's mood states in the hospital were variable. Sometimes, he was emotionally flat and showed little affect of any kind, whereas at other times, he alternated between being clearly depressed or markedly anxious. He also exhibited several episodes of panic and agitation during this hospitalization, was generally anhedonic (i.e., unable to experience enjoyment in anything around him), and had some sleep disturbance. His interpersonal functioning in the facility was marked by loneliness, dependency, and childlike efforts to establish relationships, most of which backfired. At times, he also showed lapses of control over aggressive impulses. In light of his history of suicidal behavior, which was still evident in slash marks on his wrists, there was also concern about the seriousness of his self-destructive tendencies. Although he was not overtly suicidal while in the hospital, he was preoccupied at times with thoughts of self-mutilation as a way of absolving himself from his exaggerated sense of guilt.

Larry's psychotherapist in the hospital was a psychodynamically oriented clinician who formulated Larry's disturbance as revolving around two themes. The first theme was intense concern on Larry's part about his adequacy as a man, with a powerful accompanying need to prove that he was a "real man." The second theme concerned his having suffered from a lack of stable relationships with important people in his life, beginning with his very distant father and the death of his mother when he was age 5. He was then shuffled first to his grandmother and then to his aunt, which contributed further to his deficient relatedness to others. Larry may have reacted to this deprivation with enormous underlying rage that, in turn, led him to experience a tremendous amount of guilt. It is conceivable that this guilt, stemming from a belief that his anger could harm the objects of his rage or cause bad things to happen to them, gave Larry an illusory sense of control that in reality was lacking in his life. Such an illusory sense of control would help account for his grandiosity and convictions of omnipotence, both of which served to defend him against painful awareness of the lack of control that had characterized his life.

This type of dynamic formulation illustrates the kind of case conceptualizations traditionally favored by many psychoanalytically oriented clinicians. Although based on clinical experience and a theoretical framework, these formulations are largely speculative. In Larry's case, some components of his therapist's formulation were proved by follow-up data to have been accurate, whereas other components of the formulation could neither be confirmed nor rejected based on subsequent evidence. With an increasing contemporary emphasis on evidence-based practice, psychodynamic formulations have become less common in clinical work than they were in the past. Nevertheless, aspects of these formulations can sometimes be very revealing.

Larry was diagnosed on admission to this hospital and at the time of his discharge as having chronic paranoid schizophrenia with depressive features. His condition would currently be codified as Schizophrenia, Paranoid Type, Continuous in the American Psychiatric Association (2000) *Diagnostic and Statistical Manual of Mental Disorders* (*DSM-IV-TR*). Along with his depression, he was also showing some features of mania in his grandiose delusions and poor self-control. He was initially treated with antipsychotic medications as well as psychotherapy. Midway through his hospital stay, he was also placed on lithium, a mood-stabilizing medication. However, the lithium was judged to be ineffective for him and was discontinued after several weeks.

Larry was discharged from the hospital with the expectation that he would participate in outpatient psychotherapy several times a week and would be maintained on an antipsychotic medication. At this time, the intensity of his symptoms had diminished considerably, but he still had to face the challenge of dealing with some lingering and persistent problems. These problems included a mild tendency to paranoid misinterpretations of his experience and frequently recurring depressive episodes, as well as his need to regain some modicum of adequate psychosocial functioning.

Posthospital Course

We describe the course of Larry's life following his discharge from the hospital in the context of what has been thought and learned about the course of schizophrenia. Schizophrenia was originally conceived early in the twentieth century as a condition that resulted in a steady, downhill course of deterioration and from which there was rarely, if ever, any recovery. Shortly afterward, this grim prognosis was modified by clinical scholars to allow for the possibility that, despite the inevitability of a poor outcome, some schizophrenia patients may not show steady deterioration. Instead, although their disordered thinking would remain constantly present at some level, their psychotic state might be recurrent rather than continuous. This would mean that partial recoveries could be expected for some patients, at least temporarily, even though complete recovery was viewed as unlikely.

In modern times, negative views of outcome in schizophrenia have been altered further by the availability of increasingly effective antipsychotic medications and the development of other innovative treatment methods as well, including intensive hospital-based intervention programs focused on shorter lengths of stay, and better treatment and rehabilitation programs during the post-hospital period. As a consequence, considerably fewer schizophrenia patients are hospitalized for extended stays in chronic treatment services than was the case only a generation ago. Research studies in the United States have also confirmed that partial recovery occurs in most patients who develop schizophrenia and that about half of persons with schizophrenia even show the potential for complete recovery for one or more years, often, but not always, followed by a relapse.

Despite the improved prognosis for partial recovery and temporary complete recovery, on the other hand, schizophrenia remains a chronic disorder. Its pathological effects are very difficult (although not impossible) to overcome, and it typically shows a poorer outcome than other types of psychotic disorders and a heightened risk of suicide. There is good evidence that their poor course over time is a distinguishing characteristic of schizophrenia patients compared to persons with other psychotic disorders. It may, in fact, be that recurring episodes of psychopathology distinguish patients with schizophrenia from other types of psychotic patients more clearly than the nature of their psychopathology at any time.

The majority of schizophrenia patients are vulnerable to recurrent symptoms and to depression, with more persistent symptomatic and functional impairment over time than other types of psychotic patients. With modern day treatment and a more benevolent social setting, schizophrenia patients fluctuate over time between severe disability and moderate disability, although a number enter into periodic remission or recovery, often followed by relapse, and the number improving may increase to a limited or even moderate extent as they get older.

One factor leading to the relatively poor course and outcome of schizophrenia patients, as compared to persons with other types of serious disorders, involves the concept of greater vulnerability, less resilience, and slower recoverability (see Harrow et al., 1997). This constellation of greater vulnerability and slower recovery cuts across multiple domains of psychotic and nonpsychotic symptoms, extends to psychosocial functioning, and ties together diverse findings concerning the relatively poor prognosis for schizophrenia.

With this background information on the typical course of schizophrenia in mind, we turn to Larry's life after he was discharged from the hospital. In commenting previously on his social skills, Larry had indicated that, even before his first breakdown while in the military, "I was never very good at making friends." Making friends continued to be a problem for him, perpetuated by the combination of (1) his having below-average social skills, (2) his developing paranoid concerns about most of the people he met, and (3) his experiencing awkwardness in social gatherings in relation to his having had psychiatric hospitalizations. Aside from his wife and daughter, the few other people with whom he sought social contact were former patients he had known while in the hospital. With these fellow former patients, he was able to feel relatively comfortable and not awkward about having been in mental institutions. This relative comfort in being with other former patients commonly characterizes the postdischarge social life of persons who have been hospitalized with schizophrenia, although it is not always the case among schizophrenia patients.

During most of the posthospital period during which Larry was followed, he was able to sustain a good relationship with his wife, Joan, and his daughter. His home life was accordingly serving as an important source of strength and support for him. By the time of the 7½-year follow-up, however, the quality of his marital relationship had deteriorated somewhat, mainly because of feelings on Larry's part that Joan had become too critical of him. Some of this feeling seemed to derive from his own feelings of inadequacy and from concerns that he was not supporting the family adequately. At the same time, it was probable that Joan had in fact become more critical of him and that her actions and his misperceptions were acting together to fuel his distress.

As for his work performance, Larry continued to feel responsible for the financial support of his family and tried to keep himself employed, even working overtime when possible. At first, he obtained a job as a clerk and held it for almost seven months. His wife also took a part-time job to help out with the family finances, but Larry was able to provide the bulk of their income with the combination of his salary and his veteran's benefits. After a time, however, he began to develop suspicions about his coworkers that made the job situation uncomfortable for him and interfered with the quality of his work. His declining performance led to his being fired, although he maintained that the reason for his dismissal was his posing a threat to his boss by virtue of "knowing too much inside stuff about the company."

After a brief period of unemployment, Larry found another clerical job that he kept for five months. He left this job on his own volition, but again because of discomfort with his coworkers. He then was unemployed for the next two years before finding another job, which he also held only briefly. For the ensuing seven years, Larry was mostly unemployed, although he continued periodically to find jobs that would last a few months and continued to worry about not bringing home a regular paycheck. His benefit payments still contributed to the family income, but his not working caused him considerable dismay and seemed to increase the intensity of his depressive feelings. In the meantime, Joan gradually increased her hours at work so that her income provided almost all of the family support not covered by Larry's disability payments.

Throughout the 10-year follow-up in which Larry participated, he was treated regularly on an outpatient basis. The problems that were addressed in this treatment included his paranoid concerns about his coworkers and other people as well, his depressive symptoms, and his worries about being a failure as a husband and inadequate as a provider for his family. He continued to take various psychotropic medications during this period and to participate in once-weekly psychotherapy sessions. On one occasion, Larry took an overdose of one of his medications. This was his only attempt to hurt himself during the 10-year follow-up, however, and his therapist paid little attention to it. In retrospect, given Larry's earlier history of suicidal thoughts and behavior, the overdosing incident should have been taken more seriously.

Despite his weekly psychotherapy and continued maintenance on antipsychotic medication, Larry frequently had ideas of reference, such as wondering whether the TV was trying to harm him. He also continued to experience problems with depression and anxiety, and his view that his wife had become more critical of him continued to be upsetting to him. At his final follow-up evaluation 10 years after his discharge from the hospital, Larry again showed signs of paranoid concerns and depression, although he seemed to feel a little less distraught than previously about his failure to find and keep a job.

Outcome and Commentary

A little more than a year after Larry's 10-year follow-up evaluation, we received a report that he had committed suicide by hanging himself.

He was age 37 at the time of his death. Although each schizophrenia patient is unique and each person who commits suicide is unique, the tragic end to Larry's life reflects a pattern that is shown by some patients with chronic paranoid schizophrenia. In contrast to the rate of suicide for the general adult population in the United States, which is fewer than 20 per 100,000 people per year (less than 0.02%), research findings indicate that about 10% to 12% of schizophrenia patients from middle and upper socioeconomic class backgrounds commit suicide (see Westermeyer, Harrow, & Marengo, 1991).

Factors that are involved in the high rate of suicide among schizophrenia patients and that predict suicide for persons with schizophrenia are not yet completely understood. Suicide is a complex behavioral event that can result from many different factors, and it is typically influenced by the convergence of several causative factors at a particular time. We believe that the most prominent risk factors for completed suicide among patients with schizophrenia are depression and discouragement, the latter involving a sense of hopelessness on realizing that chronic features of their disorder may lead them to live with a poorer quality of life than they had anticipated or hoped for.

As to depression, research findings indicate that, although schizophrenia patients usually do not show a fully developed depressive disorder during their first episode of breakdown and hospitalization, depression often becomes a major problem in their recovery, especially following discharge from the hospital. Posthospital depression can interfere substantially with the work and social functioning of an individual with schizophrenia, as it did in Larry's case, and increases the risk of suicide (see Sands & Harrow, 1999). As previously noted, Larry showed a full depressive syndrome during two of the four follow-up assessments in the course of our 10-year study, and at least some depressive features were present at the time of the other two follow-ups.

For Larry and many other schizophrenia patients, the posthospital period was an extremely difficult time of occupational instability, financial and social problems, and continued symptoms of various kinds. Depression in particular can lead to selective memory for unhappy previous events in the lives of persons with schizophrenia, which increases their negative views of themselves and of the world around them. Feelings of disappointment and frustration about the anticipated poor quality of their future lives increase their risk for suicide, as such feelings did for Larry. Even in the absence of pronounced depression, schizophrenia patients with characteristics or abilities associated with high expectations that may never be realized can fall prey to suicidal ideation. For this reason, relatively young, intelligent, and well-educated persons with schizophrenia are especially at risk for suicide when they recognize that once-high hopes will never be realized. Those who had looked forward to success and achievement in their lives and who now see themselves as severely impaired and without hope for the future exemplify this risk. Many of these characteristics fit Larry, who, before becoming disturbed, was a bright young man expecting to have a productive life and who became particularly severely distressed by his persistent symptoms and inability to function effectively. His chronic delusions of persecution constituted an additional risk factor that is commonly seen in schizophrenia patients who take their own lives.

Of further note, the risk for suicide appears greatest in the first 10 to 15 years of schizophrenia and then appears to decline in mid-life and older adulthood. Although schizophrenia patients are more likely than people in general to commit suicide, most adapt to their poor functioning and relatively difficult life circumstances without experiencing a profound loss of self-esteem. The key to their survival is being able to accept their moderate or episodic impairments and to avoid becoming despondent or distressingly dissatisfied with the quality of their lives.

Recommended Readings

Blaney, P. H. (1999). Paranoid conditions. In T. Millon, P. H. Blaney, & R. D. David (Eds.), *Oxford textbook of psychopathology* (pp. 339–361). New York: Oxford University Press.

Bleuler, E. (1950). *Dementia praecox of the group of schizophrenias.* New York: International Universities Press. (Original work published 1911)

Carone, J., Harrow, M., & Westermeyer, J. (1991). Posthospital course and outcome in schizophrenia. *Archives of General Psychiatry, 48,* 247–253.

Drake, R. E., Gates, C., Whitaker, A., & Cotton, P. G. (1985). Suicide among schizophrenics: A review. *Comprehensive Psychiatry, 26,* 544–559.

Fowles, D. C. (2003). Schizophrenia spectrum disorders. In G. Stricker & T. A. Widiger (Eds.), *Clinical psychology* (pp. 65–92). Volume 8 in I. B. Weiner (Editor-in-Chief), *Handbook of Psychology.* Hoboken, NJ: Wiley.

Kaplan, K., & Harrow, M. (1999). Psychosis and functioning as risk factors for later suicidal activity among schizophrenia and schizoaffective patients: An interactive model. *Suicide and Life Threatening Behavior, 29,* 10–24.

References

American Psychiatric Association. (2000). *Diagnostic and statistical manual of mental disorders* (4th ed., text rev.). Washington, DC: Author.

Harrow, M., Grossman, L., Herbener, E., & Davis, E. (2000). Ten-year outcome: Patients with schizoaffective disorders, schizophrenia, affective disorders, and mood-incongruent psychiatric symptoms. *British Journal of Psychiatry, 177,* 421–426.

Harrow, M., Sands, J., Silverstein, M., & Goldberg, J. (1997). Course and outcome for schizophrenia vs other psychotic patients: A longitudinal study. *Schizophrenia Bulletin, 23,* 287–303.

Sands, J., & Harrow, M. (1999). Depression during the longitudinal course of schizophrenia. *Schizophrenia Bulletin, 25,* 157–171.

Westermeyer, J. F., Harrow, M., & Marengo, J. T. (1991). Risk for suicide in schizophrenic and other psychotic and nonpsychotic disorders. *Journal of Nervous and Mental Diseases, 179,* 259–266.

Zorilla, L. T. E., Heaton, R. K., McAdams, L. A., Zisook, S., Harris, M. J., & Jeste, D. V. (2000). Cross-sectional study of older outpatients with schizophrenia and healthy comparison subjects: No differences in age-related cognitive decline. *American Journal of Psychiatry, 157,* 1324–1326.

AUTHOR INDEX

Abramowitz, J. S., 127

Barlow, D. H., 115
Barre, P. E., 115
Beck, A. T., 263
Blinik, Y. M., 115
Brown, G. K., 263
Brown, T. A., 115

Classen, C., 192
Coen, S., 203
Croughan, J. L., 216

Davis, E., 300
Delgado, P., 122
Derogatis, L., 216
Devins, G. M., 115

First, M. B., 122, 279
Fleischmann, R. L., 122
Foa, E. B., 126
Franklin, M. E., 126

Gibbon, M., 122, 279
Goldberg, J., 300, 305
Goodman, W. K., 122

Gorman, J. M., 115
Grossman, L., 300
Gursky, D. M., 115
Guttman, R. D., 115

Harris, M. J., 302
Harrow, M., 300, 305, 308
Heaton, R. K., 302
Helzer, J. E., 216
Heninger, G. R., 122
Herbener, E., 300
Hill, C. L., 122
Hollomby, D. J., 115
Hutchinson, T. A., 115

Jamison, K. R., 289
Jeste, D. V., 302

Katz, J., 279
Katz, R., 279
Koopman, C., 192

Marengo, J. T., 308
Mazure, C., 122
McAdams, L. A., 302
McNally, R. J., 115

Novick, J., 191, 192
Novick, K., 191, 192

Peterson, R. A., 115
Price, L. H., 122

Rasmussen, S. A., 122
Ratcliff, K. S., 216
Reiss, S., 115
Robins, L. N., 216

Sands, J., 300, 305, 308
Shaw, B. F., 279
Shear, M. K., 115
Shengold, L., 200
Sholomskas, D. E., 115

Silverstein, M., 300, 305
Spiegel, D., 192
Spitzer, R. L., 122, 279
Steer, R. A., 263
Street, G. P., 127

Tolin, D. F., 127

Wechsler, D., 216
Westermeyer, J. F., 308
Williams, J. B., 279
Williams, J. B. W., 122
Woods, S. W., 115

Zisook, S., 302
Zorilla, L. T. E., 302

SUBJECT INDEX

A

Adjustment Disorder, 17–20
  with mixed anxiety and
    depressed mood, 18
Anger, issue in treatment of
  ASPD, 68
Antisocial Personality Disorder
  (ASPD), 53–72
  assessment data, 56–61
  background, 55–56
  treatment considerations,
    64–66
  treatment methods, 66–70
Anxiety-provoking situations,
  112
Anxiety sensitivity, 109
Anxiety Sensitivity Index (ASI),
  115
Anxiety/Somatoform Disorders:
  Generalized Anxiety Disorder,
    155–161
  Obsessive-Compulsive
    Disorder, 119–136

Pain Disorder, 163–180
Panic Disorder with
  Agoraphobia, 101–117
Posttraumatic Stress Disorder,
  137–153
Assessment, in-depth, 66
Assessment methods, typical, 57
Attention-Deficit/Hyperactivity
  Disorder (ADHD), 279
Attitudes, ambivalent, 37
Atypical Gender Identity
  Disorder, 219

B

Beck Depression Inventory
  (BDI), 263, 265, 279
Beck Hopelessness Scale, 279
Behavioral chain analysis:
  consequences, 46–47
  links in the chain, 45–46
  problem behavior, 46
  prompting events, 45
  vulnerability factors, 44–45

Behavioral patterns,
    dysfunctional, 42–44
Behavioral self-management
    interventions, goal of, 179
Biopsychosocial model of health,
    175
Bipolar Disorder, 76, 267–291
    background, 274–278
    case formulation, 281–283
    case history, 270–274
    interview behavior, 278–281
    treatment, 283–290
"Black despair," 263
Borderline Personality Disorder
    (BPD), 29–52, 76, 225
    case formulation, 48–50
    history of presenting problem,
        31–33
    personal history and diagnostic
        formulation, 33–38
    treatment, 38–48, 50–51
Bulimia nervosa, 37, 239–257
    case conceptualization,
        250–251
    social history, 246–250
    treatment, 251–256

C

Characteristics, distinction
    between behavioral and
    trait, 59
Characteristics of GAD,
    59–160

Chicago Follow-up Study, 300,
    301
Chronic paranoid schizophrenia,
    308
Classification system:
    alternative, 12
    reliable, 9–10
    valid, 10
Cognitive-behavioral model,
    111
Cognitive-behavioral therapy
    (CBT), 110
Cognitive confrontation, 69
Cognitive restructuring strategy,
    252, 255
Conceptualizing
    psychopathology, 7–9
Continuous phenomena, 7–9
Cultural sensitivity, 5–6

D

Dependent Personality Disorder
    (DPD), 23–28
    case formulation, 27
    criteria, 26
    developmental history, 26
    diagnostic profile, 26–27
    interview behavior, 25–26
Depressive Disorder,
    263–266
Desensitization strategy, 253
Diagnostic Interview Schedule,
    216

Diagnostic and Statistical Manual of Mental Disorders, 10–12

Dialectical behavior therapy (DBT), 31, 33, 38–39
  behavioral chain analysis, 44–47
  controlling variables, controlling, 47–48
  primary targets, 39–41
  secondary targets, 41–44

Dimensional approach to classification, 12

Discontinuous phenomena, 7–9

Dissociative Identity Disorder, 185–205
  assessment of, 189–190
  background, 185–189
  case formulation, 190–192
  treatment, 192–199

E

Eating disorders, cognitive-behavioral formulation, 251

Ego-alien, 67

Ego-syntonic, 227
  basic character pathology of ASPD, 67

Electromyelographic (EMG) biofeedback, 178

Exploratory psychotherapy, 69

Exposure and ritual prevention (EX/RP), 125–128
  implementing, 128–133
  termination, 133–135

G

Gender dysphoria, 211

Gender Identity Disorder, 209–229
  background, 216–224
  of childhood, 219
  diagnostic impression, 224–227
  gender dysphoria, 211
  history, 201–216
  treatment, 227–228

Generalized Anxiety Disorder (GAD), 155–161
  chief characteristics of, 159–160

Global Assessment of functioning (GAF), 11

H

Habit Disorders:
  Bulimia Nervosa, 239–257
  Polysubstance Dependence, 233–238

I

Identity Disorders:
  Dissociative Identity Disorder, 183–205
  Gender Identity Disorder, 207–229

Illness Intrusiveness Rating
    Scale, 115
Implicit dependency, 27
Inpatient psychiatric facilities, 65
Interoceptive exposure, 113
Interpersonal therapy strategy,
    255

M

Major Depressive Disorder, 37,
    263
Maximum security forensic
    hospitals, 65
Millon Clinical Multiaxial
    Inventory-III (MCMI-III),
    57, 59
Millon College Counseling
    Inventory (MCCI), 17–18
Minimal brain dysfunction, 271
Minimum security forensic
    psychiatric hospitals, 65
Mood Disorders:
    Bipolar Disorder, 267–291
    Depressive Disorder, 261–266
    Schizophrenia, 293–311

N

Narcissistic, 280
Normality:
    alternative to defining, 5–7
    disadvantages of statistical
        perspective, 6
    level of adjustment criterion, 7

O

Obsessive-Compulsive Disorder
    (OCD), 119–136, 280
    assessment of, 122–125
    exposure/ritual prevention,
        125–135
Outpatient centers, 65
Overanxious Disorder, 220

P

Pain Disorder, 163–180
    background, 173–175
    case formulation, 165–167
    nature and treatment,
        175–179
    outcomes, 179–180
    seeking a cure, 167–173
Panic Disorder, 37
    with Agoraphobia, 101–117
    assessment, 106–108
    impressions, 108–110
    treatment course, 111–114
    treatment outcome,
        115–116
    treatment recommendations,
        110–111
Panic Disorder Severity Scale
    (PDSS), 115
Paranoid Personality Disorder,
    79–97
    case presentation, 81–86
    course of psychotherapy,
        90–94

diagnostic understanding, 88–89
evaluation, 89–90
reassessment, 94–96
Paranoid Personality Disorder NOS, 280
Personality characteristics, 61
Personality Disorders:
  Antisocial Personality Disorder, 53–72
  Borderline Personality Disorder, 29–52
  Dependent Personality Disorder, 23–28
  Paranoid Personality Disorder, 79–97
  Schizotypal Personality Disorder, 73–77
Polysubstance abuse, 279
Polysubstance dependence, 233–238
Posttraumatic Stress Disorder (PTSD), 37, 137–153
  evaluating the event, 142–144
  treatment, 144–149
Protective rituals, 128
Psychoeducational strategy, 253
Psychological disorders, classifying, 10
Psychological normality, identifying, 5–7
  defined, 5

Psychopathology:
  conceptualizing, 7–9
Psychopathy Checklist-Revised (PCL-R), 57–60

Q

Qualitative approach, 8, 9
Quantitative approach, 7

R

Reinforcement strategy, 255
Relapse prevention strategy, 254
Response cost strategies, 252
Rorschach Inkblot Method (RIM), 17, 19, 57, 59–61

S

Schizophrenia, 76, 293–311
  case history, 295–300
  hospitalization, 300–304
  outcome, 307–309
  posthospital care, 304–307
Schizotypal Personality Disorder (SPD), 73–77
Self-attributed dependency, 27
Self-monitoring, 128
Self-mutilating behavior, 36
Shipley Institute of Living Scale, 57
Staff, ensuring safety of, 65
Stimulus control, 252

Structured Clinical Interview,
    122, 279
Subjective Units of Distress
    (SUDS), 126, 127, 132
Symptom Checklist-90-Revised,
    216

T

Targets:
    primary of DBT, 39–41
    secondary of DBT, 41–44
    dysfunctional behavioral
        patterns, 42–44
Treatment considerations for
    ASPD, 64–66
Treatment methods for ASPD
    patients, 66–70
    essential ingredients, 69–70

V

Variables:
    controlling, 47–48
    identifying, 47

W

Wechsler Adult Intelligence
    Scale-III, 216

Y

Yale Brown Obsessive
    Compulsive Scale, 122

CPSIA information can be obtained
at www.ICGtesting.com
Printed in the USA
BVHW030312200722
642000BV00008B/54

9 780471 273400